Object Oriented Programming with Java

Object Oriented Programming with Java

Neha Kaul

ARCLER PRESS

www.arclerpress.com

Object Oriented Programming with Java

Neha Kaul

Arcler Press
2010 Winston Park Drive,
2nd Floor
Oakville, ON L6H 5R7
Canada
www.arclerpress.com
Tel: 001-289-291-7705
001-905-616-2116
Fax: 001-289-291-7601
Email: orders@arclereducation.com

ISBN: 978-1-77361-208-9 (Hardcover)

ABOUT THE AUTHOR

NEHA KAUL

Neha Kaul is an experienced Java consultant currently residing in Paris, France. She is working at BNP Paribas, one of the leading banks in France. She received her double Master's Degree in Computer and Communication Networks and Information Technology from Telecom SudParis and University Paris-Saclay in 2016. She is a recipient of the prestigious Telecom Scholarship for Excellence provided by Fondation Telecom, France. She received the Bachelor of Engineering degree in Computer Engineering from the University of Pune, India in 2011. From 2011 to 2014, she was employed as a Senior Software Engineer with Geometric Ltd, Pune, India. Her major interests include Advanced Java frameworks, Logging Frameworks, Network Security and Data Mining.

TABLE OF CONTENTS

PREFACE

Java is a language that is very well suited to object oriented programming and design. Java applications are stand-alone applications similar to the application we develop using other object oriented languages such as C++, .Net etc. This book describes the Java language as its purpose is to teach the basics of object-oriented programming. In this book, we introduce the java language as its design is clean and easy to follow. The creators of this language took a fresh, minimalistic perspective and approach towards the design of this language. They included only useful, indispensible features and eliminated features that do not add value or are redundant. This innovative approach taken by them makes Java an easier language to learn and master and provides an edge over alternative programming languages. This language is an ideal, useful instrument to teach the fundamentals of object oriented programming and hence has been chosen for this book.

This book covers the fundamentals of Java and object oriented programming and shows how well they work together. Several programming samples; tested against the latest Java version 8.0 have been provided.

CHAPTER 1

OBJECT ORIENTED PROGRAMMING

Before we dive into the study of the Java programming language let us take a look at object oriented programming in brief.

What is Object oriented Programming?

Object Oriented Programming is a programming archetype or a model firmly based on the concept of 'objects'. Objects are units that contain data in many forms. Object-oriented programming (OOP) refers to a type of computer programming (software design) in which programmers define not only the data type of a data structure, but also the types of operations (functions) that can be applied to the data structure (Webopedia.com, 2017).

Data may be possessed by the object in a wide variety of forms such as fields; also known as attributes, and code, in the form of procedures, often known as methods (Development, 2017).

As a part of object oriented programming, computer applications are designed in way that enables interaction among objects that are based on a hierarchy of classes and objects that are well defined.

To explain 'objects' in simpler terms, they are similar to people. As explained by Steve Jobs objects are like people. Below is an excerpt from an interview given by Steve Jobs (Rolling Stone, 2017)

"Objects are like people. They're living, breathing things that have knowledge inside them about how to do things and have memory inside them so they can remember things. And rather than interacting with them at a very low level, you interact with them at a very high level of abstraction, like we're doing right here.

You have no idea how I did that. You have no knowledge of the laundry place. Maybe you speak French, and you can't even hail a taxi. You can't pay for one, you don't have dollars in your pocket. Yet I knew how to do all of that. And you didn't have to know any of it. All that complexity was hidden inside of me, and we were able to interact at a very high level of abstraction. That's what objects are. They encapsulate complexity, and the interfaces to that complexity are high level."

An object is the main unit of object oriented Programming. An object in software can be any real world object that we see daily like cars, people, books, a lamp and so on. Some real world objects are shown in Figure 1.

Figure 1: Real world objects.

OBJECT ORIENTED CONCEPTS

Before diving into the Java programming language and writing some code, we need to be familiar with certain object oriented concepts that have been described below.

1. **Objects:** Formally an object represents an instance of a class (Horstmann and Cornell, 2002).

For example, consider a simple table lamp; it has two possible states: on and off. It has two behaviors: you can either turn it on or turn it off. This is similar for all real world objects which can be described in terms of behavior and state. These observations all translate into software objects in the world of object-oriented programming.

Each object is made up/constitutes different states (attributes/fields), and shared behaviors, called methods. The states of a real world object are stored in the fields of an object and the behaviors are stored and described via methods.

2. **Classes:** A class is a blueprint or a template for how an object is built. It describes the state and behavior of the object (Wu, 2006).

Building on the previous example of a table lamp, consider the following class lamp:

```
public class Lamp {
  String on;
  String off;

  void turnOff() {
  }

  void turnOff() {
  }

}
```

The above class represents the object lamp in a simple way having two states and two behaviors.

3. **Inheritance:** This is a very important concept of OOP. The acquisition of all the properties and behaviors of its parent object by a child object is known as inheritance. By means of inheritance, behaviors can be passed down to objects and the code can be reused. It enables you to create new classes that

reuse, extend, and modify the behavior that is defined in other classes. The class whose members are inherited by another class is called as the base class, and the class that inherits those members from the base class is called as the derived class (Wu, 2006).

4. **Polymorphism:** Polymorphism is known as the ability of an object to behave/react to a stimulus in different ways. It is the ability of an object to take on many behaviors. It defined as the ability of different objects to have the same interface, but different implementation of this interface.

For example consider the interface – speak.

Different real world objects can use the interface speak in different ways. For example, a cat meows, a dog barks and a duck says quack.

Figure 2: Real-world polymorphism (Javatpoint, 2017).

5. Abstraction: It is the mechanism of providing just the functionality to the user and hiding internal details of the implementation from the end user.

As explained by Steve Jobs using the laundry object example (Rolling Stone, 2017), the user just uses the functionality of cleaning, but he in unaware of the low level details or the actions performed by the laundry object to clean the clothes. The actual implementation of the laundry functionality is hidden from the user. The user is provided only with 'what' the object does, not 'how' the object does it.

6. **Encapsulation:** It is process of wrapping together the data (variables) and code that acts on the data (methods) in a single unit.

It means putting together all the variables and methods into a single unit called Class. It also means concealing data and methods within an Object. It is a way to provide security to the data and methods from changes. This process is also referred to as a "black box," or a tool that can be used without knowledge of the internal implementations and mechanisms. In this way, an end user can access and use the data and methods present inside the black box, but cannot change them.

CHAPTER 2

INTRODUCTION TO THE JAVA LANGUAGE

HISTORY OF JAVA

Java is an object oriented programming language and a computing platform that was first released by Sun Microsystems in 1995 (Gosling and McGilton, 1995). The development of this language was started in 1991 by James Gosling from Sun Microsystems. James Gosling along with Mike Sheridan, and Patrick Naughton commenced this project in June 1991. At that time, James Gosling and his team (a.k.a. The Green Team) began designing and developing the first version of this language which was mainly targeted at programming digital home appliances such as televisions, set-top boxes, etc that were controlled by a wide range of computer processors. This language needed to be available for use for by several computer processors.

But in 1994, James Gosling came to the realization that this language would be perfect for use with Internet and web browsers which led to the worldwide release of the Java language. In the following year of 1995, Netscape Incorporated released its newest version of the Netscape browser which had the functionality of running Java programs within the browser.

The naming history of this language is quite riveting. Its first name 'Greentalk' was given by James Gosling. This version provided files with the extension '.gt'. Later, it was named as Oak by the Green Team as 'Oak' represented a symbol of strength. But, unluckily this name was already a trademark for Oak Technologies. The legendary story goes as follows: The team discussed for endless hours to find a new name. They were looking for a name that reflected the very essence of the language. Certain words that were suggested were "revolutionary", "jolt", "Silk", "DNA", "dynamic" etc. They wanted something that was fun to say, cool, unique, and easy to spell. During these discussions, one of the engineers while drinking a cup of Peet's Java suggested 'Java' as a name and it was added to the list. Among the top 3 names suggested, Java was the most unique and hence it was chosen.

JAVA VERSION HISTORY

There are many java versions that have been released. The current stable release of Java is Java SE 8 (Gosling and McGilton, 1995).

- JDK Alpha: 1995
- JDK 1.0: 23rd Jan, 1996
- JDK 1.1: 19th Feb, 1997
- J2SE 1.2: 8th Dec, 1998
- J2SE 1.3 8th May, 2000
- J2SE 1.4 6th Feb, 2002
- J2SE 5.0: 30th Sep, 2004
- Java SE 6:11th Dec, 2006
- Java SE 7: 28th July, 2011
- Java SE 8 18th March, 2014

FEATURES OF JAVA

Features are a set of facilities and functionalities provided by the language that help the end users develop good applications using the programming language. Some of the features provided by Java are as follows:

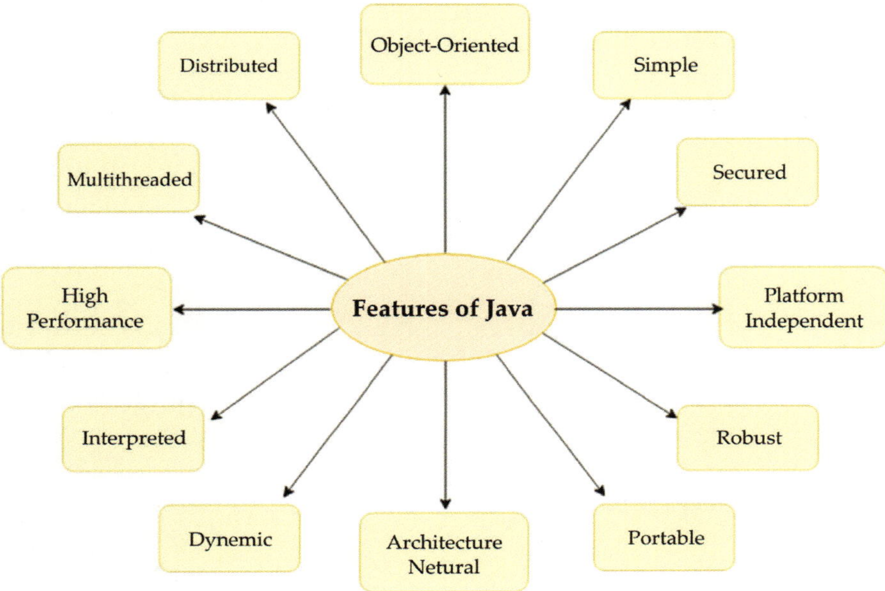

Figure 3: Features of Java (Javatpoint, 2017).

1) Simple

Java is described as a simple programming language as it has a simple user friendly syntax and hence it is quite easy to learn. Certain complex C++ concepts such as pointers and operator overloading have been eliminated in Java. Further, Java consists of an excellent memory management mechanism called the garbage collector that automatically collects unreferenced objects and frees up memory.

2) Object Oriented

In java, objects are building blocks of all its applications. As discussed in Chapter 1, Java supports all object oriented concepts and hence it is an object oriented language (Gosling and McGilton, 1995).

3) Robust

Robustness, in simple words means sturdy or strong. Java is a sturdy programming language because of its capabilities of handling exceptions

– run-time and compile time, use of an automatic garbage collector, elimination of pointers and run-time error handling.

4) Platform Independent/Architecturally Neutral/Portable

This is one of the most useful features of Java. Unlike traditional programming languages like C or ++, java code can be compiled once and run on any machines. Java follows the WORA concept, which means write-once, run-anywhere (Curtin, 1998).

A simple java file with extension .java, once compiled is converted into bytecode. This bytecode can be run on any machine be it Linux, Windows or Solaris operating system making it platform independent. Additionally, the bytecode format also provides security.

The compilation process of Java is shown below:

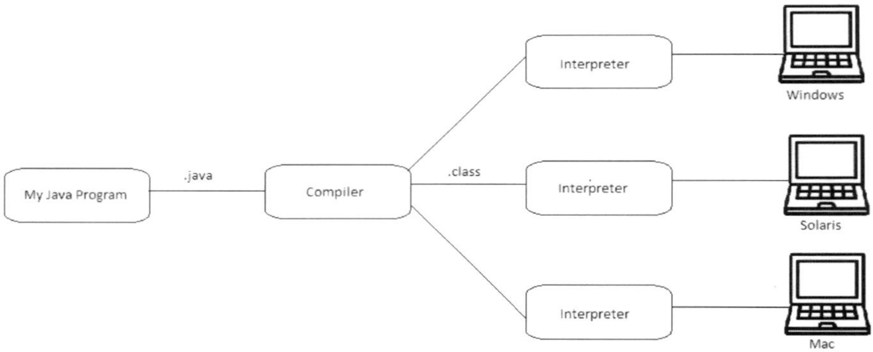

Figure 4: Compilation of a java class.

As the compiler generates bytecodes, which have nothing to do with specific or particular computer architectures, java is an architecturally neutral language.

Moreover, Java Byte code can be carried to any platform. No implementation dependent features. Everything related to storage is predefined, example: size of primitive data types

5) Secure

Java is a language that was designed keeping in mind that security is a major concern. Hence, security mechanisms and features were put in place during the development of this system which enables users to develop tamper free and virus free applications.

Some of the security features of Java are as follows:

- No pointers: As pointers have been removed from Java, it is impossible to gain access to memory locations without proper authorization. Additionally the memory allocation model is completely controlled by the run time platform and is not accessible to the programmer and hence malicious users cannot manipulate the memory.
- Static type-checking at compile time.
- Runtime checking with the security manager.

The above features, along with additional functionalities provided by Java help you create applications that are string and not susceptible to attacks.

6) Multi-Threading

Java supports the feature of multi-threading which means that using Java a program can be logically divided in parts and each part can be executed simultaneously (Gosling and McGilton, 1995). In this way, a program can complete several tasks simultaneously which reduces the execution time and enables better memory utilization.

7) High Performance

Java programs, once compiled are converted to an intermediate format known as bytecode format rather than to machine level code and this code is executed by the JVM. This unique architecture *(WORA)* of Java means that programs written in Java are faster than programs written in compiled languages such as C or C++ (Curtin, 1998). Java, being an interpreted language, makes use of an interpreter and a just in time compiler Just in time (JIT) compiler that rapidly converts Java bytecodes to native machine code.

8) Distributed

Java supports the development of distributed applications which means that multiple client server applications can be developed using Java and run on different computer networks. A sizable library of classes are provided by this language that enable communication in a distributed environment using network (TCP/IP) protocols such as FTP/HTTP/HTTPS. These features simplify the creation of distributed network applications as compared to languages such as C or C++. In this way, using Java, people separated via geographical boundaries can work together with ease.

9) Dynamic

Java supports a dynamic behaviour as on execution the end user can load the files required for execution either locally or remotely from a machine located far away just by connecting to the internet.

10) Interpreted

In contrast to most programming languages which are either compiled or interpreted, java is both. A java source file is compiled to a bytecode form by the compiler and the interpreter executes this bytecode directly on the system implementing the Java virtual machine. The combined steps of compilation and interpretation enable code checking and provide added security.

CHAPTER 3

GETTING STARTED WITH JAVA

Before we start writing java classes, the development environment needs to be setup. The system configuration recommended is as follows:

- A system that supports Java SE 8 and consists of a minimum of 2 Gigabits of memory.

The various systems that support java are: Windows®, Linux®, Mac OS and Solaris®.

- Available disk space of not less than 250 Mb which is required to install and store all the java environment software components.

COMPONENTS OF THE JAVA PLATFORM

The Java platform is made up of the JDK, JRE, JVM along with certain other components as shown in figure 5.

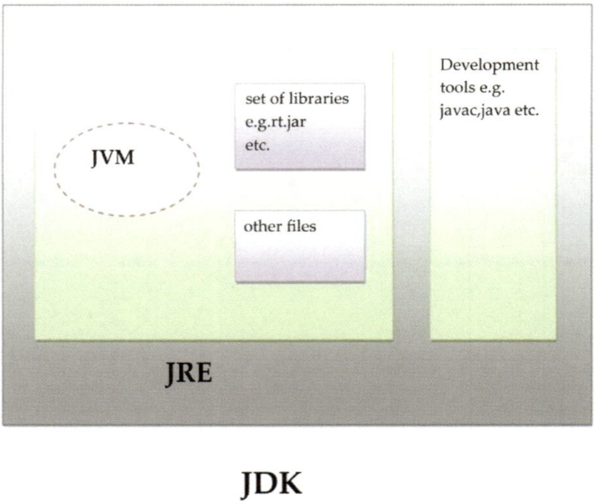

Figure 5: JDK.

1. The Java Runtime Environment

The Java Runtime Environment (*JRE*) includes the Java Virtual Machine (JVM), property settings, code libraries and components that are necessary for running java programs and is available for multiple platforms (Eckel, 2003). The JRE is a component of JDK.

2. The Java Virtual Machine (JVM)

The JVM, as its name suggests, is a virtual or abstract machine that supplies the runtime environment for executing java bytecode. At runtime it reads and interprets the .class file (the bytecode) and executes the instructions of the java program on the underlying hardware platform. This interpretation of the bytecode by the JVM is similar to that of the CPU of a computer. Hence, a JVM, JRE and JDK are platform dependent. The JVM forms the very center of the WORA principle of Java. JVMs are freely available for several software and hardware platforms (Curtin, 1998).

The main responsibilities of the JVM are as follows:

- It loads the java bytecode
- It verifies the bytecode

- It understands the instructions given by the program and executes them
- It provides a runtime environment for execution of the bytecode

3. The Java Development Kit (JDK)

This is the featured software development kit for Java. It is a development environment that helps programmers build components, applets and applications using Java. This kit tools useful for developing and testing programs written in the Java and running on the Java platform (Gong and Ellison, 2003).

The latest stable version of the Java Software environment is 8 and can be downloaded from the following link:

http://www.oracle.com/technetwork/java/javase/downloads/jdk8-downloads-2133151.html

The JDK provides you with a compiler along with a complete set of inbuilt utilities that help in software application development.

4. The Java compiler

The compiler forms a part of the JDK. The java source code is a file with an extension of .java. The java compiler checks the java source code against the language's syntax and converts the file into a .class file that contains bytecodes. These codes are a simple set of commands/instructions that are further translated/understood/interpreted and then executed by the JVM as explained above. Bytecode is a set of instructions targeted to run on a Java virtual machine (JVM).

SETTING UP YOUR LOCAL ENVIRONMENT

In this book, the environment used is: Windows 10 Enterprise Edition and Java 8.

The steps to install Java jdk 8 on windows environment are as follows:

1. Installation process of the JDK.
    - Go the Java SE downloads page and download the latest JDK.
    - Follow the instructions and run the exe file to install the JDK on your machine.

2. Once the installation of JDK is done, the environment variable 'PATH' needs to be updated with location of the Java binaries.
3. On a windows machine, if you have installed JDK at the following location: G:\java\ jdk1.8.0_131, go to Control Panel-> System and Security -> Advanced System Settings and click on Environment Variables.

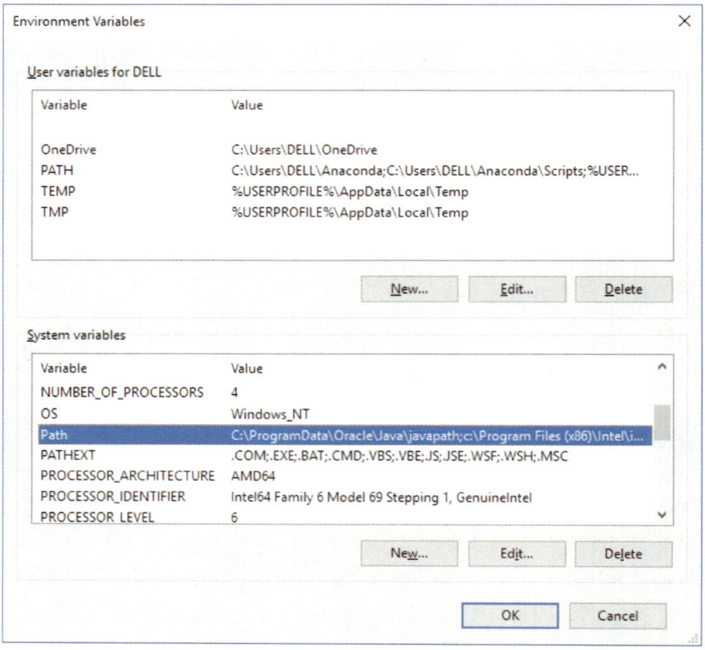

Figure 6: Environment Variables.

Now go to the list of variables and select the variable **path**. Append the path of the java binaries to the existing path by clicking on edit as follows:

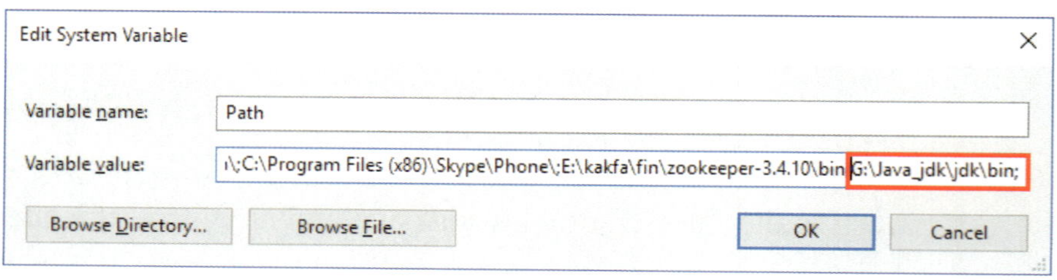

Figure 7: Setting the path variable.

1. Install the Eclipse IDE from the Eclipse Downloads page. This serves as an advanced multifunctional editor that helps you write, compile and debug Java programs (Shavor et al., 2003).
   a. Chose the platform that you are working on (Windows/ Linux/Mac, etc) along with the correct processor type (32 bit or 64 bit)
   b. Follow the default instructions and complete the installation of eclipse on your machine, maintaining the default settings while installation.
2. Setup Eclipse
   a. To setup eclipse, launch the eclipse.exe file from the directory where eclipse was installed.
   b. The setup will ask you to provide a workspace. Select the default workspace or add a workspace of your choosing.
   c. The eclipse welcome page is displayed.

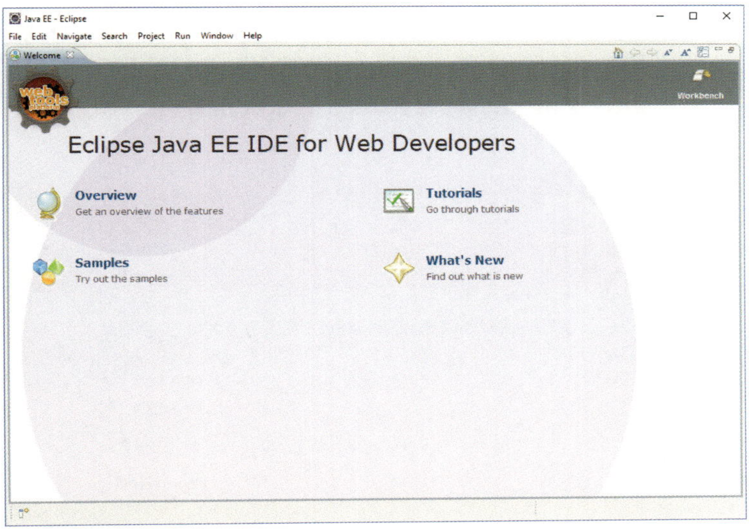

Figure 8: Eclipse Welcome page.

- Go to Windows-> Preferences -> Java -> Installed JREs as shown below:

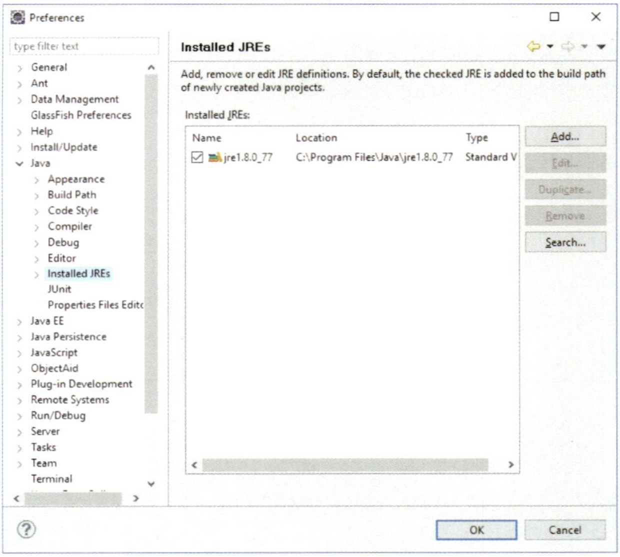

Figure 9: Adding JDK to your eclipse workspace.

- Add the newly installed JDK by clicking on the 'Add' button.
- Select the option Standard VM and click on **Next.**

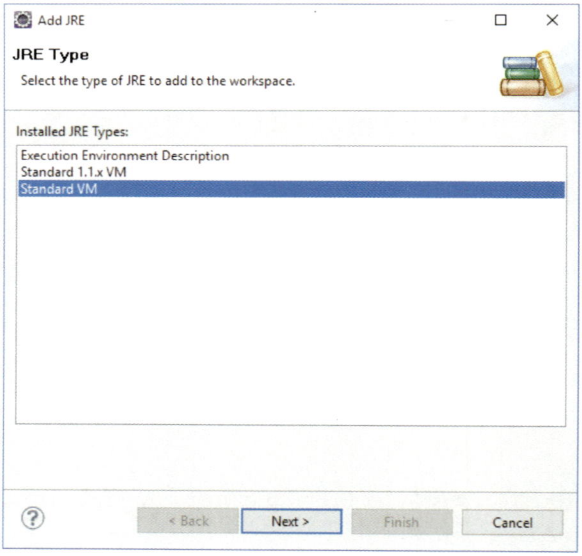

Figure 10: Adding JDK to your eclipse workspace (1).

- Specify the home directory of the installed JDK. In our case it is C:\Program Files\Java\ jdk1.8.0_131 on our Windows system.

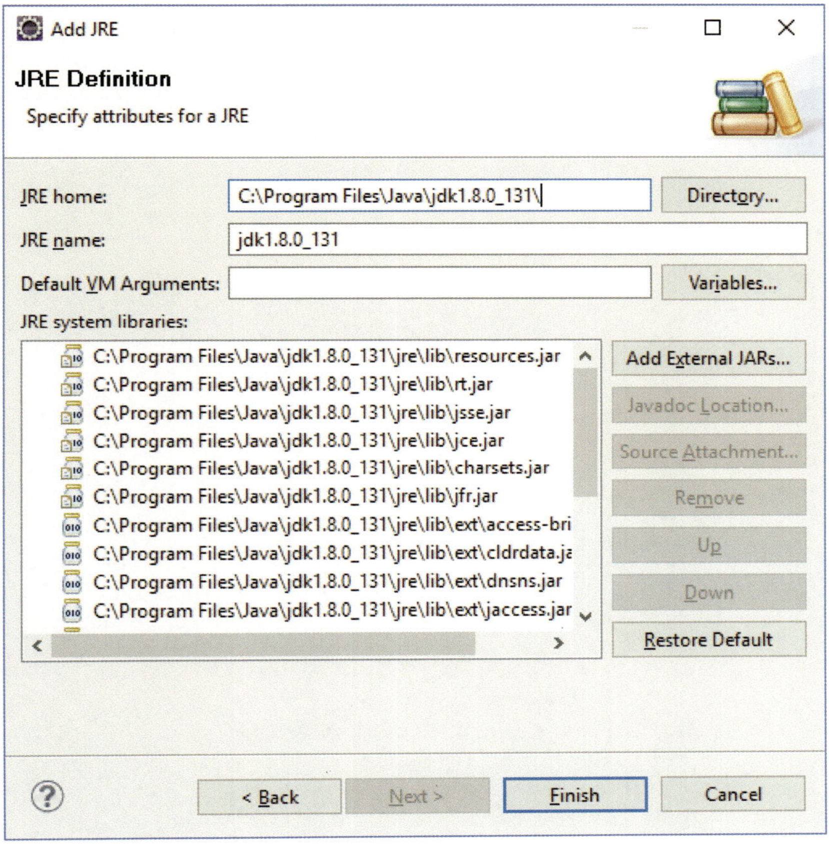

Figure 11: Adding JDK to your eclipse workspace (2).

- Click on finish.
- Verify that the JDK that you installed has been selected and click on OK.

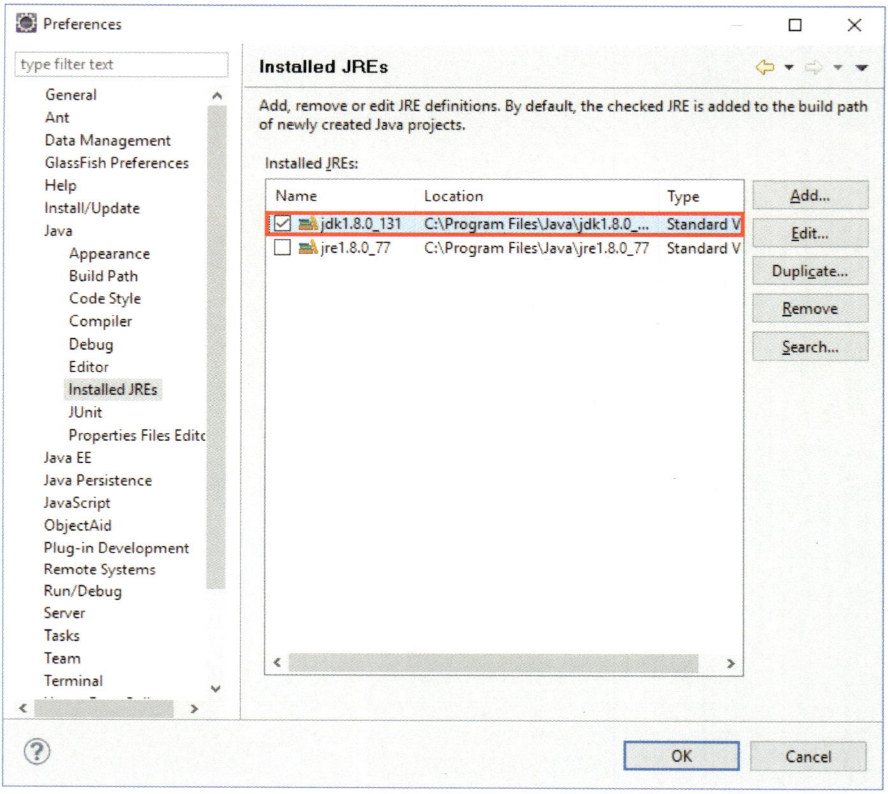

Figure 12: Adding JDK to your eclipse workspace (3).

- The setup is done!

Running your first Java Program in Eclipse

- In eclipse go to File->New -> Java Project as shown in Figure 13 below:

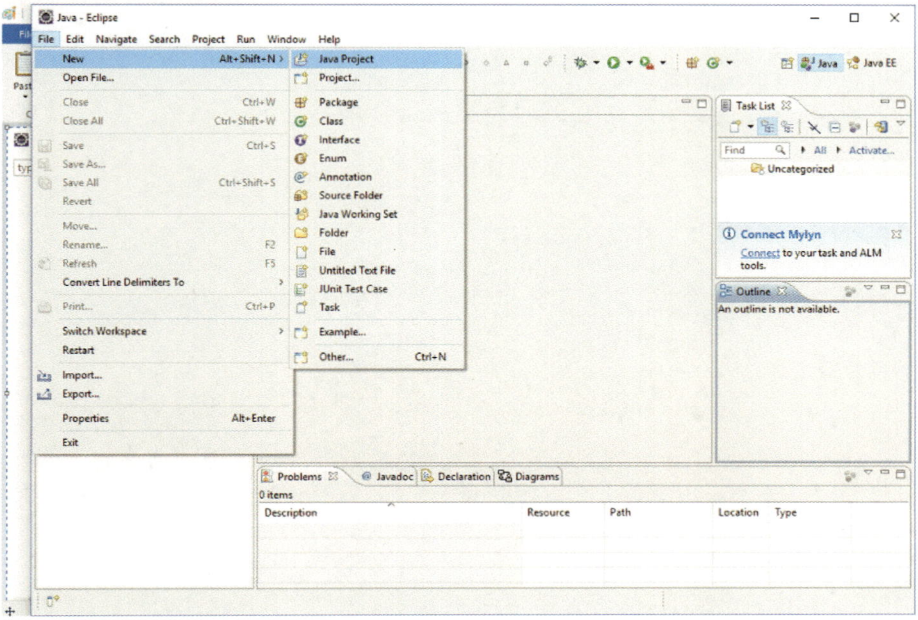

Figure 13: Creating a new Java project.

- Provide the name 'Trial' for the project and use same workspace location that you entered while starting eclipse
- Verify that the version of JDK that you're using is correct and click on Finish.

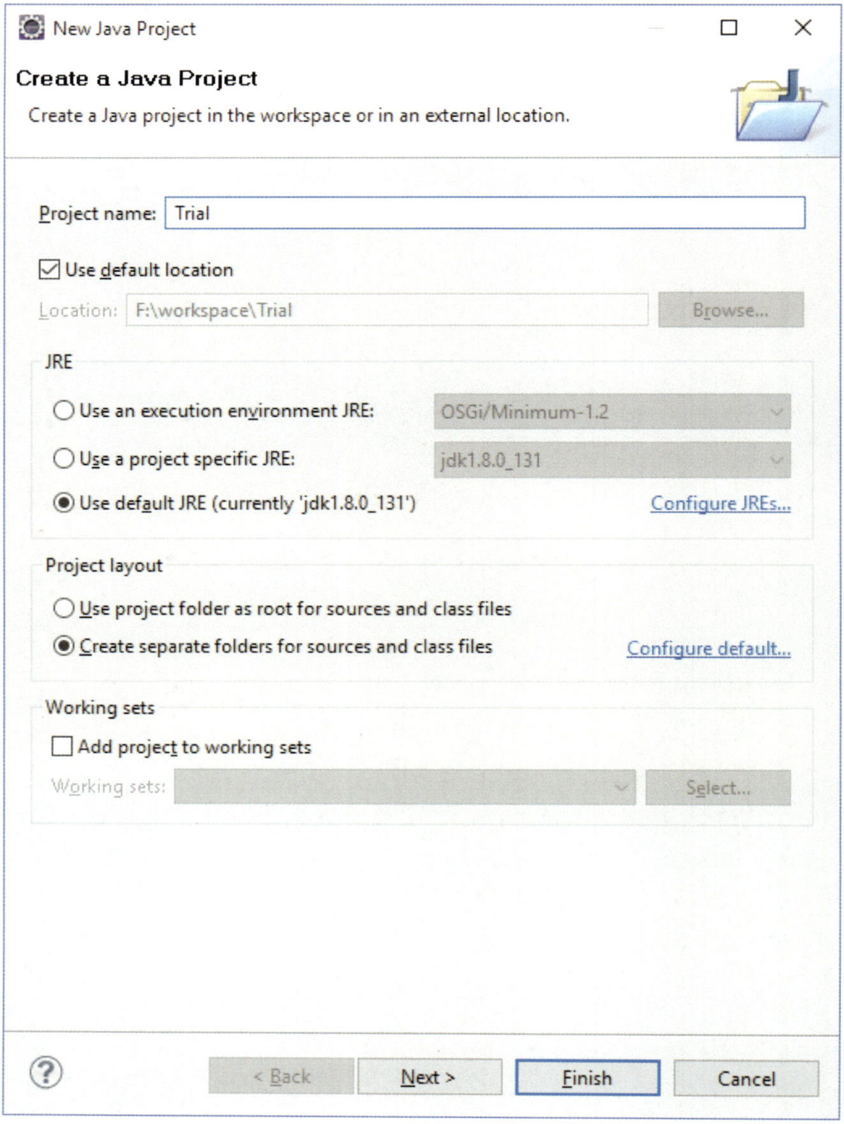

Figure 14: Creating a new Java project (1).

- Now that you have successfully created a project, we now proceed to create our very first java class.
- To create a class, right-click on the name of your project 'Trial' and go to new-> Class.

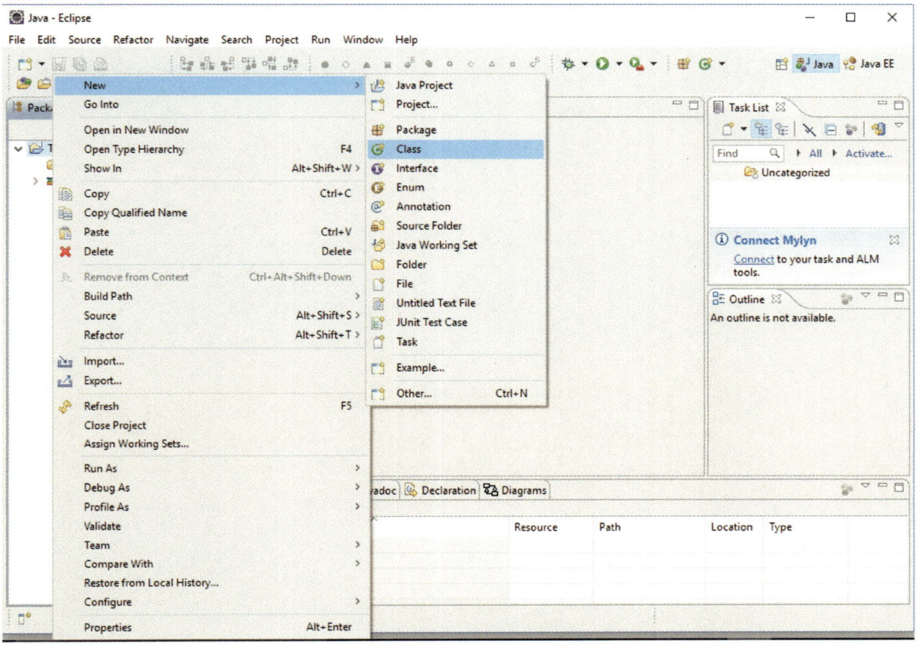

Figure 15: Adding a class to your Java project.

- The following dialog Box will appear.

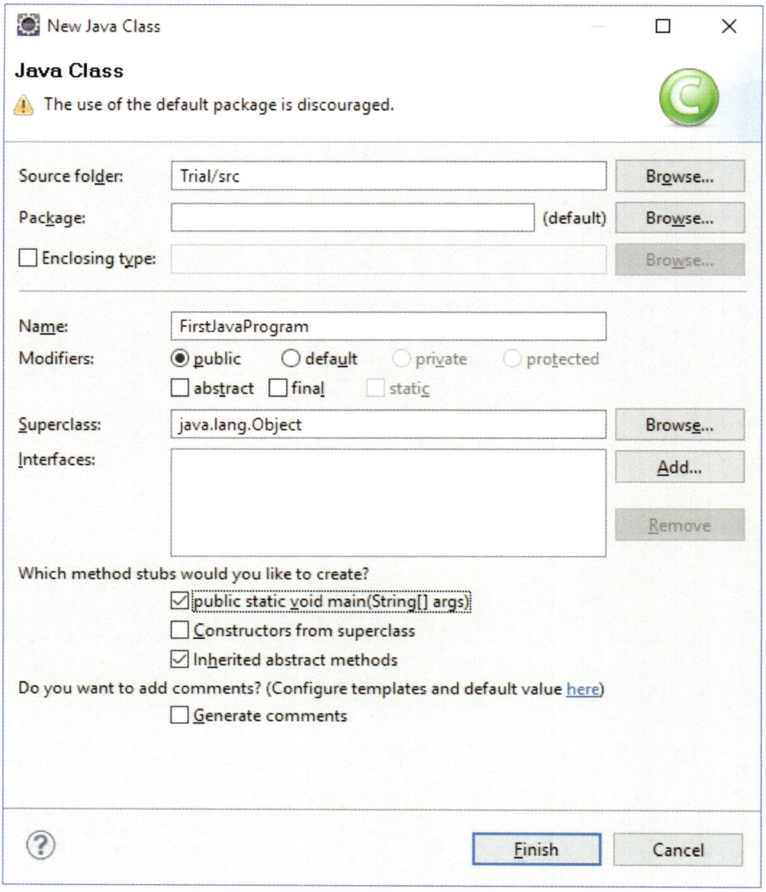

Figure 16: Adding a class to your Java project (1).

- Provide the class name as FirstJavaProgram, select the option 'provide static void main (String args[]) from the 'Which method stubs would you like to create?' section and click on Finish.
- The following screen is displayed.

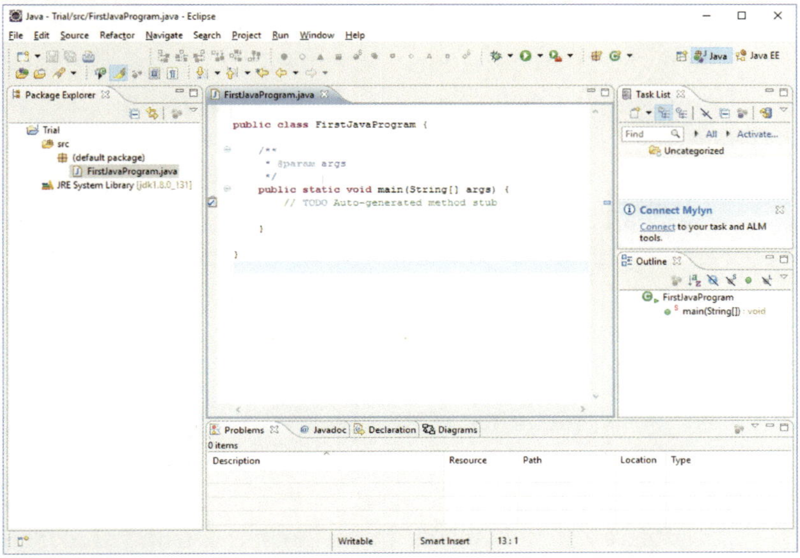

Figure 17: Adding a class to your Java project (2).

- Add the following code to print a simple output on the console.
  System.out.println("Hi! This is my first Java Program!");
- Save the file. Right-click on the file and go to Run as -> Java Application. The following output is displayed on the console.

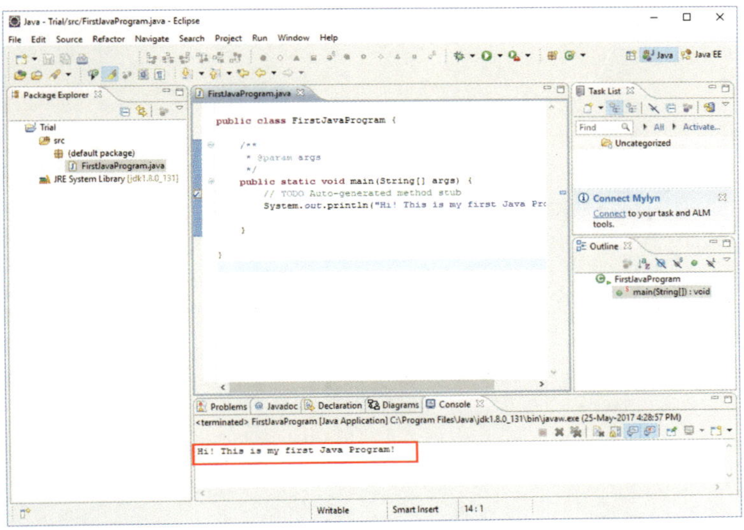

Figure 18: Running your Java program.

Here is high level breakdown of the above example:

- The name of the program/application and the class name must be identical. In our example, 'FirstJavaProgram' is the class name and hence the file name is stored as 'FirstJavaProgram.java' by default by eclipse.
- Java is a language that is case sensitive; hence the identifiers **First** and **first** are considered to be different.
- The class FirstJavaProgram has been declared as public which means it can be accessed publicly. This identifier has been discussed further in chapter 4.
- The 'class' identifier is the reserved keyword in Java that is used to create a class.
- For running stand-alone java programs the 'main' method is compulsory and it needs to be declared using the identifier 'public'. These identifiers will be discussed in detail in Chapter 4.
- 'Main' method takes an array of strings as an argument.
- To display the desired output on the console, the string is passed as an input to 'System.out.println' method which prints the given string on the console.

Running your first Java Program using the Command Prompt

Section 3.2.1 describes the process of creation and execution of a java program with the use of the Eclipse IDE. An IDE is used as it simplifies the development process. However, we can execute a java program with the use of a simple text editor for writing and the command line for executing as well.

This section describes this process.

- Open a simple text editor such as notepad and write down your code.

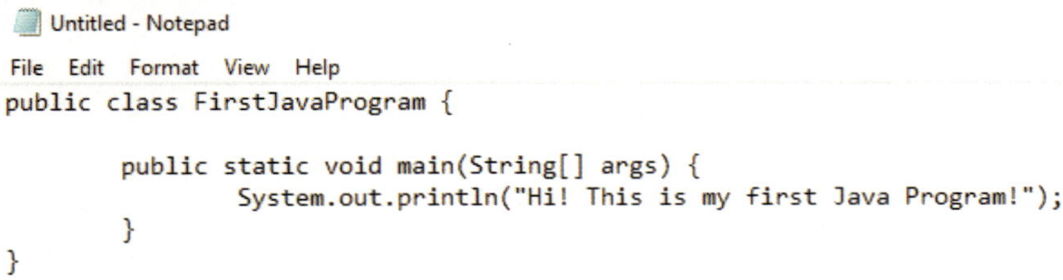

Figure 19: Write a Java program using notepad text editor.

- Save the file as a 'Java' file with the extension '.java' in the desired location on your machine. Since the name of our program is FirstJavaProgram, save the file as FirstJavaProgram.java. Make sure the file type is either set to 'All Files (*) or 'Java'.

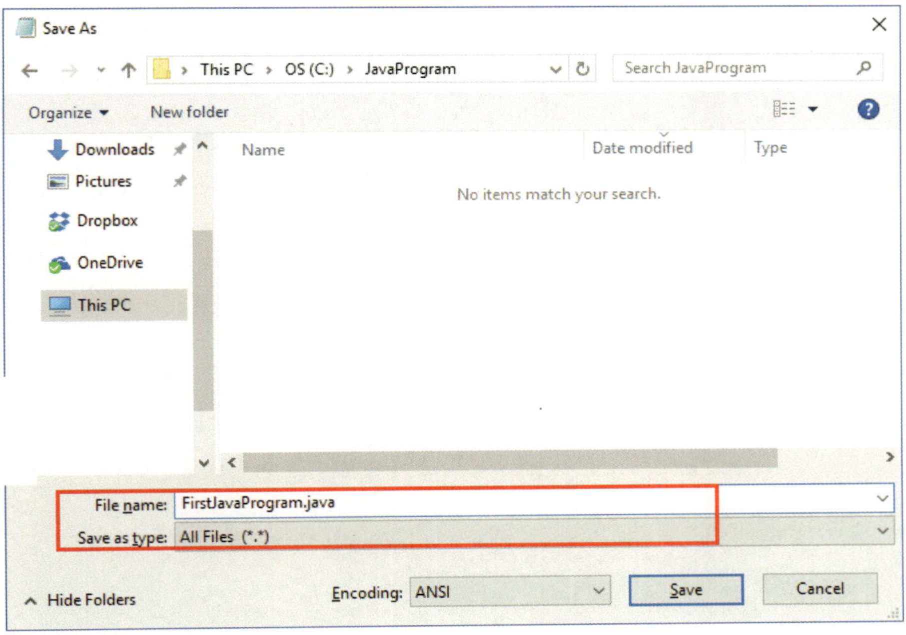

Figure 20: Save a java source file.

- Open the command prompt using the cmd command in the main menu as shown below.

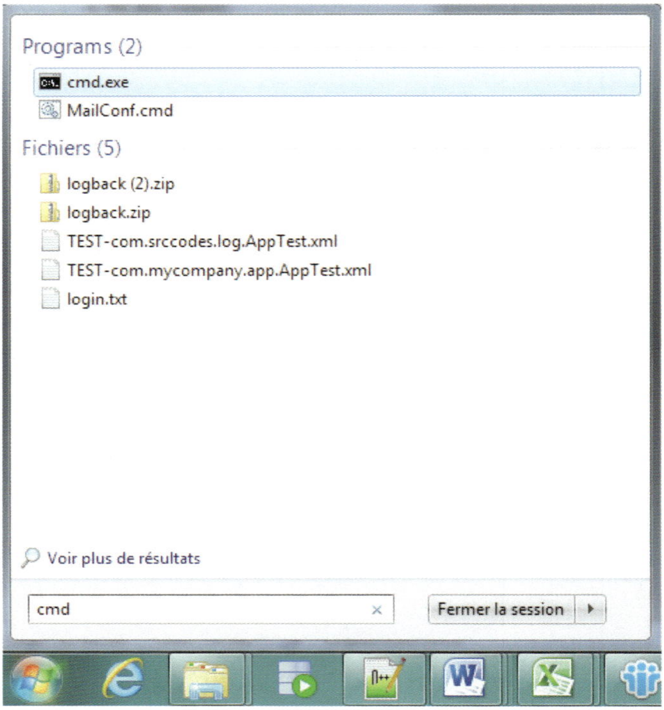

Figure 21: Launch the command prompt.

The following window showing the prompt is displayed.

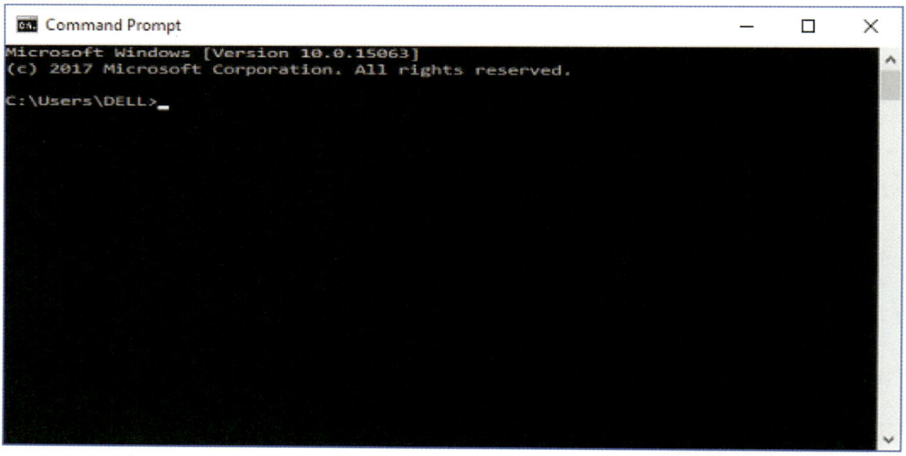

Figure 22: Command prompt .

- Traverse to the directory where you stored the file 'FirstJavaProgram.java'.
- Run the command - javac FirstJavaProgram.java
- If there are no compilation errors, nothing is displayed. This step compiles and creates a .class file in the same folder as the source file.

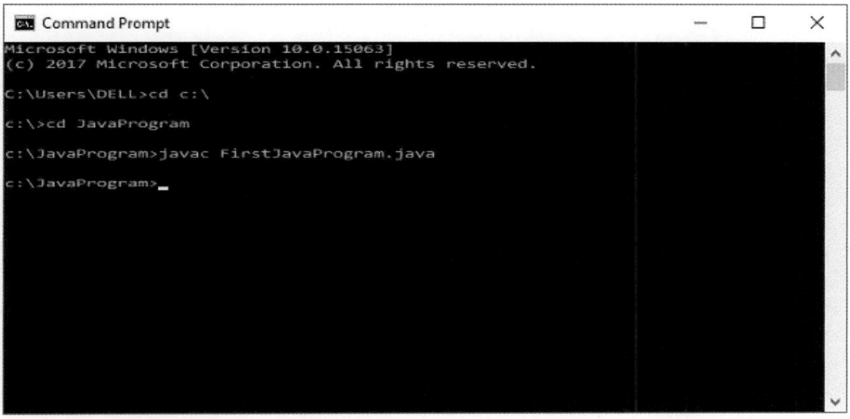

Figure 23: Running your java program from the command prompt.

- Then to run your program, run the command - java FirstJavaProgram. This command launches your application and prints the output as follows:

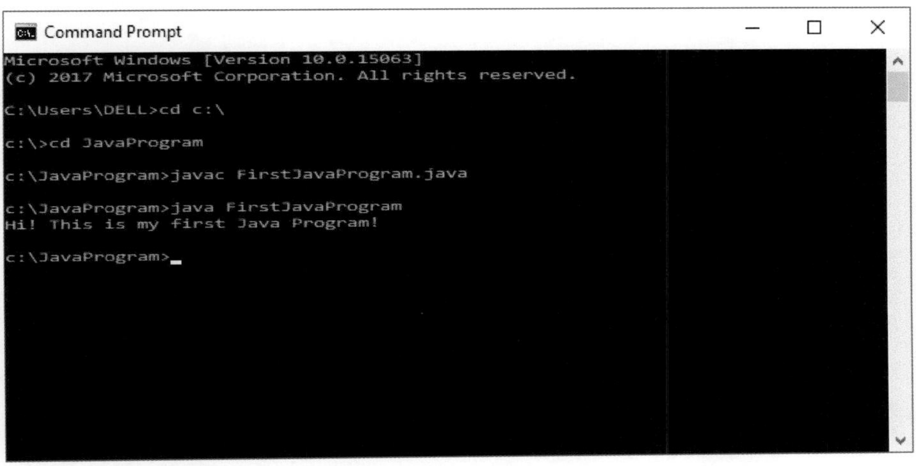

Figure 24: Running your java program from the command prompt (1).

BASIC JAVA SYNTAX

- **Identifiers** - Identifiers, in most programming languages including java are names that we give to classes, variables, packages, methods and interfaces. They must be made up of letters, numbers, the dollar sign or the connecting punctuations such as underscore(_). They can begin with a letter (a-z A-Z), the dollar sign or the underscore.

The following restrictions apply to an identifier:

a. It cannot begin with a digit

b. It cannot contain spaces

c. Should not be a reserve word

- **Variables** – These are nothing but named memory locations. Following the conventions of Java identifiers certain legal examples of variable names are as follows:

a. myVar

b. MYVAR

c. MyVar

d. MyVar1

e. $MyVar

f. _MyVar

g. i

h. j

Some examples of illegal variable names are as follows:

- 9My_Var: //begins with a digit
- My Var // Contains a space
- my+var // The plus sign is not an alphanumeric character
- variables1-2 // The hyphen is not an alphanumeric character

- O'Donald // Apostrophe is not an alphanumeric character
- My&Var // ampersand is not an alphanumeric character
- **Case Sensitivity** – Java is case sensitive, which means the identifier **Hello** and **hello** would have different meanings in this language.
- **Class Names** – In case of class names the first letter of the class name should be in Upper Case. In case the class name is made up of several words, each word's first letter should be made capital.

Example: *class FirstJavaProgram*

- **Method Names** – The naming convention in case of method name is that the method names should start with a lower case letter. In case a method name is formed from many words, all the words except the first word should have their first letter capitalized.

Example: *public void myFirstJavaMethod()*

- **Program File Name** – In java, the name of the class file, when saved should be the same as the class name. This should take into consideration the case sensitivity of java. Hello and hello do not mean the same thing.

When we save the file, it should be saved using the class name and append a '.java' at the end to specify the file type. In case of mismatch of the file name and the class name, the java program will not compile.

- **Data Types -** They stand for the different types of values that can be stored in a variable.

The primitive types of variables in java are the following:

Table 1: Primitive Data types (Wu, 2006)

Data Type	**Default Value**	**Default Size**
char	'\u0000'	2 bytes
byte	0	1 byte
Int	0	4 bytes

float	0.0f	4 bytes
long	0L	8 bytes
double	0.0d	8 bytes
boolean	false	1 bit

public static void main (PSVM) Meaning

As explained in section 3.2, the main method is the first method called when a java program begins.

To execute your program, the JVM needs to locate your program. But, JVM does not belong to the same package as any declared java class. Hence, the main method needs to be declared as public. This specifier permits accessibility across all packages.

The **static** keyword is used as it permits main( ) to be called without the need to create a particular instance of the class. This is needed as the JVM is not capable of creating class objects; hence a way to access the main method is provided by the static keyword. Any method declared as static can be called outside the class without the need for creating an object using the syntax ClassName.methodName().

In a similar way, the JVM can call the main method as <ClassName>.<main>

The keyword **void** simply tells the compiler that main( ) does not return a value.

In the main( ) method, string arguments are passed. The argument is declared as **String args[ ]**. This declaration means that a parameter named args of type stringArray is passed with the main method. These String arguments in the form of an array are necessary because the main method is called by the JVM by passing command line arguments.

Comments in java

Java has 3 different types of comments namely: Block/Traditional, end of line and documentation (Wu, 2006).

Block Comments are the ones that start with /* and end with */ and can extend upto several lines long. For example:

/* This is a long comment.

This comment is two lines long. */

End-of-Line Comments commence with a double forward slash (//) and apply just to the current line. For example:

// This is an single line comment

Documentation comments are those that are processed by the Javadoc tool that is used to generate documentation. The documentation comment is the same as block comments apart from the fact that it starts with /** and respects certain conventions that have been defined by the Javadoc tool. For example:/**

* This is a Javadoc documentation comment.

*

* @author XYZ

*/

Reserved Words/ Keywords

Similar to most languages of programming, Java has a set of special words that are recognized only by the compiler. Hence, as these words are specific to the java compiler, we are not allowed to use them for naming our Java elements. Below is the list of java keywords:

Table 2: Keywords in Java (Docs.oracle.com, 2017)

assert***	default	goto*	package	synchroni-zed
boolean	do	if	private	This
break	double	implements	protected	Throw
byte	else	import	public	Throws
case	enum****	instanceof	return	transient
catch	extends	int	short	Try
char	final	Interface	static	Void
class	finally	Long	strictfp**	volatile
const*	float	Native	super	While

Legend:

*	not used
**	added in 1.2
***	added in 1.4
****	added in 5.0

Additional literals that cannot be used are: true, false and null.

Although the list is quite short, we aren't obligated to remember this list as IDE's such as Eclipse help us identify the reserve words by use of syntax colouring.

Consider the following class:

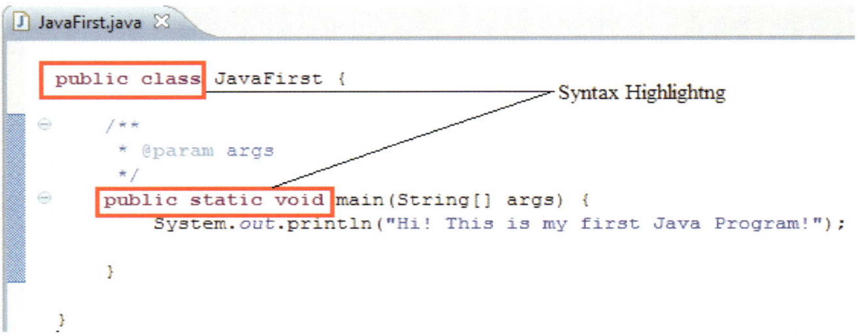

Figure 25: Syntax Highlighting.

As we can see, the keywords **public static class** and **void** have been highlighted clearly by the use of a colour.

The next chapter discusses additional fundamental concepts of Java such as objects, classes, keywords, packages, interfaces and so on.

CHAPTER 4

CLASSES AND OBJECTS

This section covers java classes and its components such as objects, methods, variables and so on.

JAVA OBJECTS

As discussed in chapter 3, an object has state and behavior. On observing real or day to day life, we can clearly see many objects such as buildings, streets, cars, houses and so on. These real life objects are similar to software objects. These objects are made up of a state and associated behaviors.

Example: Consider the object Person. It has several states such as name, address, height, weight, etc. Further, it has behaviors such as eating, breathing, walking and so on.

An object in software stores its state in fields and its behavior is exhibited by methods. In the course of software development, methods are the entities that work/operate on the object.

JAVA CLASSES

Class – Classes are nothing but blueprints that help create individual objects. A class describes the state and behavior of the object of its type.

Example: Class Person

```
public class Person {
  String firstName;
  String lastName;
  String address;
  int age;


  void eating() {
  }

  void breathing() {
  }

  void sleeping() {
  }

  void setAge(int age) {
        age= age + 1;
  }
}
```

In this example, as we can see the class Person has the states: firstName, lastName, age and address.

The behaviors are described by the following methods: eating(), sleeping() and breathing().

An important point to note is that the a single file (.java) can hold many classes, but only one class that is declared with the access modifier public. Access modifiers have been discussed in section 4.6.

METHODS

As discussed in the previous section, a method describes the behaviour of a class. A class can have several behaviours and hence several methods. The methods contain the logic for that behaviour and manipulate data and perform actions on the data.

In the above example of the class Person, eating(), breathing() and sleeping() are examples of methods.

Methods can be with or without arguments. For example, the methods eating(), breathing() and sleeping() have no arguments or parameters. But, the method **setAge** has been passed the parameter **age** which has been manipulated.

```
void setAge(int age) {

    age= age + 1;

}
```

VARIABLES TYPES

A class can contain any of the following variable types.

1. **Local variables** – These variables are those that are defined inside constructors or methods or blocks and are called local variables. They are declared and initialized within the method. Once the method has been executed, the variable will be destroyed. They are visible only within the scope of the declared method/constructor or block.

For example, consider the following method.

```
public void calculateDiscount(int sellingPrice )
{
        int finalPrice =0;
        finalPrice = 0.99 * sellingPrice;
        System.out.println("Final Selling Price is : " + finalPrice);
}
```

In the above method, the variable **finalPrice** has been declared an initialized first. Then, it has been used to store a value. This value has then been printed on the console. Once the method has been exited from, the variable **finalPrice** will be destroyed.

2. **Instance variables** - Instance variables are variables that are declared within a class but outside any of its method declarations (Wu, 2006). The minute the class is instantiated; its instance variables are initialized. These variables can be accessed from inside any of the class's constructors or method or block of the concerned class.

For example consider the class Person.

```
public class Person {
String firstName;
String lastName;
 String address;
 int age;



 void eating() {
System.out.println("This person loves ice cream. "+ firstName)
 }
```

```
void breathing() {
}

 void sleeping() {
}

        public static void main(String[] args){
        Person person = new Person();
         person.firstName = “Mark”;
        System.out.println(“First Name: “ + firstName);

        person.lastName = “Anthony”;
        System.out.println(“Last Name:” + lastName);

}

}
```

The above code on execution will print the following output on the console:

```
First Name: Mark
Last Name: Anthony
```

When we use the operator 'new' to create an object of class **Person** as shown in the example above, the instance variables are created. These variables will be destroyed when the object will be destroyed. Each object of the class Person will hold a copy of all the instance variables that have been declared. So, in case of Person class, each object of this class will hold a value of the instance variables firstName, lastName, age and address. The values held by the instance variables may be referenced or used by the methods, constructors or other blocks of code.

Access modifiers (as will be discussed in the next section) can be allotted for the instance variables. These variables have default values allotted to them.

As shown in the above code, the instance variables have been accessed in two ways:

- Directly in a defined method as follows:

```
void eating() {
System.out.println("This person loves ice cream. "+ firstName)
}
```

- By an object of the class using the dot (.) reference as seen in the main methods follows:

```
Person person = new Person();
        person.firstName = "Mark";
```

Also, if changes are made to instance variables of one object, the instance variables held by other objects are not affected. If changes are made to instance variables held by one object, they will not be reflected in the instance variables held by other objects.

3. **Class variables** - Class variables, also known as static member variables are variables declared at class level with the keyword **static**. These variables are common to and are shared by the entire class. Only one copy of this variable is created and shared by all the instances of the class. Changes made to class variables are visible to all instances of the class.

Their value can be manipulated by any class objects but these variables can be manipulated without the use of an instance of a class using the class reference.

This is demonstrated by figure 26 where the static variable has been accessed in two ways: 1. By an instance/object of the class 2. By using the class reference.

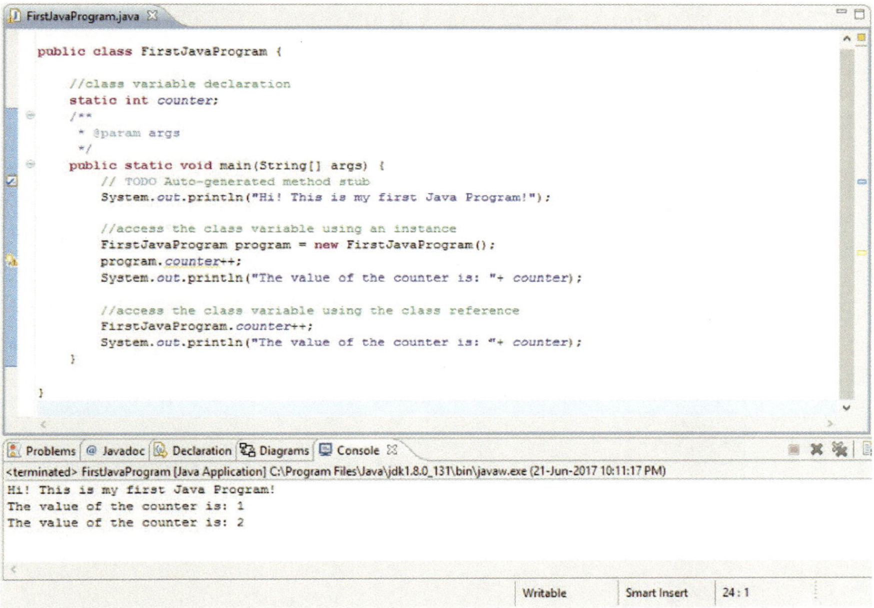

Figure 26: Static variables.

Additionally as per naming conventions, it is discouraged to access static members in a non-static way as it promotes disambiguation. When we declare a variable as static, we are saying that this variable belongs to the class. Hence, it should be accessed via the class.

4. **Class Methods** – In addition to class variables java supports class level methods as well. Class methods are also called as static methods. A method can be declared as static using the keyword static in the method declaration. These methods should be invoked using the class name and not using an instance of the class. Like static variables, these methods can also be accessed using the class instance, but this is discouraged as it results in ambiguity as to the type of method. If a method

is accessed using the Class name, it is pretty clear that the method is a static method and not a regular method.

A typical use of these static methods is to access and manipulate static fields (Figure 26).

The following combinations of instance variables and class variables are not permitted:

a. Instance methods can access and manipulate class/static methods and variables directly

b. Instance methods can access instance variables and methods directly.

c. Class methods can be accessed by class/static variables and methods directly.

d. Instance variables and methods cannot be directly accessed by class methods or variables. They must use an instance/object reference.

PACKAGES

A package is a grouping of similar/related types that help encapsulation of groups of classes, interfaces, enumerations and annotation types providing access protection and namespace management (Naughton and Schildt, 1996).

Packages in Java can be of two types: built-in and user-defined

Built-in packages are those that have been previously defined and provided by Java. Some examples are java.io, java.util. Some of these packages will be discussed in later chapters.

User defined packages are the packages created by the user/programmer. Before discussing these packages in detail, let us see certain merits of using packages in Java:

a. The use of packages promotes reusability which is an important requirement in the software industry as it helps save time and effort. With the help of packages, classes can be reused by several java programs.

b. Secondly, with the help of packages, the location of classes/files is defined which makes it easy to look for the files. This is extremely useful in case of large-scale applications that contain hundreds of classes.

c. Several times, in real world situations, there is a need for creating classes with the same name.

For example, consider an application that has an Age class that maintains the age of the Person class. Similarly, the class **Dog** can also have an Age class. In this case, the compiler will not let us create another class named **Age**. This is called a 'name-space collision'. The use of packages solves this problem and allows us to have separate packages for the Person and Dog Class; each with its own **Age** class.

Naming Conventions and points to remember:

1. In each type (class/interface/enumeration) only a single package declaration can be done.
2. The statement that declares a package must be the first statement in the class/interface/enumeration.
3. A standard for defining package names has been put into place. Most organizations use their reversed Internet domain name to define and identify their packages in a unique way.

For example, if the domain name is www.abcd.com then the package name is com.abcd.packageName

Defining and using a Package using Command Line

1. Defining and Executing via Packages

A package can be easily defined with the package keyword. If you use the notepad to edit your java code (execution using command line) as described in Chapter 3 section 3.2.2, then add the following line at the very beginning of your class.

package myJavaPackageName;

Use the following command to compile the java class that is in the package.

javac –d directory . javaClassName.java

The directory parameter specifies the destination where the compiled class files will be created. If you want to keep the destination of the compiled class files as the same directory in which the .java file is present, you can use the dot (.) operator.

Consider the class Person in package myPackage.

This class can be compiled as follows:

java –d . Person.java

The following command is used to run the class.

java myJavaPackageName.javaClassName

The Person class is run as follows:

Java myPackage.Person

2. Accessing a Package in another Class

A package can be accessed in another package in the following ways:

a. Using import

The import statement is used to access one package in another package

Consider the following example

```
Package myPackage;
Class Person{
 public void printMessage(){System.out.println(«Hello»);}
}
```

Now, if we want to use/import all the classes that fall under the package myPackage in another class named Cars, we use the following statement right after the package statement as shown below. The * after myPackage imports all the classes present under the package myPackage.

```
package carPackage;
import myPackage.*;
Class Cars{
```

```
public static void main(String args[]){
 Person person = new Person();
 person.printMessage();
 }
}
```

The output of the above program is Hello.

Additionally, if we want to import a single class or if we want to explicitly note all the classes of a package, this is possible in the following way.

```
package carPackage;
import myPackage.Person;
Class Cars{
 public static void main(String args[]){
 Person person = new Person();
 person.printMessage();
 }
}
```

The output of the above program is Hello.

b. Qualified Names

Further, if you don't want to write import statements in your current class, you can use the fully qualified package name (the package that you wish to import) when required to access the classes from this package as follows:

```
package carPackage;
Class Cars{
 public static void main(String args[]){
 myPackage.Person person = new myPackage.Person();
```

```
person.printMessage();
}
}
```

3. Subpackages and their access in Java

A package that is created within a package is called a subpackage. An interesting thing regarding the psubpackages in Java is that subpackages need to be explicitly imported. If you import the parent package, its subpackages are not imported.

Consider the following package hierarchy:

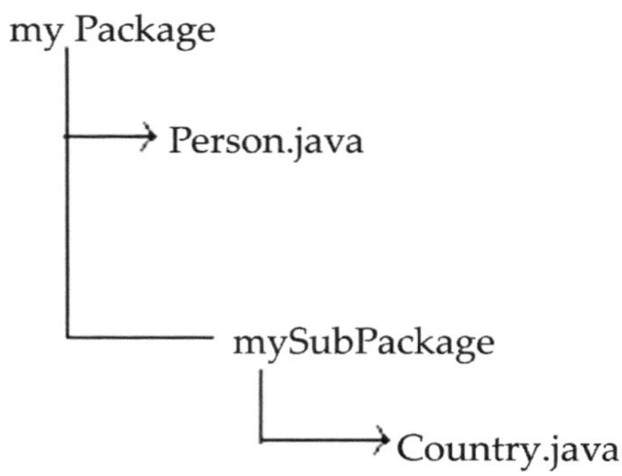

Figure 27: myPackage hierarchy.

The class Person is present in myPackage and the class Country is present in mySubPackage. So now if the class Cars want to access the class Country, another import statement must be added as shown below.

```
package carPackage;
import myPackage.*;
import mySubPackage.*;
Class Cars{
public static void main(String args[]){
Person person = new Person();
```

```
 person.printMessage();
Country country = new Country();
 }
}
```

The class country can be compiled and executed in the following way:

Javac –d . myPackage.mySubPackage.Country.java

java myPackage.mySubPackage.Country

Defining and using a Package using Eclipse IDE

In eclipse, package creation is quite simple. Once you create a project, you need to just right click on it and click on New-> Package.

The following dialog box appears:

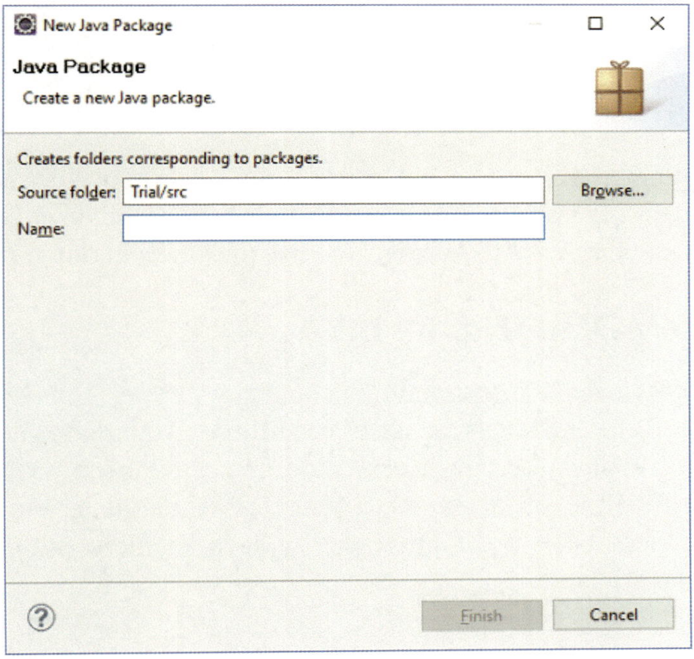

Figure 28: Creating a new package in Eclipse.

Enter the package name and click on the finish button. The package is added to your Java project as shown below.

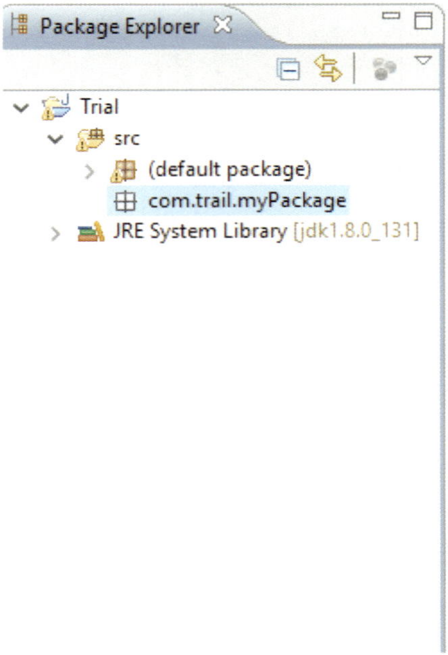

Figure 29: Creating a new package in Eclipse (1).

As explained in section 4.5.1, when we use eclipse we do not need to explicitly run the javac and java commands as Eclipse does this for us. This makes it very easy to manage and use packages in our applications.

ACCESS MODIFIERS IN JAVA

In any object oriented programming language, there is always a need to provide different levels of access to different components of your application. In java, certain access modifiers have been provided that provide different levels of access to your classes, variables and methods. Four modifiers have been provided by java; namely public private protected and default.

a. Private

This is the most restrictive access modifier. When a class/variable/ method is declared as private, it means that it is visible only within the current class. This modifier is not applicable to classes. Out of the four modifiers, only 2 are applicable to a class: public and default access.

Consider the following example:

Class Person has a private variable named age.

We try to access this variable in another class named Cars in the same package

We get a compile time error as shown in the figure below.

The class Person:

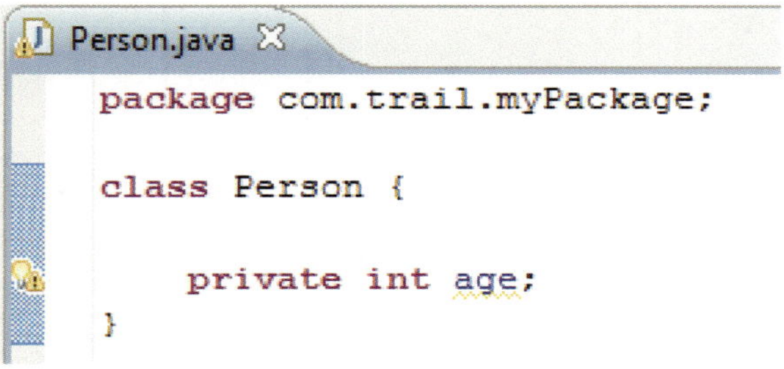

Figure 30: private modifier.

The class Cars:

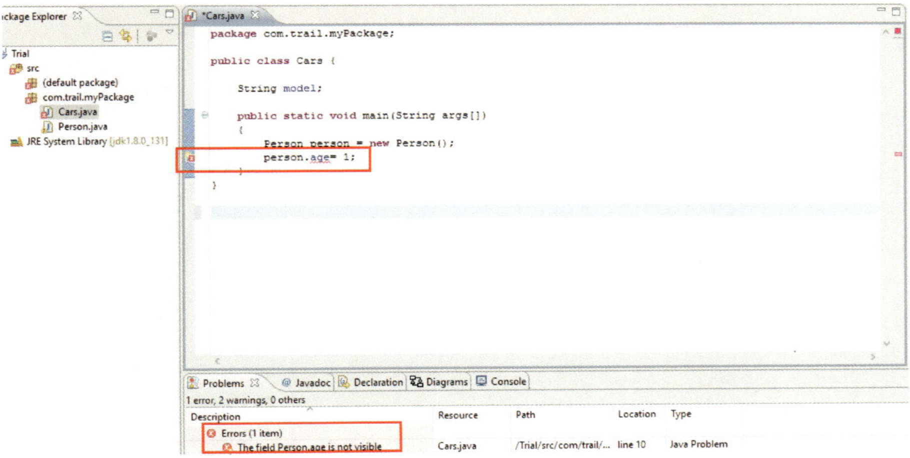

Figure 31: private modifier (1).

The private keyword restricts direct access to the variable age. To enable other classes to access and manipulate this variable, we provide methods called as getters and setters. Getters return the value of the variable and setters set the value of the variable to the value specified by the programmer.

This is demonstrated in figure 19 and 20.

Class Person with getters and setters

```
Person.java

package com.trail.myPackage;

class Person {

    private int age;

    public void setAge(int age) {
        this.age = age;
    }

    public int getAge() {
        return age;
    }
}
```

Figure 32: getters and setters.

Class Cars using the getters and setters to access the private variable age.

```
Cars.java

package com.trail.myPackage;

public class Cars {

    String model;

    public static void main(String args[])
    {
        Person person = new Person();
        //set the value of the variable 'age' with a setter
        person.setAge(10);
        //recover the value of the variable 'age' with a getter
        int age = person.getAge();
        System.out.println("Age: "+age);

    }
}
```

Figure 33: getters and setters (1).

As we can see, the getters and setters permit class Cars to indirectly access the variable age via a getter and setter. The above code produces the following output:

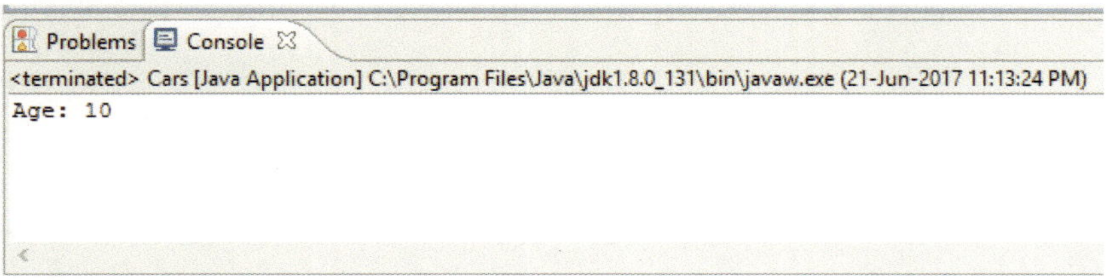

Figure 34: getters and setters (2).

Default

This level of access is allotted to the class in case no modifier has been explicitly specified.

A variable/class/package declared with this modifier is visible to all the classes in the same package.

This has been demonstrated by the following example.

Consider the class Person. The variable age has been defined with no modifier hence its access is default. As we can see, the age variable is accessible throughout this class.

```
Person.java

package com.trail.myPackage;

class Person {

    int age;

    public void displayMethod()
    {
        System.out.println("The age is: " +age);
    }

    public static void main(String args[])
    {
        Person person = new Person();
        person.age= 10;
        int age = person.age;
        System.out.println("Age is: " + age);
    }
}
```

Figure 35: default modifier.

Additionally, this variable can be accessed by other classes in the same package. This is shown by the class Cars which is able to access the variable age.

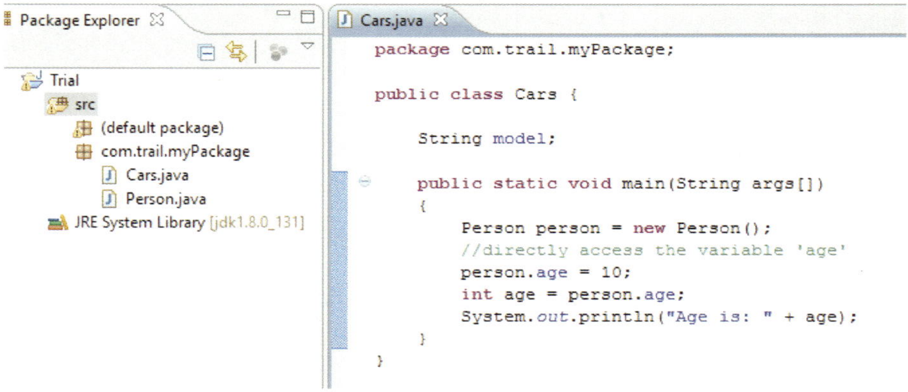

Figure 36: default modifier (1).

However, this variable is not visible to a class situated in another package. This is demonstrated by the class Country (located in package com.trial.secondPackage) that tries to create an instance of the class Person that has been declared with no modifier. We get the compile time error that says 'Person' is not visible which means that at this level, we don't have access to the class Person and its variables.

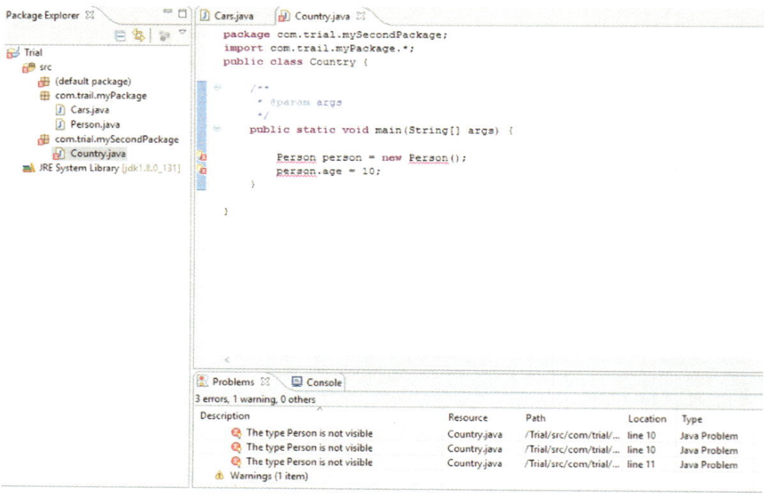

Figure 37: default modifier (2).

However if we change the access modifier of the class Person to public as follows and retry to access the variable 'age' in the class Country, we still get a compile time error. This is seen due to the fact that although the class Person is now public, its variable 'age' is still not public and hence not accessible.

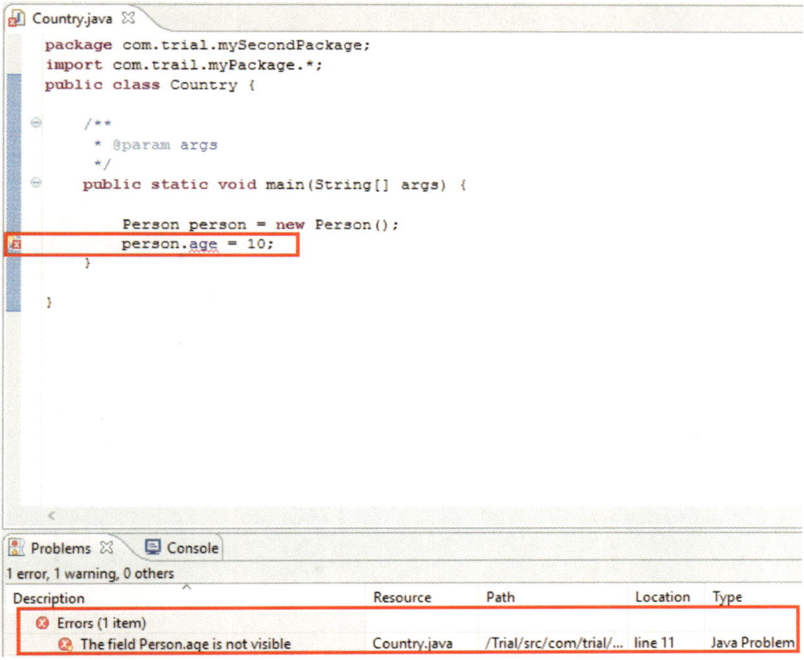

Figure 38: default modifier (3).

Protected

In java, the types (variables/methods/constructors) can be declared as protected. The protected modifier enables access in the package and its subpackages. So, all the classes in the package as well as the subclasses (child classes) in other packages have access to a field declared as protected.

Consider the following example:

The class Person with a protected variable

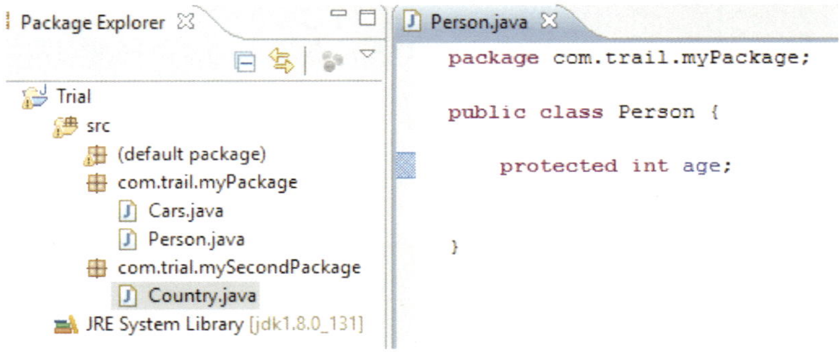

Figure 39: protected modifier.

The class Country then accesses this variable through inheritance via its instance.

Figure 40: protected modifier (1).

As we can, the variable age is accessed using an instance of the class Country. We cannot access the variable **age** of Person directly in class **Country**. This is because although the class Person has been declared as a public class, the variable **age** is protected and hence it is accessible only at the same package level and subclass-package level. The access at subclass level is achieved via Inheritance which will be discussed in Chapter 5.

d. Public

This access modifier means that the item declared as public can be accessed everywhere throughout your application. This modifier provides the widest scope among all the modifiers.

The following table shows the access to members permitted by each modifier.

Table 3: Access Modifiers and their scope (docs.Oracle.com, 2017)

Access Modifier/scope	Class	Package	SubClass	Global/outside package level
Public	Yes	Yes	Yes	Yes
Protected	Yes	Yes	Yes	No
Default/no access modifier	Yes	Yes	No	No
Private	Yes	No	No	No

The above table describes the access provided by each modifier and their visibility in a particular scope. As we see, at class level or within a class, all types (methods/variables/classes) are visible as shown in column 1, which means that a class always has access to its members. The 2nd column shows the visibility at package level. All modifiers except for the private modifier provide access at the package level. The 3rd column depicts the access at sub class level. As we can see, members declared as protected and public are the only ones that are visible at the sub class level. The 4th column shows the visibility of the member outside package level; at a global application level. At this level/scope, only public members are visible.

The instance variables of a class are visible to all the members of the class. Generally it is recommended to declare these variables private as it promotes encapsulation.

Another important point to note is that access modifiers cannot be used/assigned for local variables.

NON-ACCESS/OTHER MODIFIERS

In addition to access modifiers, java has some non-access modifiers

a. Final

This modifier is given to a member if you do not want its value to change.

It is applicable to the following types:

- Class
- Methods
- Local Variables
- Instance variables
- Method Arguments

Consider the following class that has a final method and instance variable:

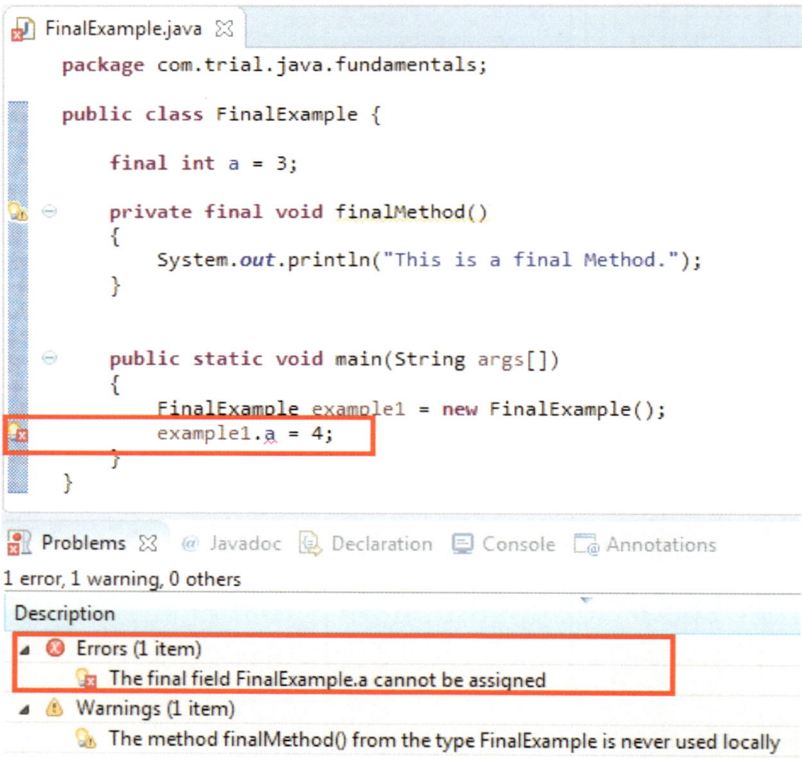

Figure 41: final modifier.

As seen in the above example, when we try to assign a new value to the variable 'a' we get a compile time error, which shows that the value of a variable declared as final cannot be modified. These variables can be used as constants in Java.

A method that is declared as final cannot be overridden in its subclass. But it can be reused by the subclass.

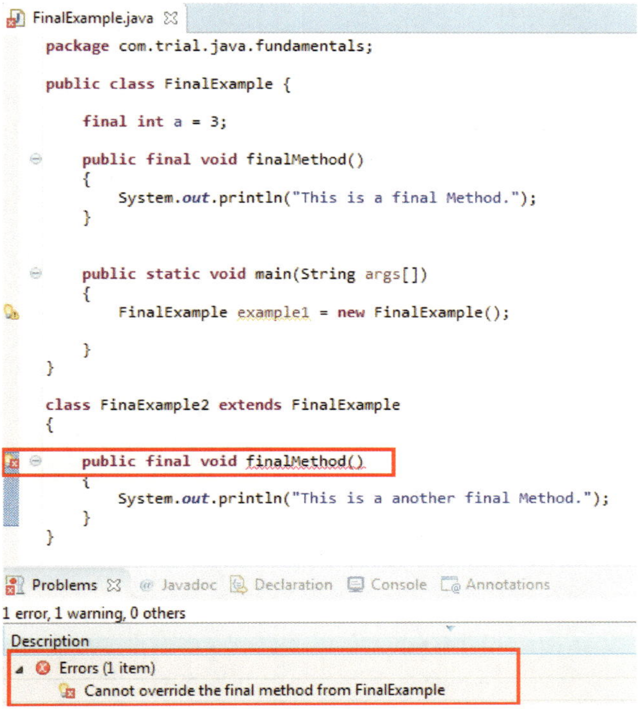

Figure 42: final modifier (1).

A class declared as final cannot be inherited and extended by any other class.

Transient

This modifier is applicable to a variable. A variable (local or instance) declared as transient will be skipped during the process of serialization. Serialization is a way to persist/save the state of an object which is discussed in Chapter 11.

Volatile

This modifier is applicable to variables. A variable marked as volatile means that its value will be modified and accessed by several threads. Further this indicates that its value should be accessed from the main memory and not cache. This comes in use in the context of multithreading which has been discussed in Chapter 16.

Synchronized

This keyword is applicable to a method or a block of code within a method. It is also applicable to static methods. This keyword is used in the context of multithreading in Java. It means that only one thread can access that block of code at one time. All the other threads have to wait for the object to be available again. This is discussed in Chapter 16.

Strictfp

This keyword is used in case floating point arithmetic. It can be applied to classes, interfaces and methods. This keyword makes sure that the results of floating point arithmetic operations are same throughout different operating systems.

Native

This keyword is applicable only to methods and it marks that the method will be implemented in a language other than Java. This works in combination with the Java provided interface called the Java Native Interface (JNI).

CONSTRUCTORS IN JAVA

A constructor in Java is a piece/block of code that helps you create objects. Every time the **new()** operator is invoked, the constructor is called. Constructors look a lot like methods, the only difference being that they don't have return types and that they have the same name as the class. A class can have 0 or more constructors.

There are classified into two types:

Default Constructor

A default constructor is the one that has no parameters. The syntax is as follows:

```
Java_Class_Name(){
    //optional block of code
```

}

For example, consider the following constructor of the Person class:

```
Person.java

package com.trial.mySecondPackage;

public class Person {


    Person()
    {
        System.out.println("A new instance created!");
    }


    public static void main(String args[])
    {
        Person person = new Person();
    }
}
```

Figure 43: Default Constructor.

The output is as follows.

```
Problems  Console
<terminated> Person (1) [Java Application] C:\Program Files\Java\jdk1.8.0_131\bin\javaw.exe
A new instance created!
```

Figure 44: Default constructor (1).

Additionally, a constructor with no method body can be passed as well. Its syntax is same the default constructor except it is empty. It is essential to note that in the absence of a user defined constructor, the compiler by default creates a no-argument/zero argument constructor at compile time. This type of constructor is used to provide default values/ default state of the object. This constructor assigns the same default value to all the objects that are created. Constructors can be assigned the access modifiers public, protected, private, or none (default).

Parameterized Constructor

This is a constructor that takes one or more arguments or parameters. This constructor is used to provide values to the object's properties. This constructor can provide values other than the default values. In this way, different values can be assigned to different objects. This is shown in figure 45.

Figure 45: Parameterized constructor.

As we can see, two objects of type Person have been instantiated and assigned different values.

An essential thing to note is that if we provide a parameterized constructor only (no default constructor), then the default constructor will not be auto-generated by the compiler.

This behavior/concept is shown by the example below:

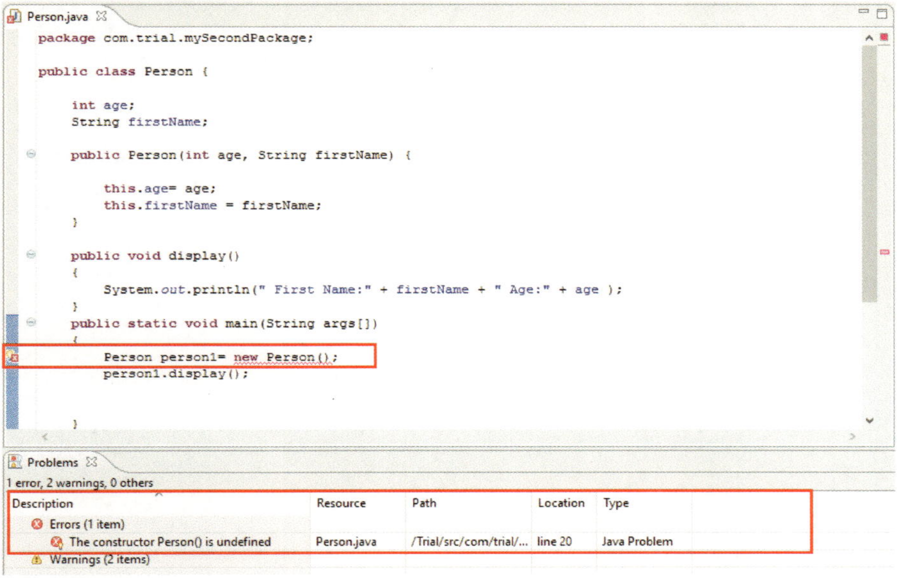

Figure 46: Parameterized constructor (1).

We get a compile time error as shown in the above figure.

Constructor Overloading

Overloading a constructor means having many constructors in a class that differ in their parameters. The parameters can differ in terms of types, count and order.

The following example shows the class Person with 3 different constructors and their respective outputs.

Person.java

```
package com.trial.mySecondPackage;

public class Person {

    int age;
    String firstName;
    String lastName;

    public Person(int age, String firstName) {

        this.age= age;
        this.firstName = firstName;
    }

    public Person(String firstName, int age) {

        this.age= age;
        this.firstName = firstName;
    }

    public Person(String firstName, String lastName, int age) {

        this.age= age;
        this.firstName = firstName;
        this.lastName = lastName;
    }

    public void display()
    {
        System.out.println(" First Name:" + firstName + " Age:" + age );
    }

    public static void main(String args[])
    {
        Person person1= new Person(20, "Alex");
        person1.display();
        Person person2= new Person("Alex", 21);
        person2.display();
        Person person3= new Person("Alex", "Smith", 22);
        person3.display();
```

Figure 47: Constructor overloading.

The output is as follows:

Console

```
<terminated> Person (1) [Java Application]
 First Name:Alex Age:20
 First Name:Alex Age:21
 First Name:Alex Age:22
```

Figure 48: Constructor overloading (1).

THIS KEYWORD

'This' keyword refers to the current instance of the class. This reference is used to refer the current instance if there is a possibility that the reference is ambiguous.

For example, consider the class Person. In the constructor, the parameters that have been provided are the same as the class variables to provide meaning names. Hence, we use the 'this' variable to separate the instance variables from the local variables.

```
public class Person {

    int age;
    String firstName;
    String lastName;

    public Person(int age, String firstName) {

        this.age= age;
        this.firstName = firstName;
    }

    public Person(String firstName, int age) {

        this.age= age;
        this.firstName = firstName;
    }

    public Person(String firstName, String lastName, int age) {

        this.age= age;
        this.firstName = firstName;
        this.lastName = lastName;
    }

}
```

Figure 49: this keyword.

Programmers may argue that in the above case the keyword doesn't need to be used and the ambiguous nature of the variables can be corrected by giving different names to the instance variables and local variables. This could be done as follows:

Person.java

```
package com.trail.myPackage;

public class Person {

    int age;
    String firstName;
    String lastName;


    Person(int a, String f, String l)

    {

        age = a;
        firstName = f;
        lastName = l;
    }

}
```

Figure 50: this keyword (1).

As we can see, the local variables of the constructor have been named differently as compared to the instance variables. In programming, a good practice is to give meaningful names to variables (Naughton and Schildt, 1996).

But, the names given in the example do not carry any meaning. The names do not explain what the parameter is. One needs to dive into the constructor and read the entire class to understand what the variables mean. In a small code, this is easy to decode. But imagine a large scale application with numerous classes and packages and projects. In that case, it is extremely difficult to process all the code in a quick way.

Hence, meaningful names must be given to all members of a class. Doing this makes the code more readable and easy to follow and understand.

An important point to note is that the 'this' keyword cannot be used by class member functions/static members as they belong to the class and not to a particular instance of that class. There is no instance for 'this' to refer to.

Additionally, the 'this' keyword can also be used in the following manner:

calling an overloaded constructor in the current class

If a class has several constructors, one constructor can be called from another constructor by means of the keyword 'this' as follows:

Person.java

```
package com.trial.mySecondPackage;

public class Person {

    int age;
    String firstName;
    String lastName;

    public Person(String firstName, int age) {

        this.age= age;
        this.firstName = firstName;
    }

    public Person(String firstName, String lastName, int age) {

        this(firstName, age);
        this.lastName = lastName;
    }

    public void display()
    {
        System.out.println(" First Name:" + firstName + " Age:" + age );
    }
    public static void main(String args[])
    {
        Person person1= new Person("Alex", 20);
        person1.display();
        Person person2= new Person("Alex", "Smith", 22);
        person2.display();
    }
}
```

Figure 51: this keyword (2).

As we can see, in the constructor with 3 arguments a this statement has been used. The statement calls the 2 argument constructor that accepts the parameters **age** and **firstName** respectively. This helps reuse the existing constructor.

Further, the default constructor can be called from a parameterized constructor using 'this' as follows.

Person.java

```java
package com.trial.mySecondPackage;

public class Person {

    int age;
    String firstName;
    String lastName;

    public Person()
    {
        this("Laurie", 25);
        System.out.println("New Instance created!");
    }

    public Person(String firstName, int age) {

        this.age= age;
        this.firstName = firstName;
    }

    public void display()
    {
        System.out.println(" First Name:" + firstName + " Age:" + age );
    }
    public static void main(String args[])
    {
        Person person1= new Person();
        person1.display();

    }
}
```

Figure 52: this keyword (3).

As shown in the class Person above, the parameterized constructor has been called from the default constructor by using the 'this' keyword. The output generated by the program is as follows:

Console

```
<terminated> Person (1) [Java Application] C:\Program Files\Java\jdk1.8.0_131\bin\javaw.exe
New Instance created!
First Name:Laurie Age:25
```

Figure 53: this keyword (4).

return current instance/object from a method

The keyword this can also be used to return an object from a method and it is a valid return value as it represents an instance of the class. This is shown as follows:

Country.java

```java
package com.trial.mySecondPackage;

public class Country {

    public Country getCountryInstance() {
        return this;
    }

    public void display() {
        System.out.println(" This is the country class! ");
    }

    public static void main(String[] args) {

        Country country = new Country();
        country.getCountryInstance().display();
    }

}
```

Figure 54: this keyword (5).

As seen in the figure above, the method getCountryInstance() returns an instance of the **country** object which is then passed on to the display method.

The output of the program is as follows:

Console

<terminated> Country (1) [Java Application]

```
This is the country class!
```

Figure 55: this keyword (6).

as an argument to a method

'This' can also be used to invoke another method by passing it as an argument. This enables method chaining. This situation arises in case we want to pass the reference of an object to several methods.

This has been explained in the following example:

Country.java

```
package com.trail.myPackage;

public class Country {

    String name;

    Country()
    {
        name = "USA";
    }

    public void display(Country country)
    {
        System.out.println("Hi! Country Name is: " + country.name);
    }

    public void displayCountry()
    {
        display(this);
    }

    public static void main(String args[])
    {
        Country country = new Country();
        country.displayCountry();
    }


}
```

Figure 56: this keyword (7).

As seen in the above figure, the method displayCountry() passes the 'this' reference which in turn calls the display() method. The output generated by the above program/code is as follows:

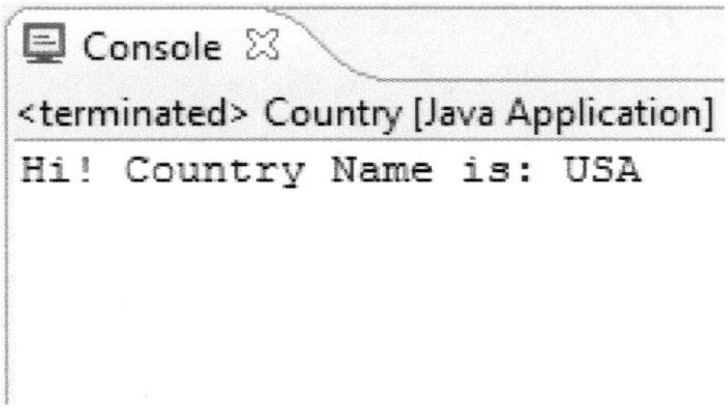

Figure 57: this keyword (8).

SUPER KEYWORD

This keyword is used to refer to the superclass/parent class of the current class. It serves to differentiate members of superclass from the subclass (Horstmann and Cornell, 2002). This keyword is used in the context of Inheritance and is discussed in detail in Chapter 5.

JAVA MEMORY MANAGEMENT

The JVM in java consists of the following sections: Stack, Heap and Data Area.

The memory is divided in the above components as follows:

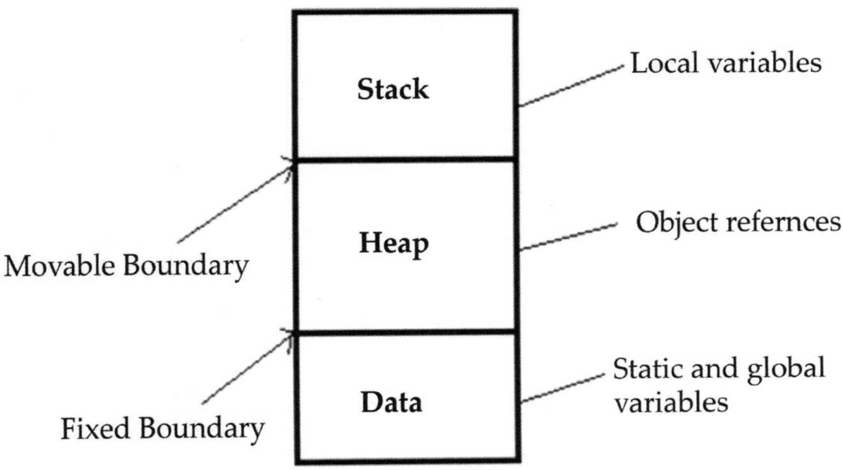

Figure 58: JVM memory.

The data area is used to store the class variables and global variables. The local variables or instance variables are always stored on the stack. The stack and heap space are dynamic with a movable boundary.

Consider the following example:

Person person;

person = new Person();

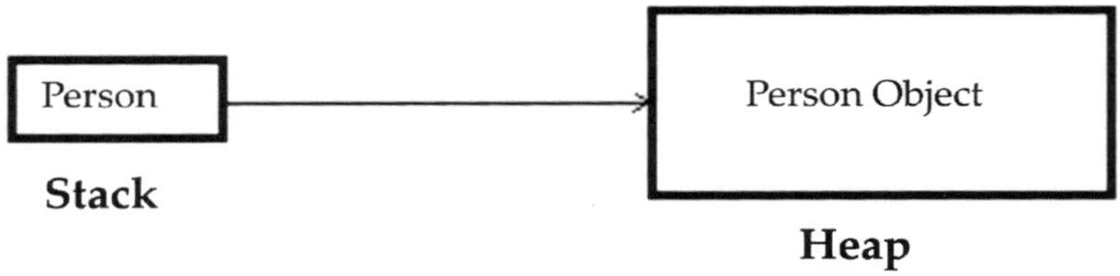

Figure 59: JVM heap and stack.

The instance variable 'person' is first created on stack. On execution of the 'new' command, the object is created and stored on the heap. The reference to this Person object is stored on the stack.

Whenever we create an object in Java using the 'new' operator or by other means, memory is allocated to the object from Heap.

The life cycle of objects on heap is longer than that of stack. The values on stack exist only within the scope of their creation.

When the object is no longer referenced its memory is released by the garbage collector. This process is discussed in Chapter 17.

CHAPTER 5

EXTENDING JAVA CLASSES

INHERITANCE

As discussed in Chapter 1, inheritance is an important pillar of object oriented programming. Using inheritance we pass properties and behaviors from one class to another.

In Java, this is achieved via the keyword extends.

The class that inherits from another class is called as the subclass or the derived class and the class whose properties are inherited is called as the parent/base/super class.

The syntax is as follows:

```
class SuperClass{
}
class subclass extends SuperClass{
}
```

A very simple example of inheritance in Java can be demonstrated by the following example:

Consider the class Vehicle:

```
Vehicle.java

public class Vehicle {

    public void display(){

        System.out.println("Hi! You are in class Vehicle!");
    }
}
```

Figure 60: Inheritance Example-1.

The class TwoWheeler inherits from the class Vehicle. Hence, it now has access to the method display of Vehicle as shown below:

```
TwoWheeler.java

public class TwoWheeler extends Vehicle {

    TwoWheeler()
    {
        System.out.println("Instance of TwoWheeler created!");
    }

    public static void main(String args[])
    {
        TwoWheeler twoWheeler = new TwoWheeler();
        twoWheeler.display();
    }
}
```

Figure 61: Inheritance Example-1 (1).

The output is as follows:

```
Console
<terminated> TwoWheeler [Java Application] C:\Program Files\Java\jdk1.8.0_131\bin\javaw.exe
Instance of TwoWheeler created!
Hi! You are in class Vehicle!
```

Figure 62: Inheritance Example-1 (2).

As we can see, the statement “Hi! You are in class Vehicle” has been printed which serves as proof that the subclass TwoWheeler has access to the method display() of its superclass Vehicle.

Here are some key points to note about inheritance in Java:

- All the members (methods and fields) of the superclass are inherited by the subclass, thereby giving the subclass the possibility of reusing them.
- The single exception to rule number 1 is that the private members of the superclass cannot be referred or used directly in the subclass.
- Each time a subclass object is created, a copy of the superclass contents is made within this object which gives the subclass access to the superclass.
- Java supports multilevel inheritance, but only upto 2 levels. This means that a class can extend upto two levels below. For example, consider the hierarchy:

Vehicle -> TwoWheeler -> Bike

The class TwoWheeler inherits from the Vehicle and the class Bike further inherits from the class TwoWheeler. But, in this case, the class Bike cannot have a subclass.

- Constructors are not inherited by the subclass. Nevertheless, they can be invoked from the subclass by means of the super keyword.
- New members (methods and fields) can be declared in the subclass that is not present in the superclass.
- An extension to point 4, we have the possibility of adding a method with the same name and signature as that of a method in the superclass inside the subclass. This phenomenon is called overriding (Wu, 2006). This principle will be discussed further in section 5.2.4.
- In addition to methods, variables/instance variables with the same name as the one in the superclass can be declared in the subclass which hides the superclass variable. This is also known as shadowing.

As mentioned in chapter 3, the super keyword is used in the context of inheritance, being primarily used to reference the parent class from the subclass. It can be used in the following scenarios:

1) Refer to immediate parent class's instance variables

In case the superclass and the subclass have the same member variable/field, super is used to get access to the superclass variable. This is shown clearly by the example in figure 63.

Vehicle.java

```
public class Vehicle {

    String color = "White";
    public void display(){

        System.out.println("Hi! You are in class Vehicle!");
    }
}
```

Figure 63: Inheritance Example-2: Super Keyword.

TwoWheeler.java

```
public class TwoWheeler extends Vehicle {

    String color = "Red";

    public void display()
    {
        //this will print the subclass color
        System.out.println("Color is:" +color);
        //this will print the superclass color
        System.out.println("Color is:" +super.color);
    }

    public static void main(String args[])
    {
        TwoWheeler twoWheeler = new TwoWheeler();
        twoWheeler.display();
    }
}
```

Console

```
<terminated> TwoWheeler [Java Application] C:\Program Files\Java\jdk1.8.0_131\bin\javaw.exe
Color is:Red
Color is:White
```

Figure 64: Inheritance Example-2: Super Keyword (1).

As we can see, on using the super keyword, the value belonging to the superclass has been displayed.

2) To invoke a method in the superclass

This keyword can be used to invoke/access a superclass method as well. It must be used if the subclass has a method with the same name as that in the superclass. This phenomenon is also called as method overriding.

This has been demonstrated in figure 65,66 and 67.

```
Vehicle.java

public class Vehicle {

    String color = "White";
    public void display(){

        System.out.println("Hi! You are in class Vehicle!");
        System.out.println("Color is:" +color);
    }
}
```

Figure 65: Inheritance Example-3: Super Keyword.

```
TwoWheeler.java

public class TwoWheeler extends Vehicle {

    String color = "Red";

    public void display()
    {
        //this will print the subclass color
        System.out.println("Color is:" +color);
        //invokes the display method of the super/parent class
        super.display();
    }

    public static void main(String args[])
    {
        TwoWheeler twoWheeler = new TwoWheeler();
        twoWheeler.display();
    }
}
```

Figure 66: Inheritance Example-3: Super Keyword (1).

The output is the following:

```
Console
<terminated> TwoWheeler [Java Application]
Color is:Red
Hi! You are in class Vehicle!
Color is:White
```

Figure 67: Inheritance Example-3: Super Keyword (2).

In the above example, Both classes Vehicle and TwoWheeler have the same method namely display(). If we call the display() method from the TwoWheeler class, it will call the display() method of the class TwoWheeler as java gives priority to the local class over the superclass. Hence, if we want to access any method that has the same name in the superclass from the subclass, the super keyword needs to be used.

3) To invoke the constructor of the superclass

The keyword can also be used to call the superclass constructor from the subclass.

Let's see a simple example;consider the class Vehicle as follows:

```java
// Vehicle.java
public class Vehicle {

    public Vehicle() {

        System.out.println("Invoked Vehicle class constructor");
    }

}
```

Figure 68: Inheritance Example-4: Super Keyword.

The class TwoWheeler inherits from class Vehicle and we instantiate an object of this class.

```
TwoWheeler.java
public class TwoWheeler extends Vehicle {

    public TwoWheeler() {
        super();
        System.out.println("Invoked TwoWheeler class constructor");
    }

    public static void main(String args[]) {
        TwoWheeler twoWheeler = new TwoWheeler();

    }
}
```

Figure 69: Inheritance Example-4: Super Keyword (1).

As we can see, in the constructor, super() has been called, which invokes the superclass constructor. The output is as follows:

```
Console
<terminated> TwoWheeler [Java Application] C:\Program Files\Java\jdk1.8.0_131\bin\javaw.exe
Invoked Vehicle class constructor
Invoked TwoWheeler class constructor
```

Figure 70: Inheritance Example-4: Super Keyword (2).

The output shows that the superclass constructor has been successfully invoked.

An important point to note is that super() has to be the first call in the constructor.

The keyword super can further be used to call/invoke the super/parent class's parameterized constructor. This is shown in the following example:

```
Vehicle.java

public class Vehicle {

    String color;
    int wheels;

    public Vehicle() {

        System.out.println("Invoked Vehicle class constructor");
    }

    public void display() {
        System.out.println("Color: " + color);
        System.out.println("Number of wheels:" + wheels);
    }

    public Vehicle(int wheels, String color) {

        this.wheels = wheels;
        this.color = color;
    }

}
```

Figure 71: Inheritance Example-5: Super Keyword.

```
FourWheeler.java

public class FourWheeler extends Vehicle {

    int numberOfSeats;

    public FourWheeler(int numberOfSeats, int wheels, String color) {

        super(wheels, color);
        this.numberOfSeats = numberOfSeats;

    }

    public void display() {
        super.display();
        System.out.println("Number of seats:" + this.numberOfSeats);
    }

    public static void main(String args[]) {
        FourWheeler car = new FourWheeler(4, 4, "Red");
        car.display();
    }
}
```

Figure 72: Inheritance Example-5: Super Keyword (1).

As we can, we have the superclass Vehicle with the parameterized constructor Vehicle(int wheels, String color). As these 2 parameters are common for all types of vehicles, the subclasses can reuse the parent class constructor instead of initializing these instance variables in the superclass FourWheeler.

Using the super keyword, the parameters have been passed to the superclass constructor as shown in figure 72.

Upcasting and downcasting in Inheritance

In java, in context of inheritance, we are allowed to treat an object of subclass type as an object of type superclass. This called as upcasting. It can be done whenever there exists and IS-A relationship between 2 classes.

This is demonstrated by the following example. Consider the class Vehicle:

Vehicle.java

```
public class Vehicle {

    String color;
    int wheels;

    public Vehicle() {

        System.out.println("Invoked Vehicle class constructor");
    }

    public void display() {
        System.out.println("Color: " + color);
        System.out.println("Number of wheels:" + wheels);
    }

    public Vehicle(int wheels, String color) {

        this.wheels = wheels;
        this.color = color;
    }

}
```

Figure 73: Upcasting in Inheritance.

Now the class, FourWheeler, which IS-A Vehcile that inherits from this class. It has been upcasted as follows:

TwoWheeler.java

```
public class TwoWheeler extends Vehicle {

    String color;

    TwoWheeler()
    {
        this.color ="Red";
    }

    public static void main(String args[]) {
        TwoWheeler twoWheeler = new TwoWheeler();
        System.out.println(twoWheeler.color);
        //upcasting
        Vehicle vehicle = twoWheeler;
        vehicle.display();

    }
}
```

Figure 74: Upcasting in Inheritance (1).

The above example shows automatic upcasting. This upcasting can be done manually as well as follows:

TwoWheeler twoWheeler = new TwoWheeler();

Vehicle vehical = (Vehicle)twoWheeler;

In java, if you want to upcast a subclass to a parent class, this is done automatically without habing the need to implicitly specify the parent class's name. This is because upcasting can never generate errors and fail as All TwoWheelers are Vehicles!

But downcasting is a little tricky. When we try to downcast a parent class to a subclass we get a compile time error as follows.

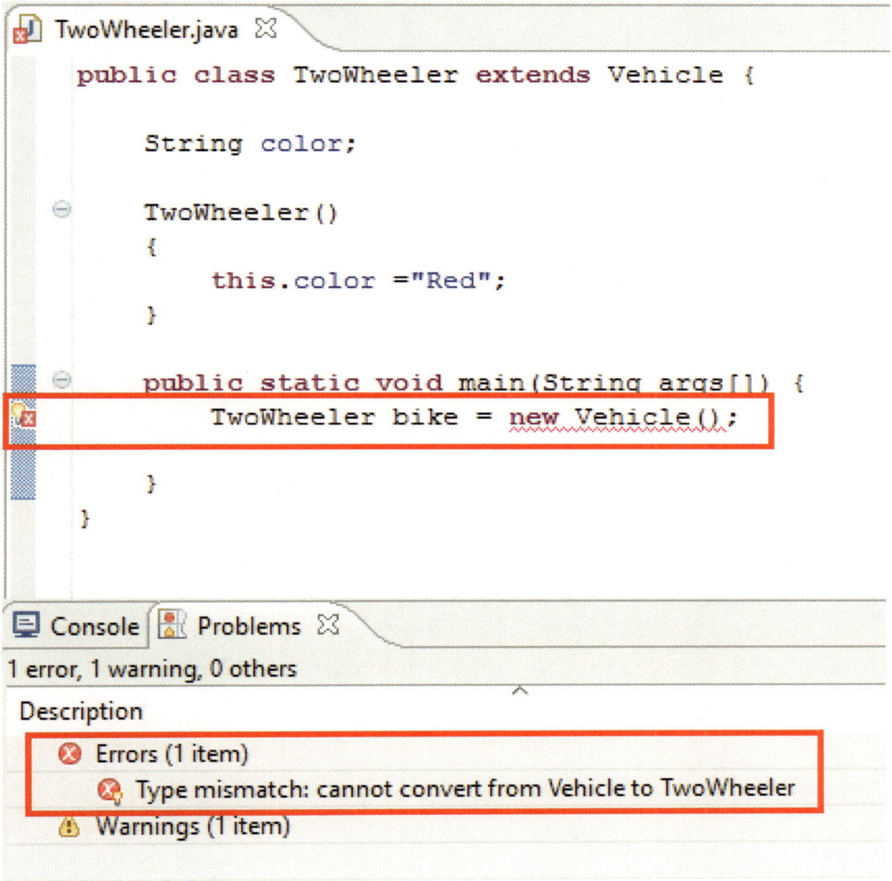

Figure 75: Downcasting in Inheritance.

This can be fixed by simple adding a cast to the instance declaration as follows:

TwoWheeler.java

```java
public class TwoWheeler extends Vehicle {

    String color;

    TwoWheeler()
    {
        this.color ="Red";
    }

    public static void main(String args[]) {
        TwoWheeler bike = (TwoWheeler) new Vehicle();

    }
}
```

Figure 76: Downcasting in Inheritance (1).

Although, the above code doesn't generate compile time errors, on execution of this code, a runtime exception called as ClassCastException is thrown as follows:

Console Problems

```
<terminated> TwoWheeler [Java Application] C:\Program Files\Java\jdk1.8.0_131\bin\javaw.exe
Invoked Vehicle class constructor
Exception in thread "main" java.lang.ClassCastException: Vehicle cannot be cast to TwoWheeler
	at TwoWheeler.main(TwoWheeler.java:11)
```

Figure 77: Downcasting in Inheritance (2).

This exception is thrown since all TwoWheelers are Vehicles, but all Vehicles aren't TwoWheelers.

Hence, downcasting should not be performed in Java.

Additional points about inheritance:

- All classes in java inherit have the Object class as their parent class, they inherit from it by default.
- Java supports multilevel inheritance upto 2 sublevels from the baseclass. As shown below, we can go down only upto levels from class A:

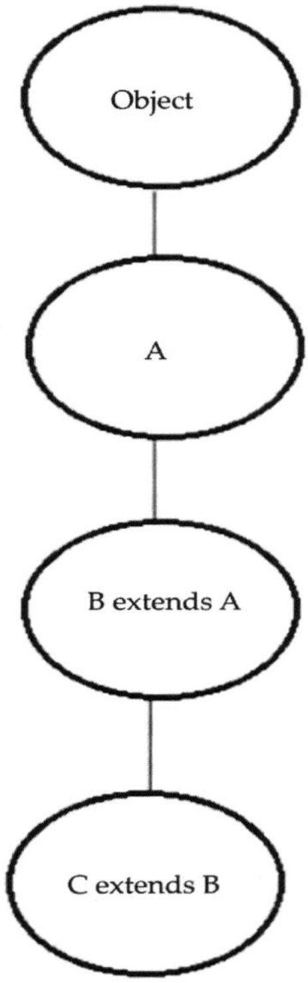

Figure 78: Multilevel Inheritance.

- Java does not support multiple inheritance. Multiple inheritance is supported by certain languages such as C++. Multiple inheritance means that a subclass can inherit from two parent classes. It is also called as diamond inheritance (Tempero and Biddle, 2000). This is depicted as follows:

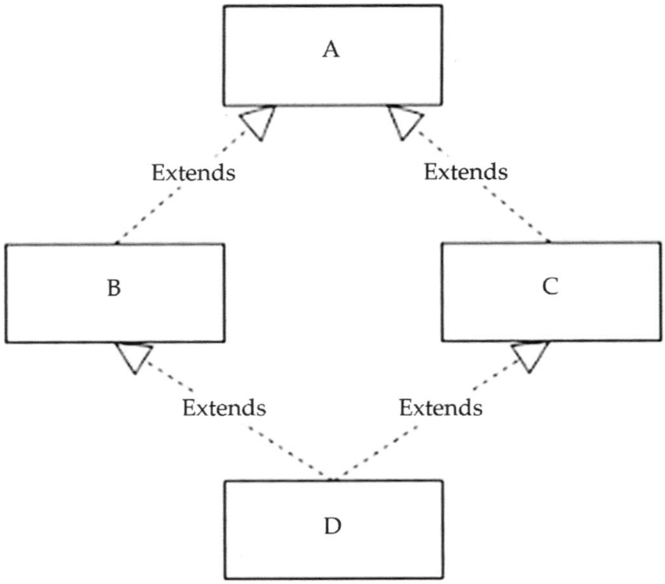

Figure 79: Multiple Inheritance (Stack Overflow, 2013).

This type of architecture causes ambiguity.

If in the above design, class B and class C have a method print() and class D does not override it, then in class D, how is one supposed to call the method print() ?

The compiler is unable to resolve this ambiguity as it does not know which parent class's print() method has been called.

Hence, Java does not support this type of inheritance. This behavior can be achieved with the help of interfaces which will be described in section 5.2.3.

Abstraction

As per dictionary, abstraction is the quality of dealing with ideas rather than events (Liskov and Guttag, 2000). For instance, when you consider the case of e-mail, complex details such as what happens as soon as you send an e-mail, the protocol your e-mail server uses are hidden from the user. Therefore, to send an e-mail you just need to type the content, mention the address of the receiver, and click send.

Likewise in Object-oriented programming, abstraction is a mechanism/process of hiding the actual implementation details from the user, providing only the functionality to the user. In other words, the user will have the information on what the object does instead of how it does it.

In Java, abstraction is achieved using Abstract classes and interfaces.

Abstract Classes

An *abstract class* is a class that is declared using the keyword abstract. An abstract class may or may not include abstract methods. These classes cannot be instantiated, but they can be inherited by other classes (Gosling and McGilton, 1995). Any class that contains the keyword 'abstract' is known as an abstract class.

A simple example of an abstract class declaration is as follows:

```
public abstract class Fruits{
}
```

A method is said to be abstract if it has been declared using the keyword abstract. An abstract method cannot have a body and it should be declared as follows:

```
Abstract void displayName();
```

Some key points about abstract classes are as follows:

- Any class that has at least 1 abstract method must be declared as abstract.
- When a class is declared as abstract we cannot instantiate it using the operator new() for instance.
- A class that is abstract can have methods that are abstract as well as methods that are regular, that is not abstract. These methods are the methods that we have been studying so far.
- In order to use an abstract class, it must be inherited by another class. In this case, the subclass needs to provide all implementations for the abstract methods of its superclass.

Here is a sample abstract class:

Fruits.java

```
package com.trial.java.fundamentals;

public abstract class Fruits {

    String name;
    String fruitType;

    public Fruits() {

    }

    public Fruits(String name, String fruitType) {

        this.name = name;
        this.fruitType = fruitType;
    }

    public String getName() {
        return name;
    }

    public void setName(String name) {
        this.name = name;
    }

    public String getFruitType() {
        return fruitType;
    }

    public void setFruitType(String fruitType) {
        this.fruitType = fruitType;
    }

    public void display() {

        System.out.println("Fruit Name:" + name+ " Fruit Type:" + fruitType);
    }
}
```

Figure 80: Abstract Classes.

As we can see, the class Fruits has been declared with the keyword abstract. Apart from this change, it is just like any other Java class.

This class can be used by way of inheritance. So we create a class Apple that inherits from this class. This is shown in figure 81.

```java
package com.trial.java.fundamentals;

public class Apple extends Fruits {

    private String appleType;

    public Apple() {
        super();
        appleType = "Green Apple";

    }

    public Apple(String name, String fruitType, String appleType) {
        super(name, fruitType);
        this.appleType = appleType;
    }

    public String getAppleType() {
        return appleType;
    }

    public void setAppleType(String appleType) {
        this.appleType = appleType;
    }

    public void display() {
        super.display();
        System.out.println("Fruit Type:" + appleType);
    }

    public static void main(String args[]) {
        Apple redApple = new Apple();
        redApple.name = "Apple";
        redApple.fruitType = "Seeded";
        redApple.display();
        Apple goldenApple = new Apple("Apple", "Seeded fruit", "Golden Apple ");
        goldenApple.display();

    }
}
```

Figure 81: Abstract Classes (1).

As we can see, the class Apple now has access to the class Fruits and its members.

The output on execution of class Apple is as follows:

```
Problems  Javadoc  Declaration  Console  Annotations
<terminated> Apple [Java Application] C:\Program Files\java\jdk1.8.0_92\bin\javaw.exe (26 juin 2017 à 10:44:50)
Fruit Name:Apple Fruit Type:Seeded
 Fruit Type:Green Apple
Fruit Name:Apple Fruit Type:Seeded fruit
 Fruit Type:Golden Apple
```

Figure 82: Abstract Classes (2).

If we try to instantiate the Fruits class in its subclass Apple, then we get the following error:

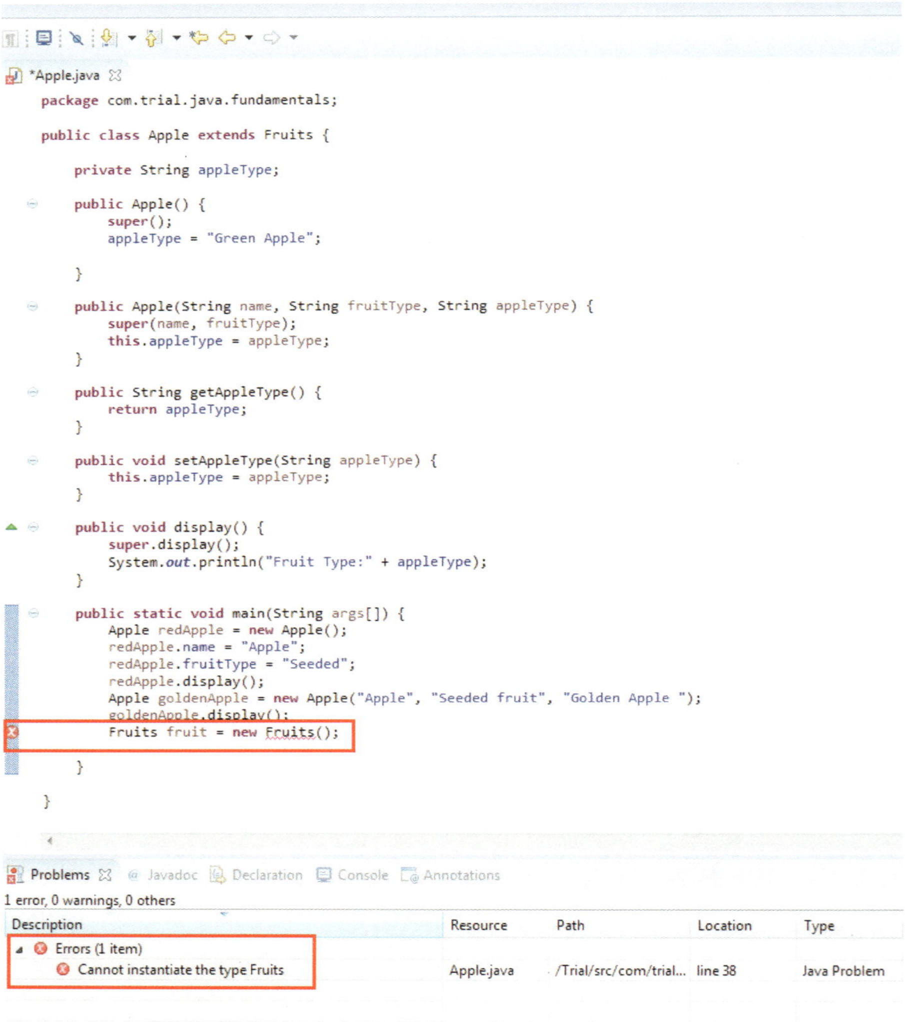

Figure 83: Abstract Classes (3).

Abstract Methods

Methods that contain the keyword abstract in their declaration are called as abstract methods. These methods are used when you want the behaviour to be defined by the subclass and not the superclass.

By way of abstract methods, the subclasses that inherit from the parent class can provide their own implementations for the abstract methods.

As shown below the syntax of an abstract method is as follows:

abstract void display();

By default, on declaring a method as abstract the class needs to be declared as abstract. Moreover, when a class inherits from the abstract class, it needs to provide the implementation of all the methods that have been declared as abstract. If the subclass doesn't provide implementations of all the abstract methods of the superclass, then it has no choice left, but to declare itself as an abstract class. But, in the end, a subclass/descendent will have to implement the methods that are abstract as you will end up with a family/hierarchy of classes that are abstract which you cannot instantiate. This is bad design as the class can never be used.

Consider the class Fruits that we used earlier. An abstract method has been added to it as follows:

Fruits.java

```
package com.trial.java.fundamentals;

public abstract class Fruits {

    String name;
    String fruitType;

    public Fruits() {}

    public Fruits(String name, String fruitType) {

        this.name = name;
        this.fruitType = fruitType;
    }

    public abstract void fruitShape();

    public String getName() {
        return name;
    }

    public void setName(String name) {
        this.name = name;
    }

    public String getFruitType() {
        return fruitType;
    }

    public void setFruitType(String fruitType) {
        this.fruitType = fruitType;
    }

    public void display() {

        System.out.println("Fruit Name:" + name+ " Fruit Type:" + fruitType);
    }
}
```

Figure 84: Abstract Methods.

As we can see, an abstract method called fruitShape() has been added to the class. The subclass Apple now needs to provide an implementation This is shown below.

```
Apple.java

package com.trial.java.fundamentals;

public class Apple extends Fruits {

    private String appleType;

    public Apple() {
        super();
        appleType = "Green Apple";

    }

    public Apple(String name, String fruitType, String appleType) {
        super(name, fruitType);
        this.appleType = appleType;
    }

    public String getAppleType() {
        return appleType;
    }

    public void setAppleType(String appleType) {
        this.appleType = appleType;
    }

    public void display() {
        super.display();
        System.out.println("Fruit Type:" + appleType);
    }

    public static void main(String args[]) {
        Apple redApple = new Apple();
        redApple.name = "Apple";
        redApple.fruitType = "Seeded";
        redApple.display();
        Apple goldenApple = new Apple("Apple", "Seeded fruit", "Golden Apple ");
        goldenApple.display();

    }

    @Override
    public void fruitShape() {

        System.out.println("Fruit Shape is round!");

    }
}
```

Figure 85: Abstract Methods (1).

Interfaces

Java includes the notion of interfaces. Interfaces are defined as reference types in Java (Gosling and McGilton, 1995).

It is, in simpler words, a collection of abstract methods. They are a collection of behaviors that can be implemented by a class. It may look and feel like a class, but it is slightly different. Principally, interfaces are made up of abstract methods.

They are declared as follows:

MyFirstInterface.java

```
package com.trial.java.fundamentals;

public interface MyFirstInterface {

    public abstract void method1();
    public abstract void method2();
    public abstract void method3();

}
```

Figure 86: Interfaces.

Similar to a java class, the extension of an interface is '.java'. Like classes, they can be stored in packages for management of namespace.

An interface is implemented by a java class. The java class that implements the interface is obligated to implement all the methods of an interface. Otherwise, similar to abstract methods, the subclass of the class implementing the interface must provide implementations for the interface methods. Else, the class needs to be declared as an abstract as well.

Implementing an interface is like signing an agreement; the class has to abide by the rules and implement the behaviour described by the interface.

Interfaces are used for providing abstraction and solving the diamond inheritance problem as discussed in section 5.1. Using interfaces multiple inheritance can be achieved and hence the diamond problem is solved.

The **implements** keyword is used to say that a class implements it.

Consider the following class the *implements* the above interface:

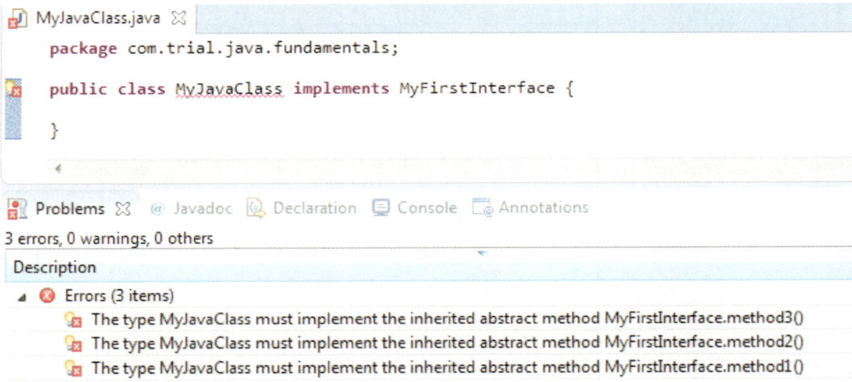

Figure 87: Interfaces (1).

But, we get a compile time error as shown above. Only using the **implements** keyword isn't enough. The implementations need to be provided as well. Once the implementation has been provided, the errors go away.

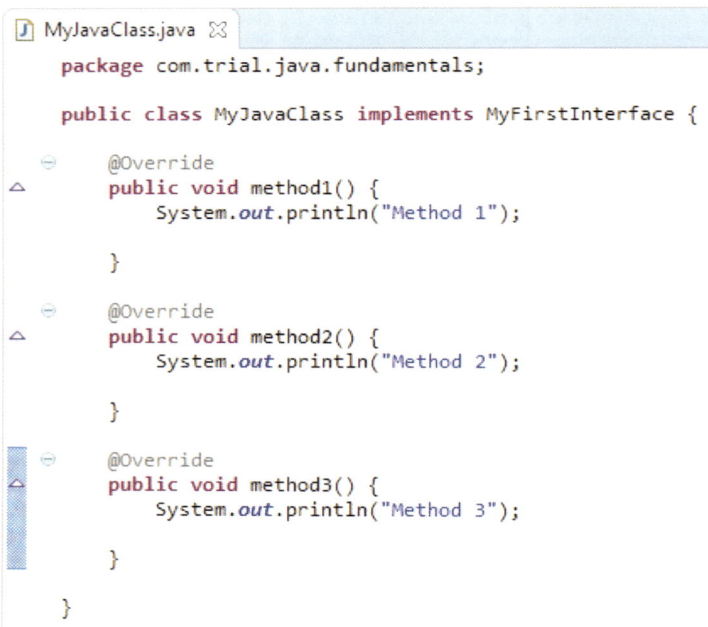

Figure 88: Interfaces (2).

Key points to know about interfaces are as follows:

- They are abstract by default. Hence, the keyword abstract isn't needed in its declaration
- Interface methods are public by default. Hence, the keyword public isn't required.
- By default, an interface is abstract and doesn't need to be declared as abstract. So, the interface that we declared above can also be declared as follows:

```
MyFirstInterface.java

package com.trial.java.fundamentals;

public interface MyFirstInterface {

    void method1();
    void method2();
    void method3();

}
```

Figure 89: Interfaces (3).

As we can see, the above declaration generates no errors.

- A class has the possibility of implementing several interfaces at a time, but a class can extend at most one class.
    - o The following declaration of a class is completely valid:

      public class Class1 implements interface1, interface2

      {

      //implementations of interface methods

      }

- An interface has the right to extend another interface; similar to classes.
- The method signature defined in the interface must be respected by the class that implements the interface.
- Like classes, interfaces can have any number of methods

- Similar to abstract classes, interfaces hold abstract methods

An interface can extend another interface as follows:

MySecondInterface.java

```
package com.trial.java.fundamentals;

public interface MySecondInterface extends MyFirstInterface {

    void display();
    void write();
}
```

Figure 90: Extending Interfaces.

As we can, the interface MySecondInterface extends from the interface that we created above. Any class that implements MySecondInterface will have to implement the methods declared in both, MySecondInterface and MyFirstInterface as well.

An interface can inherit two interfaces as well. This is shown by the example below.

Consider the interface MyThirdInterface as follows:

MyThirdInterface.java

```
package com.trial.java.fundamentals;

public interface MyThirdInterface {

    void testMethod();
}
```

Figure 91: Extending Interfaces (1).

The interface MySecondInterface extends two interfaces now: MyFirstInterface and MyThirdInterface.

This is shown in figure 92.

MySecondInterface.java

```
package com.trial.java.fundamentals;

public interface MySecondInterface extends MyFirstInterface, MyThirdInterface {

    void display();
    void write();
}
```

Figure 92: Extending Interfaces (2).

Any class that implements MySecondInterface now has to implement all the methods in MyFirstInterface, MySecondInterface and MyThirdInterface.

Suppose class X implements MySecondInterface, then I has to implement 3 methods from MyFirstInterface, 2 methods from MySecondInterface and 1 method from MyThirdInterface. So, in total class X will have to implement 6 methods.

In this way, a class can support multiple inheritance by use of several interfaces where it can implement different behaviours that can be shared among several classes.

Interfaces should be used when there is a possibility of frequent changes in your design; whereas abstract classes should be used when the design of your system is more or less stable and fixed.

For example, application frameworks can use Abstract classes as they need default services to be provided, like the Java collections framework which will be discussed in chapter 12.

Interfaces can be used when a particular behaviour is similar across classes. For example consider the class Person. A person walks; but so do many other mammals. So, instead of creating a base class for every other mammal that works such as Giraffe and so on, an interface **walk** is more practical.

Despite certain similarities between abstract classes and interfaces such as the commonality of having abstract methods and inability to instantiate them, they are different from one another in the following ways:

Table 4: Interfaces vs Abstract classes

Interfaces	Abstract Classes
Cannot have constructors	Can have constructors
All the methods are abstract	Can have non-abstract methods
It needs to be implemented using the keyword 'implements'	An abstract class needs to be inherited by another class using the keyword 'extends'
It can extend multiple interfaces	An abstract class can extend at most one class
All fields in an interface are public, final static by default	An abstract class can have non public, non static and non-final fields
Members of an interface are public by default	Abstract classes can have methods with other access modifiers such protected, private and default(no modifier)

Tagged Interfaces

Another use of interfaces is the possibility of tagging them. A tagged interface is nothing but an interface without any methods. This interface is used to carry information about the object type.

The Serialization mechanism in Java is a tagged interface. The java documentation (Serializable (Java Platform SE 8), 2015) states: "*The serialization interface has no methods or fields and serves only to identify the semantics of being serializable.*"

A tagging interface serves the following purpose:

- It helps in the creation of a common super-interface/parent. Many interfaces can extend from a particular interface which serves as their parent class. A tagging interface is understood and is meaningful only to the JVM. For example, if a class X implements the Serializable interface, it declares itself to be a member of the classes that are serializable in nature, and so when the JVM sees a class like this, it does certain operations that help in this process.
- If a class implements a tagging interface in Java, it becomes a type; like Serializable for instance.

Compile-Time and Runtime polymorphism in Java

Compile Time Polymorphism

It is nothing but method/function overloading. A method is said to be overloaded if a class consists of many methods with the same names, but different arguments. This is called as compile time polymorphism (Johnson and Foote, 1988).

An example of a class with overloaded methods is shown below:

Addtition.java

```
package com.trial.java.fundamentals;

public class Addtition {


    public void add(int a, int b)
    {
        int c= a+b;
        System.out.println("a + b = " +c);
    }

    public void add(float a, float b)
    {
        float c= a+b;
        System.out.println("a + b = " +c);
    }

    public void add(Long a, Long b)
    {
        Long c= a+b;
        System.out.println("a + b = " +c);
    }

    public int add(int a, int b, int c)
    {
        int sum = a+b+c;
        System.out.println("a + b + c = " +sum);
        return sum;
    }

    public float add(float a, float b, float c)
    {
        float sum = a+b+c;
        System.out.println("a + b + c = " +sum);
        return sum;
    }
}
```

Figure 93: Compile Time Polymorphism.

As shown in the above figure, the class Addition has several methods named **add**; each with different method parameters. This is called compile-time or static polymorphism as a method has several forms/ behaviors at compile time. This means that the compiler understands which method is being called at compile time and hence the apt name – compile time polymorphism.

An important point to note is that methods with the exact same arguments and different return types are not considered to be overloaded. The parameters need to be different else the compiler generates an error that says that the method has been duplicated.

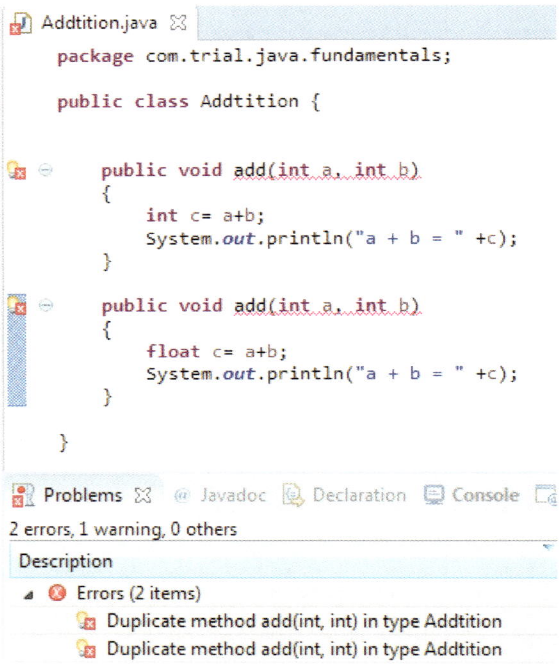

Figure 94: Compile Time Polymorphism (1).

Runtime Polymorphism

Runtime polymorphism is a way in which the call to a method is resolve dynamically. This means that the method type is determined at run-time. This is achieved by way of inheritance and method overriding. Method overriding is when a subclass implements a method present in its parent class maintaining the signature of the method. This is called as overriding the parent class implementation. The JVM determines which method it needs to call (method from the super class/subclass) at runtime.

Example:

Consider the following hierarchy

Vehicle-> TwoWheeler-> Bike

Here, the Vehicle class is the super class from which the class TwoWheeler extends and the class TwoWheeler is extended by the Bike Class.

RuntimePolymorphismTest.java

```java
package com.trial.java.fundamentals;

class Vehicle {
    public void printHello() {
        System.out.println("Hello from class Vehicle!");
    }

}

class Car extends Vehicle {
    public void printHello() {
        System.out.println("Hello from class Car!");
    }
}

class Bike extends Vehicle {
    public void printHello() {
        System.out.println("Hello from class Bike!");
    }

}

class Cycle extends Vehicle {
    public void printHello() {
        System.out.println("Hello from class Cycle!");
    }

}

public class RuntimePolymorphismTest {

    public static void main(String args[]) {

        Vehicle vehicle = new Vehicle();
        vehicle.printHello();
        Vehicle car = new Car();
        car.printHello();
        Vehicle bike = new Bike();
        bike.printHello();
        Vehicle cycle = new Cycle();
        cycle.printHello();

    }

}
```

Figure 95: Runtime Polymorphism.

As clearly seen from the above example, each of the subclasses has overridden the method printHello(). There are 4 variables/instances/ references of type Vehicle at compile time. But they hold the reference to the subclasses. Only the **object** *vehicle* truly refers to the Vehicle class. All the other instances refer to the subclasses of Vehicle class. The real 'Type' of the references **car**, **bike** and **cycle** are determined by the compiler dynamically or at run time. Hence, this is called as runtime/ dynamic polymorphism. From the output results, you can confirm that version of a method is invoked based on the actually object's type as shown below:

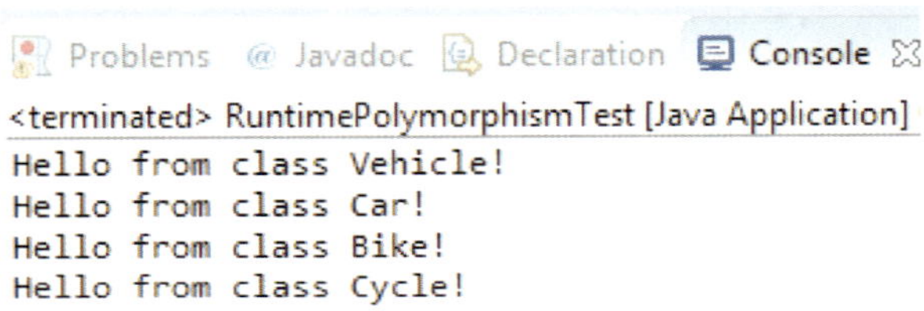

Figure 96: Runtime Polymorphism (1).

In Java, an object that has been declared to be of type X can refer to an object of class X or it can hold a reference to any of its subclasses. The compiler has the capability of resolving/invoking the right method/ function related to subclasses of class X at runtime; thereby allowing method overriding that is available in the hierarchy of class X. The compiler is able to choose which method of the subclass will be chosen based on actual 'type' of reference of the object, not the 'type' of the reference variable. This is done dynamically or at runtime, hence the apt name runtime polymorphism.

CHAPTER 6

STATEMENTS, ARRAYS AND OPERATORS

CONTROL FLOW STATEMENTS IN JAVA

In a java program, the code is generally executed in a sequential order. But, there some special statements that we can add to our code to selectively execute a block of code based on one or many conditions. These are called as control flow statements (Wu, 1996).

These statements are classified into the following types of control statements:

- Loop
- Decision
- Branch

We shall now proceed to see their definition and description in detail.

Loops

Loops help you to execute a particular piece of code in a repetitive manner until a condition has been met. In java, we have 3 types of loops.

- The for loop

For loops help you execute a block of code for a specific fixed number of times.

Consider the following example:

```
ForLoops.java

package com.trial.java.fundamentals;

public class ForLoops {

    public static void main(String args[]) {

        int i;
        for (i = 0; i < 5; i++) {
            System.out.println("Value of variable i is:" + i);
        }
    }
}
```

Figure 97: For Loop.

As we can see, we execute the loop 5 times: from index 0 to index 4

The above code produces the following output:

```
Console  Problems  Javad
<terminated> ForLoops [Java Application]
Value of variable i is:0
Value of variable i is:1
Value of variable i is:2
Value of variable i is:3
Value of variable i is:4
```

Figure 98: For Loop (1).

If you want the counter to start from 1, the 'for loop' can be manipulated as follows:

ForLoops.java

```java
package com.trial.java.fundamentals;

public class ForLoops {

    public static void main(String args[]) {

        int i;
        for (i = 1; i <= 5; i++) {
            System.out.println("Value of variable i is:" + i);
        }
    }
}
```

Figure 99: For Loop (2).

The above code produces the following output:

```
Console    Problems    Javad
<terminated> ForLoops [Java Application]
Value of variable i is:1
Value of variable i is:2
Value of variable i is:3
Value of variable i is:4
Value of variable i is:5
```

Figure 100: For Loop (3).

Furthermore, there exists 2 more variations of the 'for loop' that shall be discussed in Arrays and collections respectively.

- The while loop

This loop will execute a particular code/ block of code/statements until the given condition holds true.

This is shown by the following example:

WhileLoops.java

```
package com.trial.java.fundamentals;

public class WhileLoops {

    public static void main(String args[]) {

        int i = 1;
        while (i <= 5) {
            System.out.println("Value of variable i is:" + i);
            i++;
        }

    }
}
```

Figure 101: While Loop.

The output is as follows:

```
Console  Problems  Javadoc
<terminated> WhileLoops [Java Application]
Value of variable i is:1
Value of variable i is:2
Value of variable i is:3
Value of variable i is:4
Value of variable i is:5
```

Figure 102: While Loop (1).

As depicted by the output, the value of i has been incremented until it reaches 5, after which the control exits from the while loop.

The exit condition should be chosen carefully because if the condition is always true, we will stuck in the while loop forever. In this case the program has to be forcefully terminated else the JVM will run out of memory.

The do-while loop

This loop is an extension to the while loop. It is very similar to the while loop except that it executes the block of code at least once.

This is shown from the following example:

DoWhileLoop.java

```java
package com.trial.java.fundamentals;

public class DoWhileLoop {

    public static void main(String[] args) {

        int i=1;
         do
         {
             System.out.println("Value of i is:" + i);
             i++;
         }
         while(i<=5);


    }

}
```

Figure 103: Do-while Loop.

The output is as follows:

```
Console  Problems  Javadoc
<terminated> DoWhileLoop [Java Application]
Value of i is:1
Value of i is:2
Value of i is:3
Value of i is:4
Value of i is:5
```

Figure 104: Do-while Loop (1).

Decision Statements

Decision statements are used to make a decision to execute a particular block of code only if a particular condition or a set of conditions evaluate to true.

There are three types of decision statements:

1. If statements
2. If else statements
3. Nested If else statements
4. Switch statement

If Statements

An if statement is basically a condition that is checked before execution of a statement.

An example is as follows:

```
IfLoop.java

package com.trial.java.fundamentals;

public class IfLoop {

    public static void main(String args[]) {
        int i = 5;

        if (i == 5) {
            System.out.println(" Value of i is:" + i);
        }

        System.out.println(" Hello! ");
    }
}
```

Figure 105: If statement.

The output is as follows:

```
Console   Problems   @ Jav
<terminated> IfLoop [Java Application]
 Value of i is:5
 Hello!
```

Figure 106: If statement (1).

If else statement

This statement is an extension to the **if statement** that provides an alternate course of action in case the given condition evaluates to false.

This is demonstrated by the following example:

```
IfElseLoop.java

package com.trial.java.fundamentals;

public class IfElseLoop {

    public static void main(String args[]) {
        int i = 5;

        if (i == 5) {
            System.out.println(" Value of i is:" + i);
        } else {
            System.out.println("Value of i is not 5! ");
        }

    }
}
```

Figure 107: If-else statement.

The output is as follows:

```
Console   Problems   @ Javado
<terminated> IfElseLoop [Java Application]
 Value of i is:5
```

Figure 108: If-else statement (1).

As the value of i is 5 we get the above output. If the value of i is anything other than i we get the following statement as output.

```
Console   Problems   @ Javado
<terminated> IfElseLoop [Java Application]
Value of i is not 5!
```

Figure 109: If-else statement (2).

Nested If Else Statement

This statement is an addition to the if else where we can nest an if-else statement within another if or else statement.

This is shown by the example below:

NestedIfElseLoop.java

```java
package com.trial.java.fundamentals;

public class NestedIfElseLoop {

    public static void main(String args[]) {
        int i = 4;

        if (i > 2)
        {
            if (i == 4)
            {
                System.out.println("Value of i is equal to 4.");
            }
            else
            {
                System.out.println("Value of i is not equal to 4.");
            }
        }
    }
}
```

Figure 110: Nested If-else statements.

As shown in the above example, there is an if else loop nested inside an if loop. Depending on the value of the variable i the respective statement is printed. The output of the above program is as follows:

```
Console  Problems  Javadoc
<terminated> NestedIfElseLoop [Java Application]
Value of i is equal to 4.
```

Figure 111: Nested If-else statements (1).

Switch Statement

This type of statement provides several paths of execution for a wide variety of values. Based on the value, selective code can be executed. This statement can be used instead of complicated and long nested if else statements.

The structure of a switch statement is as follows:

switch (variable) {

case value: code to execute;

break;

case value: code to execute;

break;

default:

values_not_found_in_above_cases;

}

For instance, if we take the nested if else loop shown in figure 112, if we need to check for each value ranging from 1 to 5, the loop becomes a little tedious to handle and difficult to read as follows:

```
NestedIfElseLoop.java
package com.trial.java.fundamentals;

public class NestedIfElseLoop {

    public static void main(String args[]) {
        int i = 4;

        if (i > 0) {
            if (i == 1) {
                System.out.println("Value of i is equal to 1.");
                i++;
            }
            if (i == 2) {
                System.out.println("Value of i is equal to 2.");
                i++;
            }
            if (i == 3) {
                System.out.println("Value of i is equal to 3.");
                i++;
            }
            if (i == 4) {
                System.out.println("Value of i is equal to 4.");
                i++;
            }
            if (i == 5) {
                System.out.println("Value of i is equal to 5.");
                i++;
            } else {
                System.out.println("Value of i is 0.");
                i++;
            }
        }
    }
}
```

Figure 112: Switch statement.

This can be better done with the help of a switch statement as follows:

```
SwitchStatement.java

package com.trial.java.fundamentals;

public class SwitchStatement {

    public static void main(String args[]) {
        int i = 4;

        switch(i)
        {

            case 1: System.out.println("Value of i is equal to 1.");
            i++;
            break;

            case 2: System.out.println("Value of i is equal to 2.");
            i++;
            break;

            case 3: System.out.println("Value of i is equal to 3.");
            i++;
            break;

            case 4: System.out.println("Value of i is equal to 4.");
            i++;
            break;

            case 5: System.out.println("Value of i is equal to 5.");
            i++;
            break;

            default:
                System.out.println("Value of i is 0.");
                i++;

        }
    }
}
```

Figure 113: Switch statement (1).

The switch statement can work with the following types of primitive variables: int, byte, char and short. Starting from Java 8, switch statements work with Strings as well.

Although the above example is not very complicated and can be implemented using a nested if else loop, in real life applications, nested if else loops make the code difficult to read and understand, which is why switch cases are preferred.

Branch Statements

There are three branch statements in Java:

Break

This statement is used in the context of loops: for,while and do-while. This loop basically exits from/terminated a loop. If there are many nested loops, this statement terminates the innermost looping statement.

This is shown by the class BreakExample:

```
BreakExample.java

package com.trial.java.fundamentals;

public class BreakExample {

    public static void main(String[] args) {

        for(int i=0; i<5; i++)
        {
            System.out.println("i:" + i);
            for(int j=0;j<5; j++)
            {
                if(j==1)
                    break;
                else
                System.out.println("j:" + j);
            }
        }
    }
}
```

Figure 114: Break statement.

As shown in the example, two loops are iterating. In the inner loop a break statement has been added for a specific value of the variable j. Now, whenever the value of j is 1, the control exits from the loop.

This is evident from the output shown below:

```
Console    @ Java
<terminated> BreakExample
i:0
j:0
i:1
j:0
i:2
j:0
i:3
j:0
i:4
j:0
```

Figure 115: Break statement (1).

The output clearly shows that the value of j never goes past 0 as each time it reaches 1, the control exits from that for loop.

Continue

This statement is used in the context of a for, while or do-while loop. Basically, it skips the current iterative cycle. If the program encounters this keyword and goes back to beginning of the loop.

This is shown by the example below:

```
ContinueExample.java
package com.trial.java.fundamentals;

public class ContinueExample {

    public static void main(String[] args) {

        for (int i = 0; i < 5; i++) {
            if (i == 2)
                continue;
            else
            System.out.println("i:" + i);
        }
    }
}
```

Figure 116: Continue statement.

In the class ContinueExample, we iterate over a for loop. If the value of the variable i is 2, we call the continue statement that skips the current iteration. This is shown by the output below:

```
Console    @ Javadoc
<terminated> ContinueExample
i:0
i:1
i:3
i:4
```

Figure 117: Continue statement (1).

As seen in the output, the value of the variable i is not printed when it is 2.

Return

This statement exits from the method in which it is called or the current method. This causes the flow of the control to return back to that point in the program where the current method was called. This statement can be used in two ways: first to return a value from a method and second to return control from a method.

To return a value from a method we simply use the keyword **return** followed by the value/local variable/object to be returned.

This has been shown in the figure below:

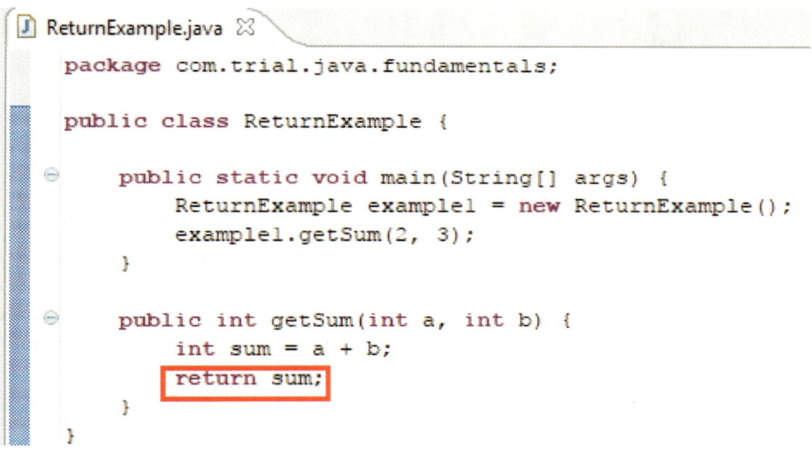

Figure 118: Return statement.

As shown by the class ReturnExample, the method getSum returns an int value. Please take a note that the data type of the value returned should always match the return type specified in the signature of the method.

To return the control from a method we simply use the return keyword without a value as follows:

```
public void method1(){
return;
}
```

ARRAYS IN JAVA

Arrays are objects in java that store many values of a particular type. The number of elements held by the array is specified at the time of creation. It is like a container that holds values of a particular type. An array has a fixed size, given at the time of creation.

An array is made up of elements and indexes that help in easy access to the individual elements of an array. The index starts from 0 in an array (Gosling, McGilton, 1995).

Each individual item held by an array is called an element and is accessed by its index. As shown below, if you want to access the 9th element in the array, its index is 8 as the indexes start with 0.

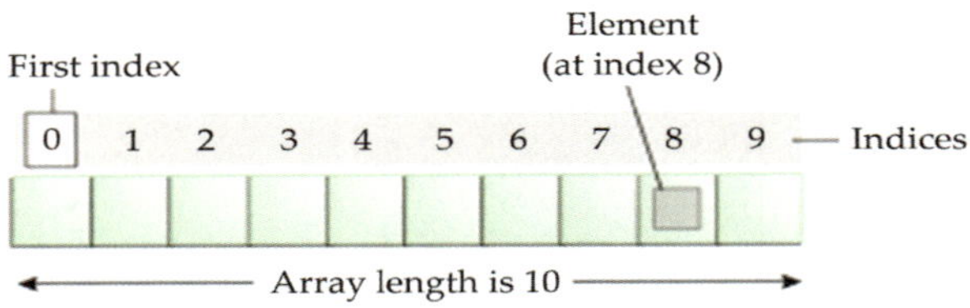

Figure 119: Array Indexes (Gosling, 2000).

The memory location of arrays is mostly contiguous which means that the blocks in memory have consecutive addresses.

Arrays have the capability of holding primitive types, objects and object references as well.

In order to create an array we need to first declare it and then create it. Upon creation, it can be initialized with the desired values. The following example shows how to create array an array of integers:

int[] arr; or int arr[]

The latter declaration is a legal way to declare an array but it is not the preferred way to declare an array as it has been adopted from C/C++.

The next step is to create the array. This is done as follows:

int arr = new int[10];

The above statement creates and array of 10 integers.

Another way to create and initialize the array at the same time is by directly providing the values it holds as follows:

int[] arr = {19, 2, 4, 35};

The above declaration both creates and initializes the array at the same time.

Arrays are advantage in terms of access and optimization. A set of data can be easily sorted and retrieved using an array. Further, any element of an array can be directly accessed using its index. But, it has a disadvantage in terms of size due to its fixed size as it does not permit us to change the size dynamically. This issue has been addressed using the collections framework that will be discussed in chapter 12.

The following example shows the declaration, creation, initialization of an array and displays its contents.

Arrays.java

```
package com.trial.java.fundamentals;

public class Arrays {

    public static void main(String[] args) {

        // declare the array
        int[] array;
        // create it
        array = new int[5];

        // the declaration and initialization can be also done in one statement
        // int [] array = new int[5];

        // initialize the array
        array[0] = 1;
        array[1] = 22;
        array[2] = 8;
        array[3] = 12;
        array[4] = 48;

        // print the contents using a for loop
        for (int i = 0; i < array.length; i++) {
            System.out.println("Element at index " + i + ":" + array[i]);
        }

        System.out.println();

        // declare and initialize in one statement
        double[] secondArray = { 1.4, 3.7, 7.2, 5.7 };

        // print the contents using a for loop
        for (int i = 0; i < secondArray.length; i++) {
            System.out.println("Element at index " + i + ":" + secondArray[i]);
        }

    }

}
```

Figure 120: Arrays.

In the above example, two arrays – one array of integers and another array of doubles have been created, initialized and displayed. The output of the example is as follows:

```
Console ⌧  Problems  @ Jav
<terminated> Arrays [Java Application]
Element at index 0:1
Element at index 1:22
Element at index 2:8
Element at index 3:12
Element at index 4:48

Element at index 0:1.4
Element at index 1:3.7
Element at index 2:7.2
Element at index 3:5.7
```

Figure 121: Arrays (1).

The above example makes use of the simple for loop to display the elements of the array. But, starting from java 5 (jdk 1.5 and above), we can use the for each loop which is shown below:

```java
Arrays.java ⌧
package com.trial.java.fundamentals;

public class Arrays {

    public static void main(String[] args) {

        // declare the array
        int[] array;
        // create it
        array = new int[5];

        // the declaration and initialization can be also done in one statement
        // int [] array = new int[5];

        // initialize the array
        array[0] = 1;
        array[1] = 22;
        array[2] = 8;
        array[3] = 12;
        array[4] = 48;

        // print the contents using a foreach loop
        System.out.println("Contents of the array of integers are: ");
        for (int element : array) {
            System.out.println (element);
        }

        System.out.println();

        // declare and initialize in one statement
        double[] secondArray = { 1.4, 3.7, 7.2, 5.7 };

        // print the contents using a foreach loop
        System.out.println("Contents of the array of doubles are: ");
        for (double element : secondArray) {
            System.out.println(element);
        }
    }
}
```

Figure 122: Arrays (2).

The output is as follows:

```
Console ⊠  Problems  @ Javadoc  D
<terminated> Arrays [Java Application] C:\Program
Contents of the array of integers are:
1
22
8
12
48

Contents of the array of doubles are:
1.4
3.7
7.2
5.7
```

Figure 123: Arrays (3).

Arrays can be used as method arguments as well. This is shown in the example below where a method that calculates the sum of all the elements in an array takes an array as an argument and returns the sum of all of its elements.

```
ArrayExample.java ⊠
package com.trial.java.fundamentals;

public class ArrayExample {

    public static void main(String[] args) {

        int[] array = { 10, 20, 30, 40 };
        ArrayExample example = new ArrayExample();
        int sum = example.calculateSum(array);
        System.out.println("Sum is:" + sum);
    }

    public int calculateSum(int[] array) {

        int result = 0;
        for (int element : array) {
            result = result + element;
        }
        return result;
    }

}
```

Figure 124: Arrays (4).

The output given by the program is as follows:

```
Console ☒  Problems  @ Javadoc
<terminated> ArrayExample [Java Application]
Sum is:100
```

Figure 125: Arrays (5).

Copying an Array

In java, we have the functionality of copying of an array that is system defined. The System class has a method called arraycopy that enables you to copy the content of one array into another.

The syntax of this method is as follows (Gosling, 2000):

public static void arraycopy(Object src, int srcPos, Object dest, int destPos, int length)

where srcPos and destPos are the source and destination positions respectively.

The following example shows the use of arraycopy method:

```
ArrayCopyDemo.java ☒
package com.trial.java.fundamentals;

class ArrayCopyDemo {
    public static void main(String[] args) {
        int[] srcArray = { 1,3,12, 4,6, 9 };
        int[] dstArray = new int[6];

        System.arraycopy(srcArray, 0, dstArray, 0, 6);
        System.out.println("The contents of the copied array are: ");
        for(int i=0; i<dstArray.length;i++)
        {
            System.out.println(dstArray[i]);
        }
    }
}
```

Figure 126: Arrays (6).

The output of the use of arraycopy is shown below:

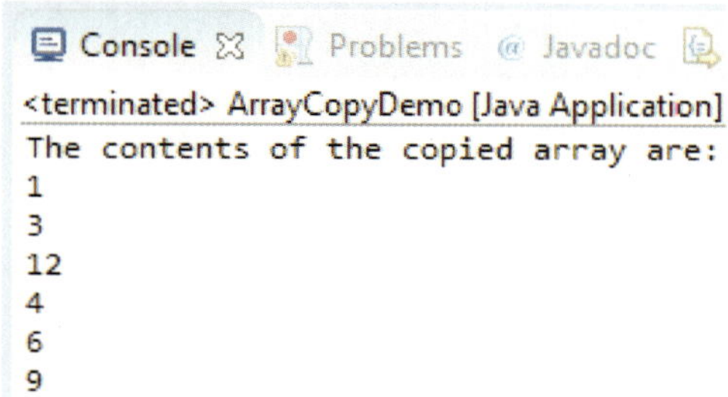

Figure 127: Arrays (7).

Multidimensional arrays

In java, we have the possibility of having arrays of arrays (embedded/nested) with the help of multidimensional arrays (Gosling, 2000). The data/information is stored in the form of rows and column; similar to a matrix or a database.

The declaration of a multidimensional array can be done in the following ways:

- int[][] array;
- int [][] array;
- int array [][];
- int []array [];

A multidimensional array can be initialized in the following way:
int[][] array = new int[2][3];// two rows and three columns:

This array can be initialized as follows:

arr[0][0]=1;

arr[0][1]=2;

arr[1][0]=3;

arr[1][1]=4;

arr[2][0]=5;

arr[2][1]=6;

The example below shows how to correctly declare, initialize and display the values of a multidimensional array.

```
MultidimensionalArray.java

package com.trial.java.fundamentals;

public class MultidimensionalArray {

    public static void main(String[] args) {

        int[][] array = new int[2][3];// array of two rows and three columns

        //initializing the array
        array[0][0] = 1;
        array[0][1] = 2;
        array[0][2] = 3;
        array[1][0] = 4;
        array[1][1] = 5;
        array[1][2] = 6;

        // printing the array
        for (int i = 0; i < 2; i++) {
            for (int j = 0; j < 3; j++) {
                System.out.print(array[i][j] + " ");
            }
            System.out.println();
        }

    }

}
```

Figure 128: Multidimensional Arrays.

The output is as follows:

```
Console  Problems  Javadoc  Declar
<terminated> MultidimensionalArray [Java Application]
1 2 3
4 5 6
```

Figure 129: Multidimensional Arrays (1).

OPERATORS IN JAVA

Operators are nothing but special characters/symbols that execute operations on one or more operands. In java, a wide variety of operators have been provided that help in manipulation of variables.

Operators in Java are divided into the following groups:

- Assignment Operators
- Arithmetic Operators
- Unary Operators
- Relational Operators
- Conditional Operators
- Bitwise Operators

We shall now see each of the operators in detail.

Assignment Operator

This is one of the most commonly used operators in any programming language. It is visible in almost all types of code.

The assignment operator assigns the value of the operand on the right side to the operand on the left side.

A simple example:

int x =20;

Here the value 20 is assigned to the variable x.

Arithmetic Operators

Java supports arithmetic operations such as addition, subtraction, multiplication, division and remainder with the help of arithmetic operators.

The subsequent example shows the use of the operators +,-,*,/ and % for the operations addition, subtraction, multiplication, division and remainder respectively.

```
ArithmeticOperators.java

public class ArithmeticOperators {

    public static void main(String[] args) {

        // additive operator
        int result = 2 + 3;
        System.out.println("The sum after addition operation is:" + result);

        // subtraction operator
        result = 5 - 2;
        System.out.println("The result after subtraction operation is:"
                + result);

        // multiplicative operator
        result = 5 * 5;
        System.out.println("The result after multiplication operation is:"
                + result);

        // division operator
        result = 10 / 2;
        System.out.println("The result after division operation is:" + result);

        // remainder operator
        result = 11 % 2;
        System.out
        .println("The result after remainder operation is: " + result);
    }

}
```

Figure 130: Arithmetic Operators.

The output of the above code is as follows:

```
Console   Problems
<terminated> ArithmeticOperators [Java Application] C:\Program Files\Java\
The sum after addition operation is:5
The result after subtraction operation is:3
The result after multiplication operation is:25
The result after division operation is:5
The result after remainder operation is: 1
```

Figure 131: Arithmetic Operators (1).

Unary Operators

Unary operators, as their name suggests work only on a single operand. The work on one operand and perform operations such as incrementing a value, decrementing a value, inverting a value and so on.

There are 5 different types of unary operators in java. They are as follows:

+ is used to describe positive values, although all values are positive without the need to specify this symbol with it

The '–' operator is used to specify that a value is negative

The '++' operator increments the value of the operand by 1

The '–'operator decrements the value of the operand by 1

The ! operator is used to negate/complement the value of the operand. In case of a Boolean value, its value is inverted from true to false or vice versa

They following class UnaryOperators tests these operators:

```
UnaryOperators.java
public class UnaryOperators {

    public static void main(String[] args) {

        // declare and initialize the variable value to negative 5
        int value = -5;
        // the value is now -5
        System.out.println(value);

        // update the variable value and make it positive
        value = +5;
        // the value is now 5
        System.out.println(value);

        // increment the value of the variable by 1
        value++;
        // the value is now 6
        System.out.println(value);

        // decrement the value of the variable by 1
        value--;
        // the value is now 5
        System.out.println(value);

        boolean isFalse = false;
        // false value
        System.out.println(isFalse);
        // update the variable isFalse to true by using the logical complement
        // operator
        System.out.println(!isFalse);
    }
}
```

Figure 132: Unary Operators.

The output produced by the program UnaryOperators is as follows:

```
Console
<terminated> UnaryOperators [Java Application]
-5
5
6
5
false
true
```

Figure 133: Unary Operators (1).

Relational Operators

These operators help determine if an operand is less than, greater than or equal to another operand. They are as follows:

== equal to

< less than

<= less than or equal to

> greater than

>= greater than or equal to

!= not equal to

The following class RelationalOperators demonstrated the use of these operators:

```
RelationalOperators.java
class RelationalOperators {

    public static void main(String[] args) {
        int x = 2;
        int y = 2;
        if (x == y)
            System.out.println("x == y");
        x = 4;
        if (x > y)
            System.out.println("x > y");
        if (x < y)
            System.out.println("x < y");
        if (x >= y)
            System.out.println("x >= y");
        if (x != y)
            System.out.println("x != y");

    }
}
```

Figure 134: Relational Operators.

The output produced by the class RelationalOperators is as follows:

```
Console    Problems
<terminated> RelationalOperators [Java Application]
x == y
x > y
x >= y
x != y
```

Figure 135: Relational Operators (1).

Conditional AND and OR Operators

These two operators perform logical AND and OR operations on two expressions of Boolean nature respectively.

The important thing to note in case of these operators is that they show 'short circuit' behaviour, which means that if the first operand is false; the second operand/expression is not evaluated.

The conditional operators have been demonstrated using the class ConditionalOperators as follows:

```java
ConditionalOperators.java
class ConditionalOperators {

    public static void main(String[] args){
        int x = 4;
        int y = 5;
        if((x == 4) && (y == 5))
            System.out.println("Both values x and y are equal");
        if((x == 4) || (y == 2))
            System.out.println("The value is either 4 or 2");
    }
}
```

Figure 136: Conditional Operators.

The output of the class is as follows:

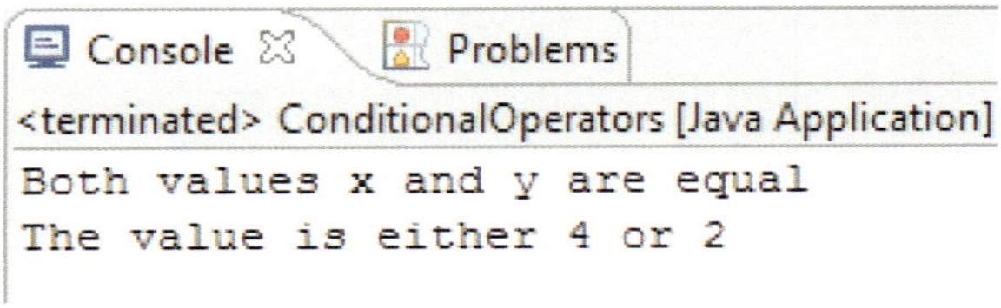

Figure 137: Conditional Operators (1).

The Bitwise Operators

In java there are operators that work on bits, performing bit by bit operations. These are defined by Java and can be applied to the following primitive types: int, long, char, short and byte.

There are four different bitwise operators and two bitshift opeartors in Java.

The bitwise opeartors are: & or AND, | or OR, ^ or EXOR and ~ Negation/complement.

The bitshift operators are: left shift (<<) and right shift (>>)

The bitwise operators work on operands that are expresses in binary such as 00000010. or 2 (it decimal).

The & opearator will perform a logical bitwise AND on two operands

The | opearator will perform a logical bitwise OR on two operands

The ^ opearator will perform a logical bitwise EXOR (exclusive OR) on two operands

The ~ opearator (unary/operates on a single operand) will perform a logical bitwise inversion of the operand

For example. Consider two values 00000010 and 00000110 (2 and 3 in decimal respectively).

The & would yield 00000010

The | would yield 00000110

The ^ would yield 00000010

The ~ for both would yield 11111101 and 11111001 respectively.

The left shift operator (<<) will shift a pattern to the left by the number of digits specified and the right shift operator (>>) will shift a pattern to the right by the number of digits specified.

For the left shift operator the syntax is **number << p** where number is the number in bits and p is the number of positions to shift.

For example consider the bit value 00000011 or 3.

The left shift 3 << 2 means that shift the bits of the number 3 by 2 positions to the left.

So, applying this on the binary value, we move the bits to the left as shown below:

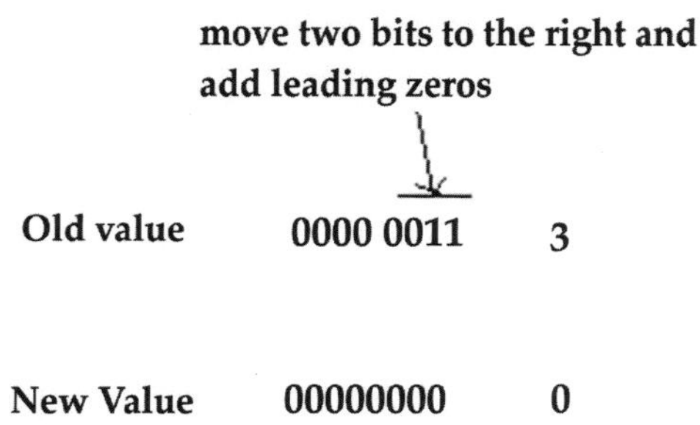

Figure 138: Bitwise Operators.

For the right shift operator the syntax is **number** >> **p** where number is the number in bits and p is the number of positions to shift.

For example consider the bit value 00000011 or 3.

The right shift 3 >> 2 means that shift the bits of the number 3 by 2 positions to the right.

Using the bit value 00000011, we get the value 00000000 which is equivalent to 0 in decimal.

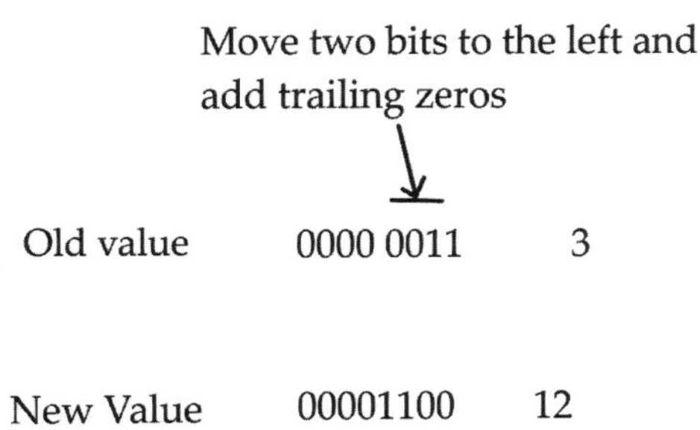

Figure 139: Bitwise Operators (1).

Shorthand Operators

We have the following shorthand assignment operators in java:

+=, -=,*=, /=,%=

1 += : This operator is used as follows: a+= b;

This translates into a= a+b;

This is a way to reduce code complexity in java.

3. -=: This operator is used as follows: a*=b;

This statement is equivalent to a=a*b;

4. /=: This operator is used as follows: a/=b;

This statement is equivalent to a=a/b;

5. %=: This operator is used as follows: a%=b;

This statement is equivalent to a=a-b;

The following program named ShorthandOperators describes the use of these operators.

ShorthandOperators.java

```
public class ShorthandOperators {

    public static void main(String[] args) {

        int a = 15;
        int b = 10;
        // += Assignment Operator
        System.out.println("+= Assignment Operator");
        a += b;
        System.out.println("value of a is:" + a);

        System.out.println("-= Assignment Operator");

        a -= b;
        System.out.println("value of a is:" + a);

        System.out.println("*= Assignment Operator");
        a *= b;
        System.out.println("value of a is:" + a);

        System.out.println("/= Assignment Operator");
        a /= b;
        System.out.println("value of a is:" + a);

        System.out.println("%= Assignment Operator");
        a %= b;
        System.out.println("value of a is:" + a);
    }
```

Figure 140: Shorthand Operators.

The output produced by the program ShorthandOperators is as follows:

```
Console
<terminated> ShorthandOperators [Java Application]
+= Assignment Operator
value of a is:25
-= Assignment Operator
value of a is:15
*= Assignment Operator
value of a is:150
/= Assignment Operator
value of a is:15
%= Assignment Operator
value of a is:5
```

Figure 141: Shorthand Operators (1).

Conditional or Ternary Operator

The conditional or ternary operator(?:) operates on 3 operands. It main functionality consists of evaluation of Boolean expressions and its aim is to decide the final value that must be assigned to the given variable.

The syntax of the conditional operator is as follows:

x = (expression to evaluate) ? value to assign if expression evaluates to true : value to assign if expression evaluates to false

The following class ConditionalOperator demonstrates the use of this operator.

```java
// ConditionOperator.java
public class ConditionOperator {

    public static void main(String[] args) {
        int x = 5;
        int y;
        // The expression evaluates to true. Hence the output is 10.
        y = (x == 5) ? 10 : 20;
        System.out.println("Value of y is : " + y);

        // The expression evaluates to false. Hence the output is 20.
        y = (x == 1) ? 10 : 20;
        System.out.println("Value of y is : " + y);

    }

}
```

Figure 142: Ternary Operator.

The output produced by the class ConditionOperator is as follows:

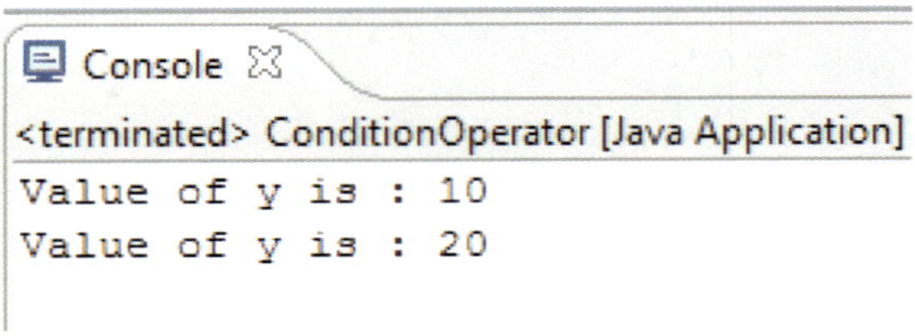

Figure 143: Ternary Operator (1).

CHAPTER 7

MISCELLANEOUS CLASSES

STRING CLASS IN JAVA

Generally strings are nothing but a sequence of characters. But in java they are objects that represent these characters. All the string manipulations are done via the String class in java. Any string declared in java is an instance of this class.

Similar to arrays a string can be declared in 2 ways:

- new operator

String str = new String("String 1 ");

- string literal

String str = "String 1";

A simple example of string declaration is as follows.

```
StringExample.java

package com.trial.java.fundamentals;

public class StringExample {

    public static void main(String args[]) {

        String string1 = new String("String 1");
        System.out.println(string1);

        String string2 = "String 2";
        System.out.println(string2);
    }

}
```

Figure 144: String Declarations.

The output of the class StringExample is as follows:

```
Console  Problems  Javadoc
<terminated> StringExample [Java Application]
String 1
String 2
```

Figure 145: String Declarations (1).

An important note about the String class is that it is immutable. Immutability means that once the objects are created, the objects cannot be changed (Gosling, 2000). Immutability has been discussed in chapter 11.

Another important concept in terms of Strings is the String pool. This is nothing but a pool of strings that is maintained that helps reusability of strings that have been created so far. By use of this pool, Strings created using literals can be reused. If a string literal has been used repeatedly in the java code, only a single copy of it is created, which save space.

For example if a string is created as follows:

String string1 = “String1”;

The value ‘String1’ is added to the pool. Now, if we create another string string2 as follows, then a new object isn’t created. The object string2 points to the value ‘String1’ in the string pool. This is depicted in figure 146:

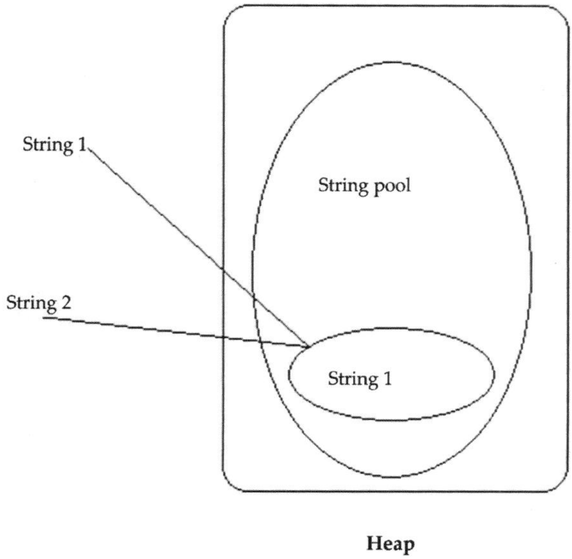

Figure 146: String Pool.

The pool cannot be used when a string is created using the new operator because this forces a brand new String instance to be allocated.

String Operations in Java

The String class in Java provides us with a range of methods that help us manipulate strings. We are now going to discuss a few of these methods (Gosling, 2000).

a. Concatenate: The concatenate method is used to concatenate two Strings. Its syntax is string1.concatenate(string2);

b. Length: The length method returns the length of a string. Syntactically is written as *String.length();*

c. Replace, replaceFirst and ReplaceAll: These methods are used to replace certain parts of the string

d. toLowerCase and toUpperCase: These methods are used to convert an uppercase string to lowercase and vice versa.

e. IndexOf: This method returns the index of the character.

f. CompareTo and compareToIgnoreCase: This method compares the values of 2 strings and returns 0 is they are equal, a value less than zero if the string is smaller and a value greater than 0 if the string is larger in size.

The use of the above methods has been demonstrated in the following class StringExample:

StringExample.java

```
package com.trial.java.fundamentals;

public class StringExample {

    public static void main(String args[]) {

        String string1 = new String("MyfirstString");
        String string2 = "Today";
        System.out.println(string1);
        // concatenate string1 and string2
        string1 = string1.concat(string2);
        System.out.println("Concatenated String: " + string1);
        int length = string1.length();
        System.out.println("Length of the String is:" + length);
        // replace only one character
        string1 = string1.replace("My", "first");
        System.out.println("The String after replace():" + string1);

        // replace the first occurrence of a substring
        string1 = string1.replaceFirst("Today", "Two");
        System.out.println("The String after replaceFirst():" + string1);

        // replace all the occurrences of a substring
        string1 = string1.replaceAll("first", "My");
        System.out.println("The String after replaceAll():" + string1);

        // convert the entire string to uppercase
        string1 = string1.toUpperCase();
        System.out.println("The String after toUpperCase():" + string1);

        // convert the entire string to lowercase
        string1 = string1.toLowerCase();
        System.out.println("The String after toLowerCase():" + string1);

        // get the first index of a character
        int index = string1.indexOf('t');
        System.out.println("The index of the character t is :" + index);

        String string3 = "mymystringtwo";
        // compare two Strings
        int result = string1.compareTo(string3);
        if (result == 0)
            System.out.println("The two strings are equal");

    }
}
```

Figure 147: String Operations.

The output generated by the class StringExample is as follows:

```
Console  Problems  @ Javadoc  Declaration  Ann
<terminated> StringExample [Java Application] C:\Program Files\java\j
MyfirstString
Concatenated String: MyfirstStringToday
Length of the String is:18
The String after replace():firstfirstStringToday
The String after replaceFirst():firstfirstStringTwo
The String after replaceAll():MyMyStringTwo
The String after toUpperCase():MYMYSTRINGTWO
The String after toLowerCase():mymystringtwo
The index of the character t is :5
The two strings are equal
```

Figure 148: String Operations (1).

The String class provides many other methods that facilitate string manipulations. They can be accessed at javadocs (Java Platform SE 8, 2015).

StringBuffer CLASS

This class is used when we need to create strings that need to be modified a lot of times. This class is exactly like the String class except that it not immutable. The string object can be changed as often as required. An advantage of this class is that it is synchronized or thread-safe.

A simple example using the method reverse() of this class to determine if a String is a palindrome is shown below:

```java
Palindrome.java

public class Palindrome {

    public static void main(String[] args) {

        Palindrome object1 = new Palindrome();
        // returns true
        object1.isPalindrome("Madam");
        // returns false
        object1.isPalindrome("Test");

    }

    public void isPalindrome(String inputString) {
        StringBuffer reverseString = new StringBuffer(inputString).reverse();
        String finalString = reverseString.toString();

        if (finalString.equalsIgnoreCase(inputString))
            System.out.println("The input string " + inputString + " is a palindrome!");
        else
            System.out.println("The input string " + inputString + " is not a palindrome!");

    }
}
```

Figure 149: StringBuffer class.

The output generated by the above class is as follows:

```
Console ✕  Problems  @ Javadoc  Declara
<terminated> Palindrome [Java Application] C:\Program
The input string Madam is a palindrome!
The input string Test is not a palindrome!
```

Figure 150: StringBuffer class (1).

StringBuilder CLASS

This class was introduced in Java 5 (jdk 1.5). This class is also used when we need to create and manipulate mutable string Strings. It is exactly similar to the StringBuffer class except for the fact that it is not thread-safe.

A simple example of the use of these classes is shown below using the StringExample class:

```java
StringBufferexample.java
package com.trial.java.fundamentals;

class StringBufferexample {

    public static void main(String args[]) {
        StringBuffer string1 = new StringBuffer("MyFirst");
        //append another string to it
        string1.append("String");
        //prints MyFirstString
        System.out.println(string1);

        String string2= "MySecondString";
        //concatenate another string
        string2.concat("Today");
        //prints MySecondString as the value needs to be assigned back to string2
        System.out.println(string2);
        //the correct way to concatenate Strings that belong to the String class
        string2 = string2.concat("Today");
        //correctly prints MySecondStringToday
        System.out.println(string2);
    }
}
```

Figure 151: StringBuffer class (2).

The results generated by the above program are:

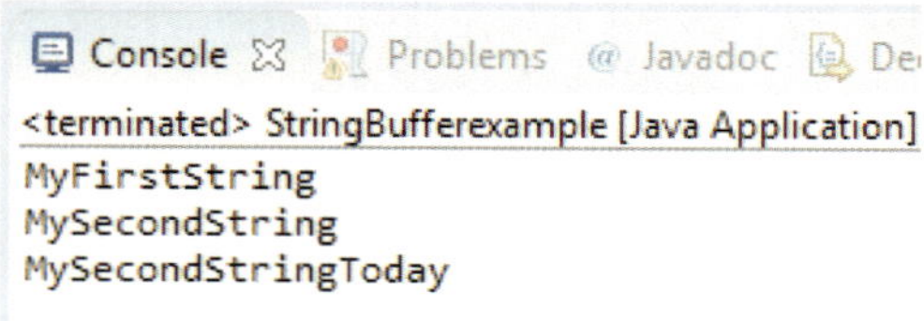

Figure 152: StringBuffer class (3).

THE OBJECT CLASS

The Object class is the superclass of all the classes in Java. Every java class is descendant (directly or indirectly) of this class. This class provides some useful methods that are inherited by every class. As a programmer, you are not obligated to use these methods, but if you do wish to incorporate them in your programs, you have to override them as per your specifications.

Some of the methods provided by this class are as follows:

Table 5: Methods of the objects class

Method	**Description**
Protected Object clone() throws CloneNotSupportedException	This methods creates a copy/clone of the object that invokes it and returns the copy
public boolean equals(Object obj)	This method compares two objects and returns true if the objects are equal
public final Class getClass()	This method returns the runtime class of an object
public int hashCode()	This method returns the hashcode value for the object invoking it
public String toString()	This method returns the object in the form of a string
protected void finalize() throws Throw-able	This method is called by the garbage collector on an object when the object is not referenced anymore

These methods have been explained below.

a. The toString Method()

The method toString() in java is used to represent an object as a string (Wu, 1996). This method is a method of the object class. On overriding this method, an object can be represented in a customized way. This is shown as below:

```java
ToStringExample.java

package com.trial.java.fundamentals;

public class ToStringExample {

    int variable1;
    String variable2;


    public ToStringExample(int variable1, String variable2) {

        this.variable1 = variable1;
        this.variable2 = variable2;
    }

    //return a String representation of the object in a customized way
    public String toString()
    {
        return "Variable1:" + variable1 + " Variable2:" + variable2;
    }

    public static void main(String[] args) {

        ToStringExample obj1 = new ToStringExample(1, "Hi!");
        System.out.println(obj1);

    }

}
```

Figure 153: toString() method.

As shown by the program ToStringExample above, the object can be printed directly in the System.out statement similar to other variables. The output generated by this program is shown in figure 22:

```
Console  Problems  @ Javadoc
<terminated> ToStringExample [Java Application]
Variable1:1 Variable2:Hi!
```

Figure 154: toString() method (1).

If we do not override the toString() method the output is as follows:

```
ToStringExample.java

package com.trial.java.fundamentals;

public class ToStringExample {

    int variable1;
    String variable2;

    public ToStringExample(int variable1, String variable2) {

        this.variable1 = variable1;
        this.variable2 = variable2;
    }

    public static void main(String[] args) {

        ToStringExample obj1 = new ToStringExample(1, "Hi!");
        // without overriding the toString() method
        System.out.println(obj1);
    }
}
```

```
Console  Problems  Javadoc  Declaration  Annotations
<terminated> ToStringExample [Java Application]
com.trial.java.fundamentals.ToStringExample@15db9742
```

Figure 155: toString() method (2).

As seen by the output, the toString() method of the object class is invoked and a hashcode is printed. If we want to print the actual values of the objects, the toString() method needs to be overridden.

b. clone()

This method creates a copy and returns a copy of the object that invokes it. It throws a CloneNotSupported Exception if the invoking class doesn't support the Cloneable interface.

```
CloneExample.java

package com.java.collections;

public class CloneExample implements Cloneable {

    int x = 0;

    public static void main(String[] args) throws CloneNotSupportedException {

        // create an object
        CloneExample object1 = new CloneExample();
        // clone the object
        CloneExample object2 = (CloneExample) object1.clone();

        // print both the objects
        System.out.println(object1);
        System.out.println(object2);
    }

    public Object clone() throws CloneNotSupportedException {

        return super.clone();
    }

    public String toString() {
        return "x:" + this.x;
    }

}
```

Figure 156: clone() method.

The output is as follows:

```
Console  Problen
<terminated> CloneExample
x:0
x:0
```

Figure 157: clone() method (1).

c. finalize(): This is a method that may or may not be invoked/called on an object when the object is no longer in use (Goetz and Peierls, 2006). This method may or may not be called by the garbage collector. We can use this method in our java class to send a request to the jvm to clean up/ free memory, but there is no sure guarantee that it will be called/invoked.

This method can be invoked using a simple object.finalize() method call.

As there is no guarantee that this method will be called, it is advised to close up all the resources that we use in our program before exiting. This is valid for file description and input streams which will be discussed in Chapter 9.

d. getClass(): This method returns an instance object of the java type/class **Class.** The object of type Class has several methods that can be used to obtain information about the invoking class itself such as the methods of the class, the members, variables and so on.

GetClassExample.java

```
package com.java.collections;

public class GetClassExample {

    public static void main(String[] args) {

        GetClassExample object1 = new GetClassExample();
        // get the class of the object
        System.out.println(object1.getClass());
        // get full name of the class
        System.out.println(object1.getClass().getCanonicalName());
        // get the class of the object
        Integer i = 3;
        System.out.println(i.getClass());

    }

}
```

The output is as follows:

Console Problems

```
<terminated> GetClassExample [Java Application] C:\Pro
class com.java.collections.GetClassExample
com.java.collections.GetClassExample
class java.lang.Integer
```

e. equals(): This method returns true if the invoking object and the object passed as a parameter are the same. It uses the equals operator (==) to compare two objects and determine their equality. This works well in case of primitive data types. But in case of objects, this is not correct. The '===' operator checks if the references of the two objects under consideration are equal, which isn't correct. The desired behaviour is that the method should return true if the two objects contain the same information. Hence, in case of Objects, if you want to check the equivalence of two objects this method should be overridden.

A simple java program demonstrating the use of the equals() method is shown below:

EqualsExample.java

```
package com.java.collections;

public class EqualsExample {

    int x;
    int y;

    public EqualsExample(int x, int y) {
        this.x = x;
        this.y = y;
    }

    public static void main(String[] args) {

        Integer a = 4;
        Integer b = 4;

        if (a.equals(b))
            System.out.println("The Intergers are equal");
        else
            System.out.println("The Tntegers are not equal");

        EqualsExample obj1 = new EqualsExample(1, 2);
        EqualsExample obj2 = new EqualsExample(1, 2);

        if (obj1.equals(obj2))
            System.out.println("The objects are equal");
        else
            System.out.println("The objects are not equal");

    }
}
```

In the example, we use the equals() method to compare Integers and objects.

In case of integers, it returns true; but in case of the objects it returns false as the equals() method has not been overridden in the class.

The output is:

Console Problems

<terminated> EqualsExample [Java Application]

```
The Intergers are equal
The objects are not equal
```

To correctly check if the objects are equal, we override the method as shown below:

EqualsExample.java

```
package com.java.collections;

public class EqualsExample {

    Integer x;
    Integer y;

    public EqualsExample(int x, int y) {
        this.x = x;
        this.y = y;
    }

    public static void main(String[] args) {

        Integer a = 4;
        Integer b = 4;

        if (a.equals(b))
            System.out.println("The Intergers are equal");
        else
            System.out.println("The Tntegers are not equal");

        EqualsExample obj1 = new EqualsExample(1, 2);
        EqualsExample obj2 = new EqualsExample(1, 2);

        if (obj1.equals(obj2))
            System.out.println("The objects are equal");
        else
            System.out.println("The objects are not equal");

    }

    public boolean equals(EqualsExample o)

    {
        if (o == null)
            return false;
        else
            return ((this.x).equals(o.x)) && ((this.y).equals(o.y));

    }
}
```

Now that the method has been properly overridden, we get the desired output as follows:

Console Problems

```
<terminated> EqualsExample [Java Application]
The Intergers are equal
The objects are equal
```

Another important point to note is that if your class overrides the equals method, then it should override the hashcode() method as well. The hashCode() method is described next.

f. hashcode(): This method returns the hash code value of the object invoking it which is the memory address of the object in hexadecimal. According to the Java definitions and documentation, if two objects are equal, so is their hashcode (Gosling, 2000).

Hence, if you override the method equals(), then you change the way the objects are compared for equality and hence the default hashcode() method and its implementation is no longer valid for your class. As a result of this behaviour, the hashcode() methd must be overridden if you override the equals() method in your class.

An example demonstrating the use of the hascode() method along with the equals() method is shown below:

```
HashCodeExample.java
package com.java.collections;

public class HashCodeExample {

    Integer x;
    Integer y;

    public HashCodeExample(int x, int y) {
        this.x = x;
        this.y = y;
    }

    public static void main(String[] args) {

        HashCodeExample obj1 = new HashCodeExample(1, 2);
        HashCodeExample obj2 = new HashCodeExample(1, 2);

        if (obj1.equals(obj2))
            System.out.println("The objects are equal");
        else
            System.out.println("The objects are not equal");

    }

    public boolean equals(HashCodeExample o)

    {
        if (o == null)
            return false;
        else
            return ((this.x).equals(o.x)) && ((this.y).equals(o.y));

    }

    public int hashCode() {
        int code = 31;
        return ((code * x.hashCode() * y.hashCode()));
    }
}
```

The output generated is as follows:

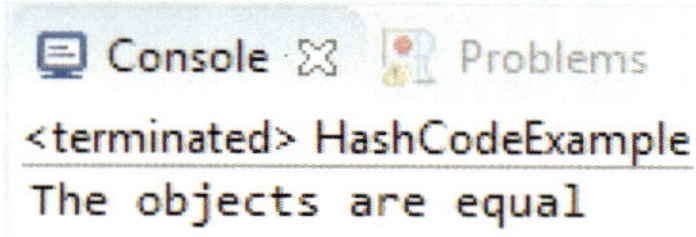

The hashcode() method can be overridden in any way that you want. Generally, the use of prime numbers along with recursive calls to the hashcode method by the members of the class is suggested.

An important point is that if two objects have the same hashcode they may or may not be equal, but if two objects are equal they must have the same hashcode.

Another simple way to override the equals() and the hashcode() method is by using the Eclipse IDE. Eclipse offers this functionality. This can be obtained in the menu obtained when you right-click on the page. This is shown below:

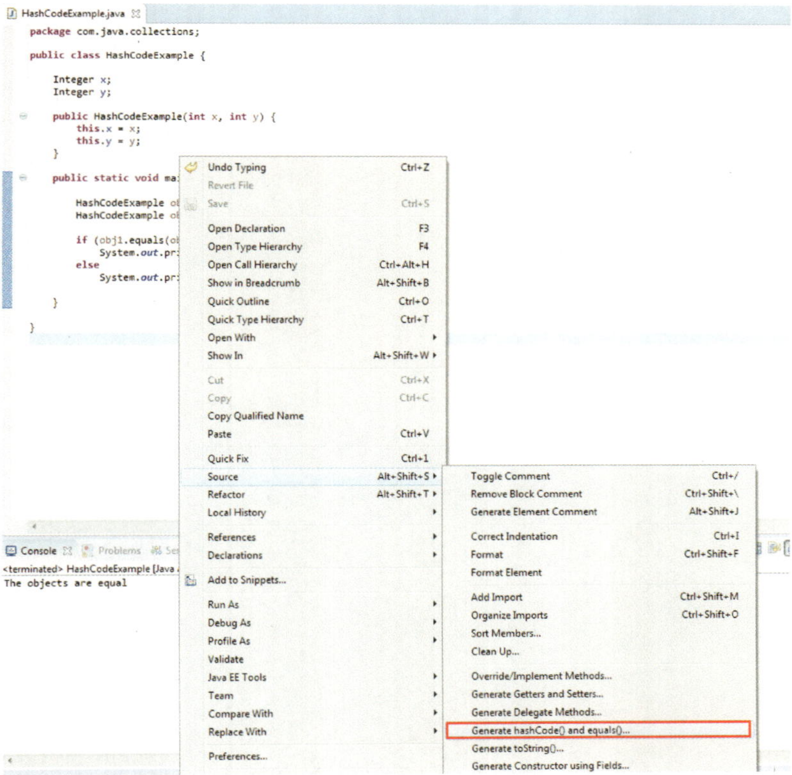

A dialog pops up and you can click on Ok. The equals() and hashcode() method are generated as follows:

HashCodeExample.java

```
package com.java.collections;

public class HashCodeExample {

    Integer x;
    Integer y;

    public HashCodeExample(int x, int y) {
        this.x = x;
        this.y = y;
    }

    public static void main(String[] args) {

        HashCodeExample obj1 = new HashCodeExample(1, 2);
        HashCodeExample obj2 = new HashCodeExample(1, 2);

        if (obj1.equals(obj2))
            System.out.println("The objects are equal");
        else
            System.out.println("The objects are not equal");

    }

    @Override
    public int hashCode() {
        final int prime = 31;
        int result = 1;
        result = prime * result + ((x == null) ? 0 : x.hashCode());
        result = prime * result + ((y == null) ? 0 : y.hashCode());
        return result;
    }

    @Override
    public boolean equals(Object obj) {
        if (this == obj)
            return true;
        if (obj == null)
            return false;
        if (getClass() != obj.getClass())
            return false;
        HashCodeExample other = (HashCodeExample) obj;
        if (x == null) {
            if (other.x != null)
                return false;
        } else if (!x.equals(other.x))
            return false;
        if (y == null) {
            if (other.y != null)
                return false;
        } else if (!y.equals(other.y))
            return false;
        return true;
    }

}
```

DATE CLASS IN JAVA

This class is present in the java.util package and represents a real time date. This utility class in Java provides us with methods and constructors that help us manipulate Date and time constructs in java. This class implements the Serializable, Cloneable and Comparable interface.

Some important methods and constructors of this class are as follows:

Table 6: Methods of the Date class

Method/Constructor	**Description**
Date()	Creates a date object with current date and time
Date(long milliseconds)	Creates a date object with an argument. This argument is the time elapsed in milliseconds after January 1 1970 at midnight.
long getTime()	Returns the time that has elapsed since January 1, 1970.
setTime(long time)	Updates the current date and time to specified time
boolean after(Date date)	Checks if the current date comes after the specified date and returns true if it does
boolean before(Date date)	Checks if the current date comes after the specified date and returns true if it does
int compareTo(Date date)	Compares two dates. Returns : -0 if dates are equal -Positive value if the first Date is after the specified date -Negative value if the first Date is before the specified Date

We shall now take a look at some examples demonstrating the use of the Date class.

Example 1: Create a Date object

DateExample.java

```java
package com.java.utilities;

import java.util.Date;

public class DateExample {

    public static void main(String[] args) {

        // Creation of date objects
        //create a date object with the current date and time
        Date date1 = new Date();
        System.out.println("Date1 : " + date1);

        //create a date object with long parameter
        Date date2 = new Date(999999999);
        System.out.println(date2);

    }
}
```

The output is as follows:

Console | Problems

```
<terminated> DateExample [Java Application] C:\Proc
Date1 : Mon Jul 17 11:23:30 CEST 2017
Mon Jan 12 14:46:39 CET 1970
```

Example 2: Manipulate date objects

DateExample1.java

```
package com.java.utilities;

import java.util.Date;

public class DateExample1 {

    public static void main(String[] args) {

        Date date1 = new Date();
        Date date2 = new Date(1234567899);
        Date date3 = new Date();

        // check if date1 is after date2
        boolean isAfter = date1.after(date2);
        if (isAfter)
            System.out.println("date1 comes after date2");
        else
            System.out.println("date1 does not come after date2");

        // check if date2 is before date1
        boolean isBefore = date2.before(date1);
        if (isBefore)
            System.out.println("date2 comes before date1");
        else
            System.out.println("date2 does not come before date1");

        // compare date1 and date3
        int isEqual = date1.compareTo(date3);
        if (isEqual == 0)
            System.out.println("date1 and date3 are equal");
        else if (isEqual > 0)
            System.out.println("date1 is after date3");
        else
            System.out.println("date1 is before date3");

        // get time elapsed since January 1, 1970
        System.out.println("Time elapsed in miliseconds from Jan 1 " + "1970 until present is: " + date1.getTime());

        // Modify a date
        System.out.println("Before updating date2: " + date2);
        date2.setTime(205589422121L);
        System.out.println("After updating date2: " + date2);

    }
}
```

The output is as follows:

Console Problems

```
<terminated> DateExample1 [Java Application] C:\Program Files\java\j
date1 comes after date2
date2 comes before date1
date1 and date3 are equal
Time elapsed in miliseconds from Jan 1 1970 until present is: 1500284600491
Before updating date2: Thu Jan 15 07:56:07 CET 1970
After updating date2: Wed Jul 07 14:10:22 CEST 1976
```

SimpleDateFormat Class

This class is present in the java.text package and is composed of methods that help in parsing and formatting date and time in Java.

As evident from the examples of the Date class, the date is represented in th format: "dd mm yy hh:mm:ss timezone" such as

Thu Jan 15 07:56:07 CET 1970

But, if want the date to be displayed in another format, we can make use of the SimpleDateFormat class.

A use case demonstrating the use of this class is shown below:

```
SimpleDateFormatExample.java
package com.java.utilities;

import java.text.SimpleDateFormat;
import java.util.Date;

public class SimpleDateFormatExample {

    public static void main(String[] args) {

        Date date1 = new Date();
        System.out.println(" The Date is: " + date1);
        // provide the desired format using SimpleDateFormat
        SimpleDateFormat simpleDateFormatter1 = new SimpleDateFormat("dd/MM/yyyy");
        // format the date
        String formattedDate1 = simpleDateFormatter1.format(date1);
        System.out.println(" The formatted Date(dd/MM/yyyy) is: " + formattedDate1);
        // provide the desired format using SimpleDateFormat
        SimpleDateFormat simpleDateFormatter2 = new SimpleDateFormat("yyyy/dd/MM");
        String formattedDate2 = simpleDateFormatter2.format(date1);
        // format the date
        System.out.println(" The formatted Date(yyyy/dd/MM) is: " + formattedDate2);

    }
}
```

The output generated is as follows:

```
Console  Problems
<terminated> SimpleDateFormatExample [Java Application] C:
 The Date is: Mon Jul 17 12:01:53 CEST 2017
 The formatted Date(dd/MM/yyyy) is: 17/07/2017
 The formatted Date(yyyy/dd/MM) is: 2017/17/07
```

Calendar Class in Java

This class is a special abstract class in Java that helps manipulate dates. Using this class, a date can be expressed as calendar terms/fields such as months, days, years etc. For example, using this class, we can find out which day of the week it is, or which day of the month it is and so on. This class implements the Comparable interface. This class represents a simple date in the Gregorian calendar format that is used worldwide.

The Calendar class has a concrete subclass called as the GergorianCalendar class that represents the date in the Gergorian calendar format.

Some useful methods from the Calendar class are as follows:

Table 7: Methods of the Calendar class

Method	**Description**
Date getTime()	This method returns a Date object that represents the time value of the Calendar class
void setTime(Date date)	This method sets the time of the Calendar to the specified Date
static Calendar getInstance()	This method is used to get an instance of the Calendar class based on the current time, the default locale zone in the current time zone
void setFirstDayOfWeek(int **value)**	This method sets the first day of the week
int getFirstDayOfWeek()	This method gets the first day the week
int getWeekYear()	This method returns the week year of the calendar instance
void add(int **field,** int **amount)**	This method adds or subtracts a value from the given instance
void set(int **year,** int **month,** int **date)**	This method sets the values for the year, month and date of a calendar instance
int getWeeksInWeekYear()	This method returns the number of weeks in a particular year that are present in the calendar instance
int get(int field)	This method returns the value of a particular calender field (day/month/year)
abstract int getMaximum(int field)	This method returns the maximum value of a given field (day/month/year) of the Calendar instance
abstract int getMinimum(int field)	This method returns the minimum value of a given field (day/month/year) of the Calendar instance
boolean **before(**Object **object)**	This method is similar to the before() method of the Date class
boolean **after(**Object **object)**	This method is similar to the after() method of the Date class

The before() and after() methods are analogous to the compareTo() method only when the object is an instance of the calendar class.

Let us now take a look at some examples demonstrating the use of the Calendar class.

Example 1: Displaying current date and time

CalendarExample1.java

```
package com.java.utilities;

import java.util.Calendar;

public class CalendarExample1 {

    public static void main(String[] args) {

        Calendar calendar = Calendar.getInstance();
        System.out.print("Current Date and Time: " + calendar.getTime());
    }

}
```

The output is:

Console Problems Javadoc Declaration Ann

```
<terminated> CalendarExample1 [Java Application] C:\Program Files\ja
Current Date and Time: Wed Jul 19 15:13:59 CEST 2017
```

Example 2: The get() method

CalendarExample2.java

```
package com.java.utilities;

import java.text.SimpleDateFormat;
import java.util.Calendar;

public class CalendarExample2 {

    public static void main(String[] args) {

        Calendar calendar = Calendar.getInstance();
        SimpleDateFormat sdf = new SimpleDateFormat("yyyy/MM/dd HH:mm:ss");
        int year = calendar.get(Calendar.YEAR);
        // months are counted starting from 0 for January to 11 for December
        int month = calendar.get(Calendar.MONTH);
        int dayOfTheMonth = calendar.get(Calendar.DAY_OF_MONTH);
        int dayOfTheWeek = calendar.get(Calendar.DAY_OF_WEEK);
        int weekOfTheYear = calendar.get(Calendar.WEEK_OF_YEAR);
        int weekOfTheMonth = calendar.get(Calendar.WEEK_OF_MONTH);

        // get 24h format for hour
        int hourOfTheDay = calendar.get(Calendar.HOUR_OF_DAY);
        int minute = calendar.get(Calendar.MINUTE);
        int second = calendar.get(Calendar.SECOND);
        int millisecond = calendar.get(Calendar.MILLISECOND);

        System.out.println(sdf.format(calendar.getTime()));

        System.out.println("The year is: " + year);
        System.out.println("The month is: " + month);
        System.out.println("It is the " + dayOfTheMonth + "th day of the month");
        System.out.println("It is the " + dayOfTheWeek + "th day of the week");
        System.out.println("It is the " + weekOfTheYear + "th week of the year");
        System.out.println("It is week " + weekOfTheMonth + " of the month");
        System.out.println("The hour of the day is: " + hourOfTheDay);
        System.out.println("Minutes: " + minute);
        System.out.println("Seconds: " + second);
        System.out.println("Milliseconds: " + millisecond);

    }
}
```

The output is as follows:

Console ☒ Problems @ Javadoc D

<terminated> CalendarExample2 [Java Application]

```
2017/07/19 15:28:37
The year is: 2017
The month is: 6
It is the 19th day of the month
It is the 4th day of the week
It is the 29th week of the year
It is week 3 of the month
The hour of the day is: 15
Minutes: 28
Seconds: 37
Milliseconds: 121
```

Example 3: Convert a Calendar instance to Date and vice versa

```
CalendarExample3.java
package com.java.utilities;

import java.text.ParseException;
import java.text.SimpleDateFormat;
import java.util.Calendar;
import java.util.Date;

public class CalendarExample3 {

    public static void main(String[] args) throws ParseException {

        // convert calendar to date
        System.out.println("------------------------------Convert Calendar Instance to Date------------------------------");
        Calendar calendar = Calendar.getInstance();
        display(calendar);
        Date date = calendar.getTime();
        System.out.println("Date is:" + date);

        // convert date to calendar
        System.out.println("------------------------------Convert Date Instance to Calendar------------------------------");
        SimpleDateFormat sdf = new SimpleDateFormat("dd-M-yyyy hh:mm:ss");
        String dateInString = "01-01-2017 10:10:10";
        Date dateToConvert = sdf.parse(dateInString);
        System.out.println("Date is:" + dateToConvert);
        Calendar calendarToSet = Calendar.getInstance();
        calendar.setTime(dateToConvert);
        display(calendarToSet);
    }

    private static void display(Calendar calendar) {

        SimpleDateFormat sdf = new SimpleDateFormat("yyyy-MM-dd HH:mm:ss");
        System.out.println("The Calendar date is:" + sdf.format(calendar.getTime()));
    }
}
```

The output generated is:

```
Console  Problems  Javadoc  Declaration  Annotations
<terminated> CalendarExample3 [Java Application]
------------------------------Convert Calendar Instance to Date------------------------------
The Calendar date is:2017-07-19 16:06:04
Date is:Wed Jul 19 16:06:04 CEST 2017
------------------------------Convert Date Instance to Calendar------------------------------
Date is:Sun Jan 01 10:10:10 CET 2017
The Calendar date is:2017-07-19 16:06:04
```

Example 4: The add()

```
CalendarExample4.java
package com.java.utilities;

import java.text.SimpleDateFormat;
import java.util.Calendar;
import java.util.GregorianCalendar;

public class CalendarExample4 {

    public static void main(String[] args) {

        SimpleDateFormat formatter = new SimpleDateFormat("yyyy/MM/dd");

        Calendar calendar = new GregorianCalendar(2015, 10, 11);
        System.out.println("Date:" + formatter.format(calendar.getTime()));

        // add 2 months to the current date
        calendar.add(Calendar.MONTH, 1);
        System.out.println("Date after adding 2 months:" + formatter.format(calendar.getTime()));

        // add a year to the current date
        calendar.add(Calendar.YEAR, 1);
        System.out.println("Date after adding a year:" + formatter.format(calendar.getTime()));

        // subtract 4 days from the current date
        calendar.add(Calendar.DAY_OF_MONTH, -4);
        System.out.println("Date after subtracting 4 days:" + formatter.format(calendar.getTime()));

    }
}
```

The output generated is:

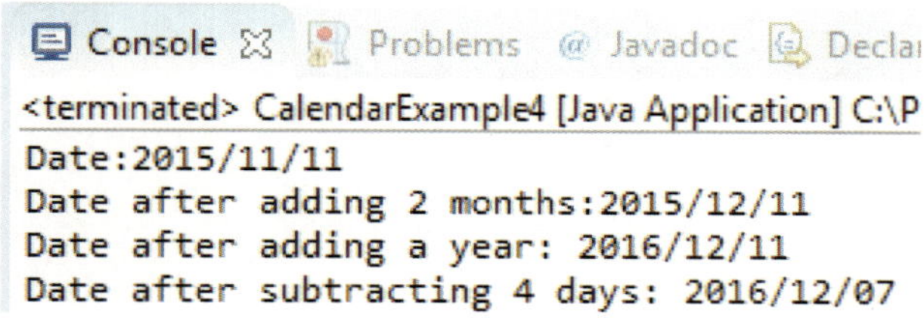

CHAPTER 8

EXCEPTIONS IN JAVA

An exception is defined as an event that occurs during the execution of a program which disrupts the usual execution of the program's instructions (Horstmann and Cornell, 2002).

When an exception occurs the program is interrupted and it terminates abruptly, which is not desirable. Hence, it is advisable to handle the exceptions if possible.

Certain examples of exceptions are: invalid input given by the user, divide by zero, etc

In java when an error occurs in a program method the following steps take place:

- The method containing the error generates an object, called an exception object and gives it to the runtime system.
- This object holds data regarding the error, its type and the program's state when the said exception occurs. This process is referred to as "throwing an exception".
- After this, an attempt is made to look for a method/something that can handle the exception. The list of possible things that

can handle the exception is the list of methods called before the method that threw the exception; also called as the method call stack.

- The java runtime looks for a method that handles the exception in the reverse order of the call stack. This means that this method contains a piece of code that knows how to deal with the exception. This is called an exception handler.
- When a method that handles the exception is found, the runtime passes the control to this method/handler. This means that the method 'catches' an exception.
- In case the java runtime is unable to find a method that 'handles' the exception, the program terminates abruptly.

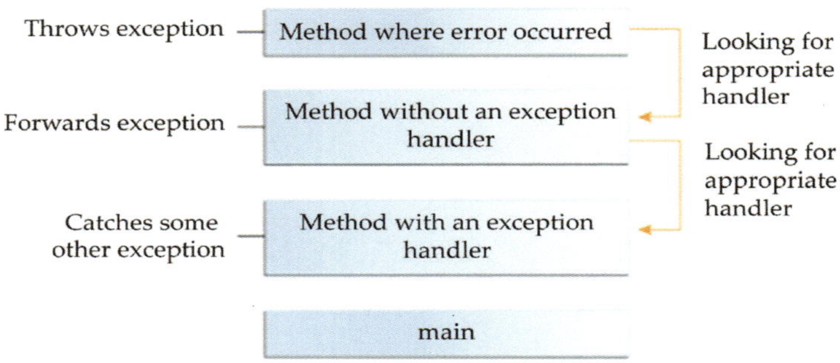

Figure 158: Call Stack (Exceptions, 1995).

Exception handling is a mechanism to control/administer runtime and compile time exceptions that a java program can possibly throw. This is extremely useful when we want to maintain the flow of the programs we write. Suppose we have code of 5 statements. If an exception occurs at the very first statement of the code, statements 2-5 are not executed. But if the exception is handled, then all the following statements are executed and a meaningful message is given to the end user stating that something has gone wrong.

There exist 3 categories of exceptions:

a. **Checked Exceptions**: These occur at compile time and need to be handled at compile time; else a compile time exception will be thrown.

b. **Unchecked Exceptions**: These exceptions are checked at execution/runtime and not at compile time.

c. **Errors**: These events are not exceptions but issues that come up during program execution, which cannot be controlled by the programmer or end user. They are nothing but abnormal events that occur in case of major failures of the runtime environment. For example, java out of memory exceptions.

The Exception classes all inherit from the Throwable class which is the parent class. The hierarchy is as follows:

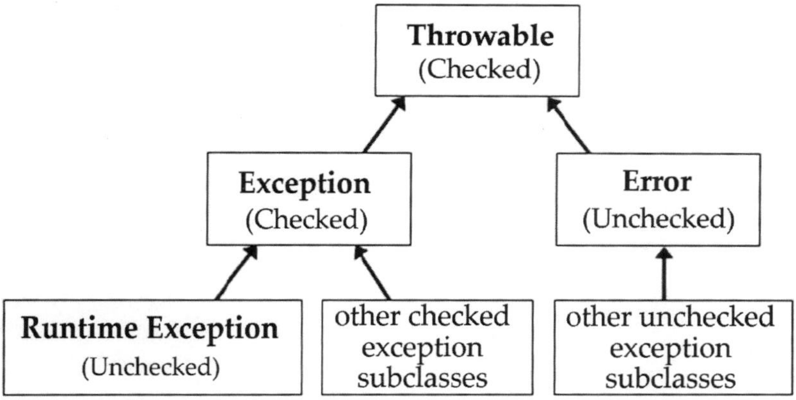

Figure 159: (Apps, 2017).

All runtime and compile exceptions descend from the class Exception. The class Error is another subclass of class Throwable.

Certain examples of errors and exceptions are:

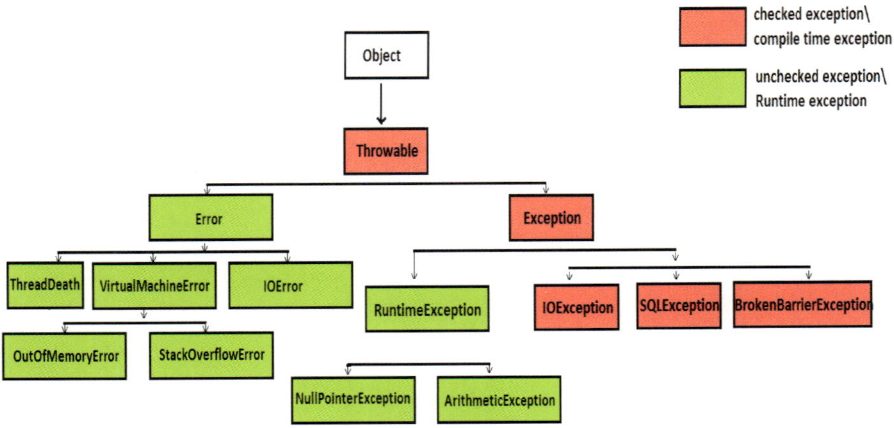

Figure 160: (Javamadesoeasy.com, 2017).

HANDLING EXCEPTIONS

Java has provided us with certain keywords that are part of the exception handling mechanism. They are: try, catch, throw, throws and finally.

The try-catch block

The bare minimum requirement of exception handling is a try-catch block. The try block consists of the code that is likely to throw an exception and the catch block handles this exception. In other words, the code likely to thrown an exception is surrounded by this block.

The basic syntax is as follows:

```
try{

}

catch (Exception e){

}
```

A try block needs to be followed by a catch or a finally block. It cannot exist on its own. It can be followed by one/more catch blocks but only one finally block (Horstmann and Cornell, 2002).

A simple program with the implementation of a try catch block is shown below:

```
ExceptionHandling.java

package com.trial.java.fundamentals;

public class ExceptionHandling {

    public static void main(String args[]) {

        ExceptionHandling exceptiionTest = new ExceptionHandling();

        exceptiionTest.method1();

    }

    public void method1() {

        int a = 10;
        int b = 0;

        try {
            int result = a / b;
            System.out.println(result);
        } catch (ArithmeticException e) {
            System.out.println("Exception caught: " + e);
        }

    }

}
```

The above sample code tries to divide an integer by zero in method1. This is an arithmetic exception in Java. The code handles this exception and gives a meaning message to user without causing an abrupt termination of the program.

The output of the above program ExceptionHandling is as follows:

```
Console  Problems  Javadoc  Declaration  Annotation
<terminated> ExceptionHandling [Java Application] C:\Program Files\java\jdk1
Exception caught: java.lang.ArithmeticException: / by zero
```

A try block can be accompanied by one/more catch blocks. It can be written syntactically as:

```
try{

}
```

```
catch(Exception1 e1){
}
catch(Exception2 e2){
}
catch(Exception3 e3){
}
```

When an exception is thrown, if it isn't caught by the first catch block, it is passed on to the next until the appropriate block that handles that exception is reached. If the exception is not caught by any of the catch blocks, it is passed to the runtime and the program ends.

The next example demonstrates the use of multiple catch blocks.

ExceptionHandling.java

```java
package com.trial.java.fundamentals;

public class ExceptionHandling {

    public static void main(String args[]) {

        ExceptionHandling exceptiionTest = new ExceptionHandling();

        exceptiionTest.method1();

    }

    public void method1() {

        int a = 10;
        int b = 0;
        int[] arr= new int[4];
        try {
            int result = a / b;

            System.out.println(result);
            System.out.println(arr[5]);
        } catch (ArrayIndexOutOfBoundsException e) {
            System.out.println("Exception caught: " + e);
        }
        catch (ArithmeticException e) {
            System.out.println("Exception caught: " + e);
        }
        catch(Exception e)
        {
            System.out.println("Exception caught: " + e);
        }
    }

}
```

The output of the above code is as follows:

```
Console ⊠  Problems  @ Javadoc  Declaration  Annotation
<terminated> ExceptionHandling [Java Application] C:\Program Files\java\jdk1
Exception caught: java.lang.ArithmeticException: / by zero
```

As the arithmetic exception has been thrown before the ArrayIndexOutofBounds exception, it is the only one handled by the code.

In case of multiple try blocks, it is paramount to know that they must be ordered in a particular way; from the most specific exception to the most general. Hence, arithmetic exception has been caught before the general type 'Exception'.

```
ExceptionHandling.java ⊠
package com.trial.java.fundamentals;

public class ExceptionHandling {

    public static void main(String args[]) {

        ExceptionHandling exceptiionTest = new ExceptionHandling();

        exceptiionTest.method1();

    }

    public void method1() {

        int a = 10;
        int b = 0;

        try {

            try {

                int[] arr = new int[4];
                System.out.println(arr[5]);

            } catch (ArrayIndexOutOfBoundsException e) {
                System.out.println("Exception caught: " + e);
            }
            int result = a / b;
            System.out.println(result);
        } catch (ArithmeticException e) {
            System.out.println("Exception caught: " + e);
        }

        catch (Exception e) {
            System.out.println("Exception caught: " + e);
        }

        System.out.println("Code after the try block");
    }

}
```

In java it is also possible to have one try block inside another. This is called as nesting of try blocks or nested try blocks. This may be employed when a particular section of code is likely to throw an exception that is completely unrelated to the exception thrown by the entire block.

The class ExceptionHandling demonstrates the use of nested try catch blocks. We have a nested try catch block that handles an ArrayIndexOutOfBounds Exception and the outer block that handles an arithmeticException.

The generated output is the following:

```
Console ⊠  Problems  @ Javadoc  Declaration  Annotations
<terminated> ExceptionHandling [Java Application] C:\Program Files\java\jdk1.8.0_92\bin\
Exception caught: java.lang.ArrayIndexOutOfBoundsException: 5
Exception caught: java.lang.ArithmeticException: / by zero
Code after the try block
```

As we can see, both the exceptions have been caught and the code following the outer try block has been executed as well.

Keywords throw and throws

The keyword throw is used when a method wants to explicitly throw/ invoke an exception.

The use of the keyword throw has been demonstrated in the program ExceptionHandler below:

```java
// ExceptionHandler.java
package com.trial.java.fundamentals;

public class ExceptionHandler {

    public static void main(String args[]) {

        ExceptionHandler exceptiionTest = new ExceptionHandler();

        exceptiionTest.method1();

    }

    public void method1() {

        int a = 10;
        int b = 0;

        if(b==0)
            throw new ArithmeticException();
        else
        {
            int result = a/b;
            System.out.println(result);
        }

    }

}
```

The output of the above program is as follows:

```
Console  Problems  Javadoc  Declaration  Annotations
<terminated> ExceptionHandler [Java Application]
Exception in thread "main" java.lang.ArithmeticException
	at com.trial.java.fundamentals.ExceptionHandler.method1(ExceptionHandler.java:19)
	at com.trial.java.fundamentals.ExceptionHandler.main(ExceptionHandler.java:9)
```

The throws keyword is generally used by a method when it doesn't want to manage an exception that is checked. By using this keyword, it passes on the job of exception handling to the class further up in the call stack.

The caller has to handle the exceptions thrown by that method.

The syntax for a method is as follows:

public void method1() throws ArrayIndexOutOfBoundsException, NullPointerException {

}

Sometimes throws is used in combination with throw as follows:

```
ExceptionHandler.java

package com.trial.java.fundamentals;

public class ExceptionHandler {

    public static void main(String args[]) {

        ExceptionHandler exceptiionTest = new ExceptionHandler();

        exceptiionTest.method1();

    }

    public void method1() throws ArithmeticException {

        int a = 10;
        int b = 0;

        if(b==0)
            throw new ArithmeticException();
        else
        {
            int result = a/b;
            System.out.println(result);
        }

    }

}
```

The output/result is the same as before; the class throws and arithmetic exception like in the previous example.

The Finally Block

The finally block is a block that can be written after a try block. This block is always executed even if an exception occurs.

When exceptions are thrown by methods in a program, the regular flow of code is interrupted and the method may not execute completely. Based on the manner in which the method has been coded, it is highly possible that an exception may cause the method to terminate prematurely, which could be an issue in case of certain methods. A simple example is that if a method opens a file at its very beginning and closes it in the end, if an exception occurs somewhere in the middle, then the code that closes the file is bypassed. The finally keyword helps in this situation serving as a contingency plan.

This is a block of code that is executed after a try or catch block even if an exception doesn't occur. So, if the method throws and exception, this block is executed even if there are not surrounding catch clauses that match the exception thrown. When a method is about to return the control from within a try or catch block, or through an uncaught exception the finally block is executed just before the return from the method.

This block can be useful for closing up resources that have been used/allocated during the course of the program with the intention of freeing them before the method ends. The block finally is not compulsory, but if there are not catch clauses following a try block, the finally block is obligatory. In simpler terms, a try block must be followed by a catch block or a finally block. Further, a try block can be followed by any number of catch blocks but only a single finally block.

Even in case no exceptions are thrown, the addition of cleanup code to prevent leakage of resources in this block is considered to be a good practice.

Some examples of the use of this block are shown by the class FinallyExample below:

Example 1: Class implementing the try/catch/finally

FinallyExample.java

```
package com.trial.java.fundamentals;

public class FinallyExample {

    public static void main(String[] args) {
        FinallyExample example = new FinallyExample();
        example.method1();

    }

    public void method1() {

        int a = 10;
        int b = 0;

        try {
            int result = a / b;
            System.out.println(result);
        } catch (ArithmeticException e) {
            System.out.println("Exception caught: " + e);
        } finally {
            System.out.println("In finally block!");
        }
    }
}
```

In this example, the method method1() throws an exception which is caught by the catch clause after which the finally block is executed. The output generated is as follows:

Console | Javadoc | Declaration | Problems

```
<terminated> FinallyExample [Java Application] C:\Program Files\Java\jdk1.8.0_131\bin\javaw.exe
Exception caught: java.lang.ArithmeticException: / by zero
In finally block!
```

Example 2: Class implementing only the try/finally block:

FinallyExample.java

```java
package com.trial.java.fundamentals;

public class FinallyExample {

    public static void main(String[] args) {
        FinallyExample example = new FinallyExample();
        example.method1();

    }

    public void method1() {

        int a = 10;
        int b = 0;

        try {
            int result = a / b;
            System.out.println(result);
        } finally {
            System.out.println("In finally block!");
        }
    }
}
```

In the above example, the exception is not caught in a catch block, but the finally block is still executed. Hence, the output is as follows:

Console | Javadoc | Declaration | Problems

<terminated> FinallyExample [Java Application] C:\Program Files\Java\jdk1.8.0_131\bin\javaw.exe

```
In finally block!
Exception in thread "main" java.lang.ArithmeticException: / by zero
	at com.trial.java.fundamentals.FinallyExample.method1(FinallyExample.java:17)
	at com.trial.java.fundamentals.FinallyExample.main(FinallyExample.java:7)
```

Two important points to note about the finally blocks are:

- In rare situations, there is a chance that the JVM may exit during the execution of the try/catch block. In such cases the finally block is not executed.
- If a thread that is executing the try/catch block is killed/ interrupted, there is a chance that the finally block may not execute, even though the rest of the application is still executing.

CHAPTER 9

INPUT OUTPUT

A program may need to communicate to the external world from time to time via a network, file storage or even a simple keyboard input. Like most programming languages, java supports input/output operations via the file system and the byte streams, providing us with the java.io package.

This package consists of a number of classes and interfaces that help in performing I/O operations. The main concept in case of I/O operations is called a stream. A stream is nothing but a continuous sequence of information/data. In java, a stream is made up bytes; each stream consisting of an input and output or a source and destination. In java, streams support several data types as follows: integer, characters and other primitive data types, objects and so on.

A stream is further divided into an input and output stream. The input stream reads the input from a source, whereas the output stream writes the data to a particular destination (Gosling and McGilton, 1995). Streams basically carry data to and from the source to the destination. Data flowing into the program comes via the input stream whereas data flowing from the program to another destination travels via an output stream.

Some possible sources and destination could as follows:

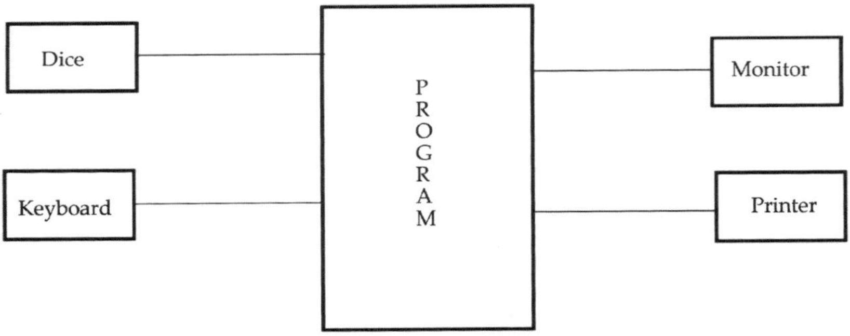

The Input output streams in java are classified as follows:

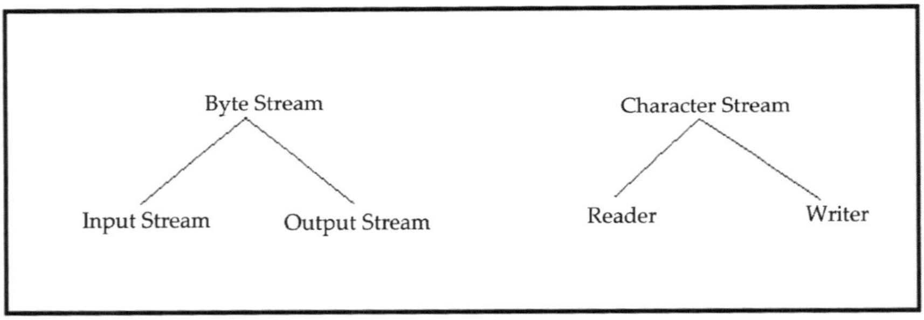

Classification of streams in Java

BYTE STREAMS

Byte Streams are used by Java programs to perform I/O operations on bytes of 8 bits. All the classes that help in perfuming byte operations descend from the Input Stream and Output Stream classes.

There exist several classes that support byte operations. We shall focus on the classes FileInputStream and FileOutputStream classes.

The following class FileExample.java demonstrates the use of these streams. The class shows how to read a file and copy the contents of the file into another file.

FileExample.java

```java
package com.trial.java.fundamentals;

import java.io.FileInputStream;
import java.io.FileNotFoundException;
import java.io.FileOutputStream;
import java.io.IOException;

public class FileExample {

    public static void main(String[] args) {

        FileInputStream inputStream = null;
        FileOutputStream outputStream = null;

        try {
            //Create an input Stream to read a file and specify the file location
            //In this case, file is present in the current project hierarchy
            inputStream = new FileInputStream("inputFile.txt");
            //Create an output stream to write the file
            outputStream = new FileOutputStream("outputFile.txt");

            int byteChar;
            //read byte by byte
            while ((byteChar = inputStream.read()) != -1) {
                //write to the output stream
                outputStream.write(byteChar);
            }
        } catch (FileNotFoundException e) {

            System.out.println("File Not Found: " + e);
        } catch (IOException e) {

            System.out.println("I/O Exception Thrown: " + e);
        } finally {
            if (inputStream != null) {
                try {
                    inputStream.close();
                } catch (IOException e) {

                    System.out.println("I/O Exception Thrown: " + e);
                }
            }
            if (outputStream != null) {
                try {
                    outputStream.close();
                } catch (IOException e) {
                    System.out.println("I/O Exception Thrown: " + e);
                }
            }
        }
    }

}
```

}

The file inputFile.txt has the following content in it:

Hello! How are you doing?

Have a good day!!

On execution of the program, a new File called outputFile.txt is generated and the contents of the input file are copied to this file as shown below:

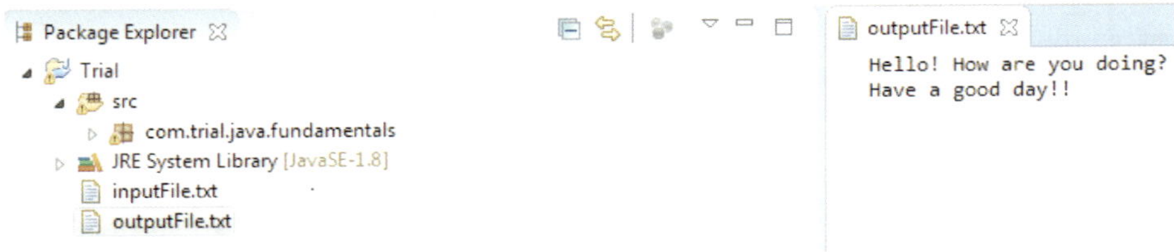

We now proceed to look at character streams and examples of their use.

CHARACTER STREAMS

Character streams are used to handle Unicode inputs and output. This is not supported by Byte Streams. Byte Streams do not support any encoding stream. So, if we try to work on a character set that is not 8 bits (like ASCII), the output would be not be correct as the byteStream just treates the input bitwise. A simple example is a file that employs UNICODE encoding system. This means that 2 bytes are used per character whereas the Byte Streams only use 1 byte. The Byte Streams split the data while reading into a single byte and this could result in bad data.

This is avoided by the use of character streams that automatically adapts to the local character set, being able to read characters in a wide variety of languages. It supports internationalization without added development work for the programmer to accommodate new languages.

The classes belonging to the character stream support Unicode characters (16-bit) and enable the user to perform operations on simple characters, arrays of characters, strings and so on. As shown below, they are further divided into a Reader and a Writer class. The reader reads 2 bytes at a time and the Writer writes 2 bytes at a time. All the character classes descend from the Reader and Writer abstract classes.

The use of the character streams is demonstrated by the class FileExample which copies the contents of a UNICODE file into another file.

FileExample.java

```
package com.trial.java.fundamentals;

import java.io.FileNotFoundException;
import java.io.FileReader;
import java.io.FileWriter;
import java.io.IOException;

public class FileExample {

    public static void main(String[] args) {

        FileReader fileReader = null;
        FileWriter fileWriter = null;

        try {
            // Create a reader to read a file and specify the file location
            fileReader = new FileReader("inputFile.txt");
            // Create an output stream to write the file
            fileWriter = new FileWriter("outputFile.txt");

            int byteChar;
            // read byte by byte
            while ((byteChar = fileReader.read()) != -1) {
                // write to the output stream
                fileWriter.write(byteChar);
            }
        } catch (FileNotFoundException e) {

            System.out.println("File Not Found: " + e);
        } catch (IOException e) {

            System.out.println("I/O Exception Thrown: " + e);
        } finally {
            if (fileReader != null) {
                try {
                    fileReader.close();
                } catch (IOException e) {

                    System.out.println("I/O Exception Thrown: " + e);
                }
            }
            if (fileWriter != null) {
                try {
                    fileWriter.close();
                } catch (IOException e) {
                    System.out.println("I/O Exception Thrown: " + e);
                }
            }
        }
    }

}
```

As we can see, this example is very similar to the previous example. The only difference is that a FileReader and a FileWriter has been used. The only difference in the 2 examples is that the variable byteChar holds a character value in the last 16 bits in this example. In the previous example, this variable holds the value in the last 8 bits. The output/results generated are the same as that of the previous example.

BUFFERED STREAMS

The buffered streams make use of buffers to read/write data. Buffers are helpful in increasing program speed and performance. Generally, in an unbuffered stream, each read and write operation is handled by the OS every time it is called, which means that multiple native method calls are done. This can result in inefficiency of the program as each native call to the OS requires time, access to the disk or file system and so on. To help fix this issue, we make use of buffered streams. Programs feed the data to a buffer and these streams read data from the buffer. The native methods for the read operation are called only when the buffer is empty. In case of the write operation, these streams write data to a buffer until it is full, after which the native method call is executed to write the data. The buffered streams are like wrapper classes that wrap the stream objects.

There are 4 buffered classes:

BufferedInputStream and BufferedOutputStream for byte streams

BufferedReader and Buffer for character streams

The following class BufferedStreamExample, using the concept of buffered streams is shown below:

BufferedStreamExample.java

```
package com.trial.java.fundamentals;
import java.io.*;

public class BufferedStreamExample {

    public static void main(String[] args) {

        try (

                Reader reader = new FileReader("inputFile.txt");
                Writer writer = new FileWriter("outputFile.txt");


                //Buffered Streams wrap the character streams into Buffered Streams

                BufferedReader bufferReader = new BufferedReader(reader);
                BufferedWriter bufferWriter = new BufferedWriter(writer);
            ) {

            String line = "";

            while (null != (line=bufferReader.readLine())) {

                bufferWriter.write(line); // writing to output buffer
                bufferWriter.write("\n");
            }
        } catch (FileNotFoundException e) {
            System.out.println("Input file is not found");
        } catch (IOException e) {
            System.out.println("Error in Reading and writing operations");
        }
    }
}
```

As shown by the class BufferedStreamExample, Reader and Writer objects have been wrapped inside the BufferedReader and writer objects.

JAVA STANDARD I/O STREAMS

Java provides us with the following standard i/o streams via the System class that are attached to the console.

- **Standard Input** – This is the standard input stream. This generally refers to the keyboard input and is this input is consumed as **System.in**.
- **Standard Output** – This is the output standard output stream that displays the program output. The output is generally the monitor/console of a computer. This output is well known and is depicted as **System.out.**
- **Standard Error** – This stream is for the errors produced by the program and is displayed using the **System.err** statement.

A simple program ConsoleExample demonstrates the use of the standard streams. The class ConsoleExample reads input from the keyboard and displays it on the console. The program will read the input until the user inputs the letter 'e'.

ConsoleExample.java

```java
package com.trial.java.fundamentals;

import java.io.IOException;
import java.io.InputStreamReader;

public class ConsoleExample {

    public static void main(String args[]) throws IOException {
        InputStreamReader inputReader = null;

        try {
            inputReader = new InputStreamReader(System.in);
            System.out.println("Enter data. Press 'e' to quit.");
            char c;
            do {
                c = (char) inputReader.read();
                System.out.print(c);
            } while(c != 'e');
        }finally {
            if (inputReader != null) {
                inputReader.close();
            }
        }
    }

}
```

The output generated is as follows:

Console | Problems | Javadoc

```
<terminated> ConsoleExample [Java Application]
Enter data. Press 'e' to quit.
a
a
b
b
c
c
d
d
e
e
```

The input is shown in green and the same value is displayed on console in black.

I/O HIERARCHY

The hierarchy of the I/O classes with some I/O classes in Java is as shown below:

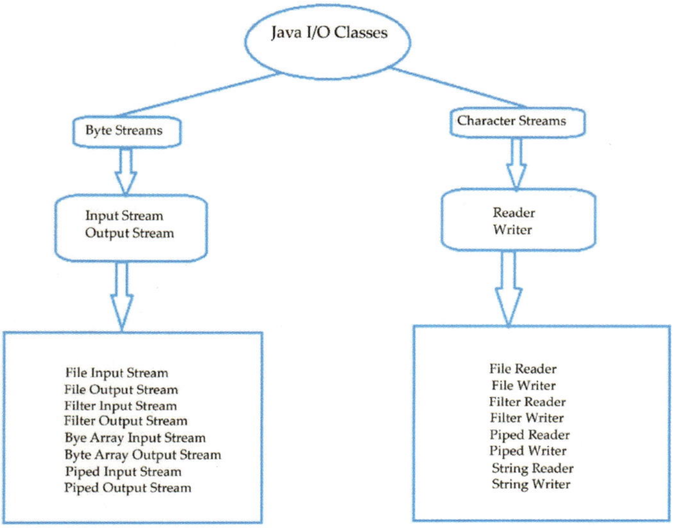

We shall now take a look at some of these byte and character stream classes using examples.

FilterInputStream and FilterOutputStream

The FilterInputSream class is a subclass of the InputStream class and this class contains other input streams that inherit from it. This class overrides the methods from its parent class and its subclasses further override methods from this class. Similar to the FileInputStream, this class has the standard read() method to help read inputs sent to the I/O ((Naughton and Schildt, 1996). Some implmenetations/subclasses of this class are:

BufferedInputStream, CheckedInputStream, DataInputStream, DigestInputStream, etc.

The FilterOutputStream class, like its counterpart FilterInputStream descends from the OutputStream class. It too overrides the methods of its parent class and its subclasses further override the methods of this class. Similar to the traditional writer classes this class has the write() method that writes output to the desired destination.

Some implementations of this class are:

BufferedOutputStream, CheckedOutputStream, DataOutputStream, DigestOutputStream, etc

The use of these two classes is shown below:

FilterInputOutputStream.java

```
package com.trial.java.fundamentals;

import java.io.BufferedInputStream;

public class FilterInputOutputStream {

    public static void main(String[] args) throws IOException {

        System.out.println(
                "--------------------------Writing to a file using FilterOutputStream--------------------------");
        // create an input file
        File inputFile = new File("inputFile.txt");
        // create an object of type FileOutputStream
        FileOutputStream outputStream = new FileOutputStream(inputFile);

        // wrap the FileOutputStream object in an object of FilterOutputStream
        FilterOutputStream filterOutputStream = new FilterOutputStream(outputStream);
        // string to write to the file
        String inptString = "Hi! Adding a line to the input file!";
        // get the input as a sequence of encoded bytes
        byte byetsToAdd[] = inptString.getBytes();
        // write the bytes to the file
        filterOutputStream.write(byetsToAdd);

        // flush and close the output streams
        filterOutputStream.flush();
        filterOutputStream.close();
        outputStream.close();
        System.out.println("Data successfully written to the file");
        System.out.println(
                "--------------------------Reading from a file using FilterInputStream-------------------------");
        // create an object of type FileInputStream
        FileInputStream inputStream = new FileInputStream(inputFile);

        // wrap the FileInputStream object in an object of FilterInputStream
        FilterInputStream filterInpurtStream = new BufferedInputStream(inputStream);
        System.out.println("The contents of the file are:");
        int inData = 0;

        // get the data from the input file
        while ((inData = filterInpurtStream.read()) != -1) {
            // display the contents of the file
            System.out.print((char) inData);
        }

        // close the input streams
        inputStream.close();
        filterInpurtStream.close();

    }
}
```

We use the FilterOutputStream to wrap a FileOutputStream object to write to a file. The FilterInputStream is used to read the contents of the file. This class wraps an object of the BufferedInputStream.

The output generated is:

```
Console  Problems  Javadoc  Declaration  Annotations  Call Hierarchy
<terminated> FilterInputOutputStream [Java Application]
--------------------------Writing to a file using FilterOutputStream--------------------------
Data successfully written to the file
--------------------------Reading from a file using FilterInputStream-------------------------
The contents of the file are:
Hi! Adding a line to the input file!
```

ByteArrayInputStream and ByteArrayOutputStream

The ByteArrayInputStream is a subclass of InputStream that accepts a byte array as a source of input. It contains an internal buffer that is made up of bytes that can be read from the stream (Friesen, 2015).

The ByteArrayOutputStream is a subclass of OutputStream that writes data into an array of bytes (internal buffer). The size of the Buffer grows as the data is written into it (Friesen, 2015).

```
ByteArrayInputOutputStream.java

package com.trial.java.fundamentals;

import java.io.ByteArrayInputStream;
import java.io.ByteArrayOutputStream;
import java.io.IOException;

public class ByteArrayInputOutputStream {

    public static void main(String[] args) throws IOException {

        // string to write to the byte array
        String inputString = "Hello! How are you?";
        // create a ByteArrayOutputStream object of size 12
        ByteArrayOutputStream byteArrayOutputStream = new ByteArrayOutputStream(12);

        System.out.println("Writing the contents to the byte stream");

        // write to the stream
        byteArrayOutputStream.write(inputString.getBytes());
        System.out.println("Data successfully written to the byte stream");

        // retrieve the contents to display from the output stream
        byte bytesToAdd[] = byteArrayOutputStream.toByteArray();

        int inData;
        ByteArrayInputStream byteArrayInputStream = new ByteArrayInputStream(bytesToAdd);
        System.out.println("Reading and displaying the contents");
        // display the contents
        while ((inData = byteArrayInputStream.read()) != -1) {
            System.out.print((char) inData);
        }
    }
}
```

The output is:

```
Console   Problems   Javadoc   Declaration
<terminated> ByteArrayInputOutputStream [Java Application]
Writing the contents to the byte stream
Data successfully written to the byte stream
Reading and displaying the contents
Hello! How are you?
```

DataInputStream and DataOutputStream

These streams are used to read and write primitive data types (int, double, float, etc) into an input and output stream respectively. A DataInputStream object wraps an InputStream object whereas a DataOutputStream object wraps an OutputStream objects.

```
DataInputOutputSream.java
package com.trial.java.fundamentals;
import java.io.DataInputStream;
import java.io.DataOutputStream;
import java.io.FileInputStream;
import java.io.FileOutputStream;
import java.io.IOException;

public class DataInputOutputSream {
    public static void main(String[] args) throws IOException {

        FileOutputStream fileOutputStream = new FileOutputStream("inputFile.txt");
        DataOutputStream dataOutputStream = new DataOutputStream(fileOutputStream);
        // write primitive data types to the DataOutputStream object
        System.out.println("Writing data to the file");
        dataOutputStream.writeInt(23);
        dataOutputStream.writeFloat(3.4f);
        dataOutputStream.writeUTF("How are you?");
        dataOutputStream.flush();
        dataOutputStream.close();
        System.out.println("Data successfully written to the file");

        FileInputStream fileInputStream = new FileInputStream("inputFile.txt");
        DataInputStream dataInputStream = new DataInputStream(fileInputStream);
        System.out.println("Reading data from the file");
        //read primitive data types from the DataInputStreamObject
        int myInt = dataInputStream.readInt();
        float myFloat = dataInputStream.readFloat();
        String myString = dataInputStream.readUTF();
        System.out.println("Int Value:" + myInt + " Float Value: " + myFloat
                + " String Value: " + myString);
    }
}
```

The output is as follows:

```
Console   @ Javadoc   Declaration   Problems
<terminated> DataInputOutputSream [Java Application] C:\Program Files\Java\jdk1.7.
Writing data to the file
Data successfully written to the file
Reading data from the file
Int Value:23 Float Value: 3.4 String Value: How are you?
```

ObjectInputStream and ObjectOutputStream

An ObjectOutputStream extends from the InputSream class and is used to write primitive data types and graphs of Java objects to an OutputStream in binary format. These objects can further be read using its counterpart Input Stream class ObjectInputStream. An ObjectInputStream reads primitive data types and objects that have been written using an ObjectOutputStream. The state of an object can be persisted by using a

File object to store the data (Naughton and Schildt, 1996).

A few examples demonstrating the use of the ObjectOutputStream and the ObjectInputStream have been provided below.

Example 1: Using File objects for persistence

```
ObjectInputStreamExample.java

package com.trial.java.fundamentals;

import java.io.*;

public class ObjectInputStreamExample {

    public static void main(String[] args) {
        String inputString = "Hello, How are you doing today? ";

        try {

            // create a new file using a FileOutputStream
            FileOutputStream fileOutputStream = new FileOutputStream("inputFile.txt");
            // wrap the FileOutputStream object within an ObjectOutputStream
            // object
            ObjectOutputStream objectOutputStream = new ObjectOutputStream(fileOutputStream);

            // write data (as an object) to the file
            System.out.println("Writing the following data to the file: " + inputString);
            objectOutputStream.writeObject(inputString);

            // flush and close the output streams
            objectOutputStream.flush();
            objectOutputStream.close();

            // create an ObjectInputStream for the previously created file
            ObjectInputStream objectInputStream = new ObjectInputStream(new FileInputStream("inputFile.txt"));

            // read and print the object as a String
            System.out.println("The contents of the file: " + (String) objectInputStream.readObject());

            // close the input stream
            objectInputStream.close();

        } catch (Exception ex) {
            ex.printStackTrace();
        }
    }
}
```

The output is:

```
Console  Problems  @ Javadoc  Declaration  Annotations  Call Hierar
<terminated> ObjectInputStreamExample [Java Application] C:\Program Files\java\jdk1.8.0_
Writing the following data to the file: Hello, How are you doing today?
The contents of the file: Hello, How are you doing today?
```

Example 2: Reading and Writing user-defined objects

ObjectInputStreamExample1.java

```java
package com.trial.java.fundamentals;

import java.io.FileInputStream;
import java.io.FileOutputStream;
import java.io.IOException;
import java.io.ObjectInputStream;
import java.io.ObjectOutputStream;
import java.io.Serializable;

//create a user defined class that is Serializable
class MyClass implements Serializable {

    private static final long serialVersionUID = 1L;
    int age;
    String name;

    MyClass(int age, String name) {
        this.age = age;
        this.name = name;
    }

    public String toString() {
        return "Age:" + age + " Name:" + name;
    }
}

public class ObjectInputStreamExample1 {

    public static void main(String[] args) throws IOException, ClassNotFoundException {

        // Store a serialized MyClass Object in a File using the
        // FileOutputStream
        FileOutputStream fileOutputStream = new FileOutputStream("myClass.txt");

        MyClass myClassObject = new MyClass(25, "Anna");
        // wrap the FileOutputStream object within an ObjectOutputStream object
        ObjectOutputStream objectOutputStream = new ObjectOutputStream(fileOutputStream);
        System.out.println("Writing MyClass Object: " + myClassObject);

        // write the custom class object to the file
        objectOutputStream.writeObject(myClassObject);
        // close the output stream
        objectOutputStream.close();

        // create an ObjectInputStream for the previously created file
        FileInputStream fileInputStream = new FileInputStream("myClass.txt");

        // wrap the FileInputStream object within an ObjectInputStream object
        ObjectInputStream input = new ObjectInputStream(fileInputStream);

        // read and print the object as a String
        MyClass myClassObject2 = (MyClass) input.readObject();

        System.out.println("Reading MyClass Object: " + myClassObject2);
        input.close();

    }
}
```

The output is:

```
Console  Problems  @ Javadoc  Declaration
<terminated> ObjectInputStreamExample1 [Java Application]
Writing MyClass Object: Age:25 Name:Anna
Reading MyClass Object: Age:25 Name:Anna
```

Note that in the above example the user defined class MyClass has to be declared to implement the interface Serializable as we save its state. The Serializable interface has been discussed in Chapter 11.

StringReader and StringWriter

The StringReader and the StringWriter classes take character streams. The StringReader class extends the Reader class and the StringWriter class extends the Writer class respectively.

The StringReader class takes in a String as an input and converts it into a character stream.

The StringWriter class is a character stream that takes in input in the form of a string buffer which is used to build a String (Naughton and Schildt, 1996).

StringReaderWriter.java

```
package com.trial.java.fundamentals;

import java.io.IOException;
import java.io.StringReader;
import java.io.StringWriter;

public class StringReaderWriter {

    public static void main(String[] args) {

        // input string
        String input = "Hello, How are you doing today ?";
        // create an object of type StringWriter
        StringWriter stringWriter = new StringWriter();
        // write the input to the object
        stringWriter.write(input);
        System.out.println("Writing input string:" + input);
        // create a StringReader object and read the input
        StringReader stringReader = new StringReader(stringWriter.toString());
        System.out.print("Reading input string:");
        int charToRead;
        try {
            while ((charToRead = stringReader.read()) != -1) {
                System.out.print((char) charToRead);
            }
        } catch (IOException e) {
            e.printStackTrace();
        }
    }
}
```

As seen from the class StringReaderWriter we have not closed the resouces stringReader and stringWriter. This is because when we use these classes the system resources like files, sockets, etc are not used and hence it is not necessary to close these resources.

The output is:

FilterReader and FilterWriter

The FilterReader class is an abstract class that helps read input from different character streams.

The FilterWriter class, is the counterpart of the FilterReader class, is another abstract class that is used to write data to different character output streams.

The classes that subclass the FilterReader and FilterWriter class must provide overridden implementations of their respective superclass.

A basic example that makes use of these classes is shown below. The class below wraps a StringWriter object within a FilterReader object for writing and into a FilterReader object for reading purposes.

```java
package com.trial.java.fundamentals;
import java.io.FilterReader;
import java.io.FilterWriter;
import java.io.IOException;
import java.io.Reader;
import java.io.StringReader;
import java.io.StringWriter;
import java.io.Writer;

public class FilterReaderWriter {
    public static void main(String[] args) throws IOException {
        // create a writer object
        Writer writer = new StringWriter(7);
        // wrap it in an object of type FilterWriter
        FilterWriter filterWriter = new FilterWriter(writer) {};
        // write data to the FilterWriter object
        filterWriter.write('A');
        filterWriter.write('B');
        filterWriter.write('C');
        filterWriter.write('D');
        filterWriter.write('E');
        filterWriter.write('F');
        filterWriter.write('G');
        // convert input data to String
        String s = writer.toString();
        System.out.println("Data written is:" + s);
        // create an object of type Reader
        Reader reader = new StringReader(s);
        // create a new filter reader object
        FilterReader filterReader = new FilterReader(reader) {};
        int byteToRead;
        // read the data and print it
        System.out.print("Data read is:");
        while ((byteToRead = filterReader.read()) != -1) {
            System.out.print((char) byteToRead);
        }
    }
}
```

The output is:

```
<terminated> FilterReaderWriter [Java Application]
Data written is:ABCDEFG
Data read is:ABCDEFG
```

These classes can also be used to create custom reader and writer classes. A custom Reader and Writer class has been shown below.

Custom Reader Example:

CustomFilterReaderExample.java

```
package com.trial.java.fundamentals;
import java.io.*;
//Create a custom Reader class that replaces all white spaces with underscores
class MyFilterReader extends FilterReader {
    MyFilterReader(Reader in) {
        // invoke super class constructor
        super(in);
    }
    // override the read() method of superclass FilterReader
    public int read() throws IOException {
        int charToRead = super.read();
        if ((char) charToRead == ' ')
            return ((int) '_');
        else
            return charToRead;
    }
}
public class CustomFilterReaderExample {
    public static void main(String[] args) throws IOException {

        // create a reader object
        Reader reader = new StringReader("Hello how are you doing today ?");
        // wrap it in an object of your custom reader class
        MyFilterReader fr = new MyFilterReader(reader);
        // read the input
        int charToRead;
        System.out.print("Output String:");
        while ((charToRead = fr.read()) != -1) {
            System.out.print((char) charToRead);
        }
    }
}
```

The output is:

```
Console  @ Javadoc  Declaration  Problems
<terminated> CustomFilterReaderExample [Java Application] C:\Progra
Output String:Hello_how_are_you_doing_today_?
```

Custom Writer Example:

CustomFilterWriterExample.java

```
package com.trial.java.fundamentals;
import java.io.Writer;
import java.io.FileWriter;
import java.io.FilterWriter;
import java.io.IOException;

//create a custom Writer class that replaces all white spaces with underscores
class MyFilterWriter extends FilterWriter {

    MyFilterWriter(Writer out) {
        // invoke super class constructor
        super(out);
    }
    //override the write() method of superclass FileWriter
    public void write(String str) throws IOException {
        if (str.contains(" ")) {
            super.write(str.replaceAll(" ", "_"));
        }
    }
}
public class CustomFilterWriterExample {
    public static void main(String[] args) throws IOException {
        //create a writer object that will write to a file
        FileWriter filterWriter = new FileWriter("outputFile.txt");
        //wrap the writer object in an object of your custom writer class
        MyFilterWriter myWriter = new MyFilterWriter(filterWriter);
        //write to the file
        myWriter.write("Hello How are you doing today ?");
        //close the writer streams
        myWriter.close();
        filterWriter.close();
    }
}
```

The output written to the file outputFile.txt is:

outputFile.txt

```
Hello_How_are_you_doing_today_?
```

CharArrayReader and CharArrayWriter

The CharArrayReader and the CharArrayWriter class are used to read and write a character array respectively. Both these classes implement a character buffer. The character array serves as a source of input for the CharArrayReader class.

In case of the CharArrayWriter class, the buffer size grows automatically when some data is written to the stream (Chan, Kramer and Lee, 1999).

A couple of examples demonstrating the use of these classes have been provided.

Example 1: A simple program demonstrating the use of the CharArrayReader and the CharArrayWriter classes.

CharArrayReaderWriterExample.java

```
package com.trial.java.fundamentals;

import java.io.CharArrayReader;
import java.io.CharArrayWriter;
import java.io.IOException;

public class CharArrayReaderWriterExample {

    public static void main(String[] args) throws IOException {

        String inputString = "Hello, How are you doing today?";

        // create an object of type CharArrayWriter
        CharArrayWriter charArrayWriter = new CharArrayWriter();

        System.out.println("Writing input string:" + inputString);
        // write the input string to the writer object
        charArrayWriter.write(inputString);

        // get the array of characters from the writer object
        char[] charArray = charArrayWriter.toCharArray();

        // create an object of type CharArrayReader
        CharArrayReader charArrayReader = new CharArrayReader(charArray);

        int charToread;
        // read the data written to the writer object
        System.out.print("Reading input string:");
        while ((charToread = charArrayReader.read()) != -1) {
            System.out.print((char) charToread);
        }

        // close the reader and writer objects
        charArrayWriter.close();
        charArrayReader.close();
    }
}
```

The output is:

Console | Problems | Javadoc | Declaration | Ann

```
<terminated> CharArrayReaderWriterExample [Java Application] C:\Pro
Writing input string:Hello, How are you doing today?
Reading input string:Hello, How are you doing today?
```

Example 2: Writing data to multiple files using the CharArrayWriter class

The CharArrayWriter class can also be used to write data to multiple files which can save time if we want to replicate data across many files. This is shown by the class CharArrayWriterExample.

```
CharArrayWriterExample.java

package com.trial.java.fundamentals;

import java.io.CharArrayWriter;
import java.io.FileWriter;
import java.io.IOException;

public class CharArrayWriterExample {

    public static void main(String[] args) throws IOException {

        // declare the input String
        String inputString = "Hello, How are you doing today?";

        // create an object of type CharArrayWriter
        CharArrayWriter charArrayWriter = new CharArrayWriter();

        // write the input string to the writer object
        charArrayWriter.write(inputString);

        // create 3 different files
        FileWriter file1 = new FileWriter("file1.txt");
        FileWriter file2 = new FileWriter("file2.txt");
        FileWriter file3 = new FileWriter("file3.txt");

        System.out.println("Writing the the following input to 3 files: " + inputString);

        // write the same input string to 3 different files
        charArrayWriter.writeTo(file1);
        charArrayWriter.writeTo(file2);
        charArrayWriter.writeTo(file3);

        // close the writer objects
        file1.close();
        file2.close();
        file3.close();
        charArrayWriter.close();

    }
}
```

The output generated is as follows:

```
Console  Problems  Javadoc  Declaration  Annotations  Call Hierarchy
<terminated> CharArrayWriterExample [Java Application] C:\Program Files\java\jdk1.8
Writing the the following input to 3 files: Hello, How are you doing today?
```

The content of the 3 files generated by the above program is shown below:

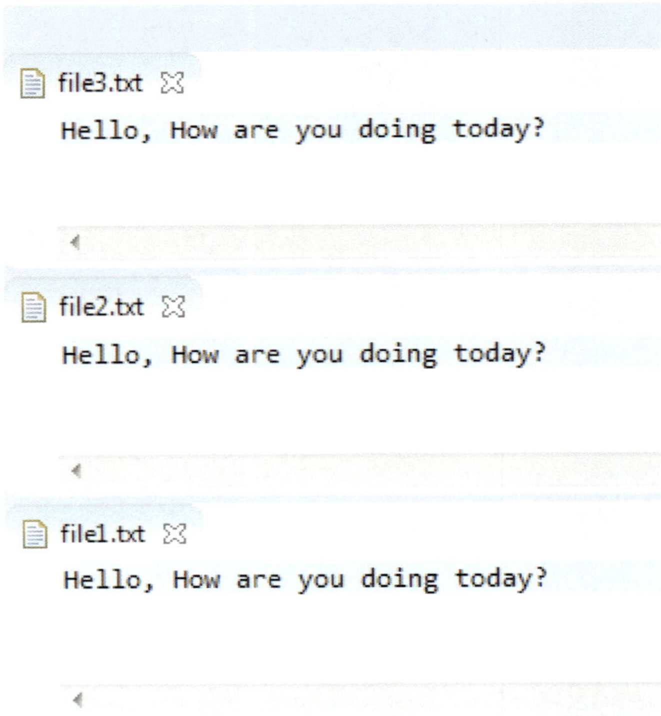

As shown by the content written in the files, the same content has been successfully written to 3 different files.

PipedInputStream and PipedOutputStream

These classes implement the input and output components of a traditional Operating System pipe operation. A pipe is basically a way to pass output from one process/program as an input to another program. A PipedOutputStream must be connected to a PipedInputStream and vice versa.

They both are connected to one other to create a communication pipe (Friesen, 2015). These classes can further be used to perform read and write operations at the same time as the streams are connected.

The data is sent via the PipedOutputStream (it serves as the sending end) and is fed as an input to the PipepInputStream (it serves as the receiving end).

PipedInputOutputStream.java

```java
package com.trial.java.fundamentals;

import java.io.IOException;
import java.io.PipedInputStream;
import java.io.PipedOutputStream;

public class PipedInputOutputStream {
    public static void main(String[] args) throws Exception {

        // declare the input String
        String inputString = "Hello, How are you doing today?";

        // create a PipedInputStream object
        PipedInputStream pipedInputStream = new PipedInputStream();

        // create a PipedOutputStream object
        PipedOutputStream pipedOutputStream = new PipedOutputStream();

        try {
            // connect the input and output stream
            pipedOutputStream.connect(pipedInputStream);

            // write data to the PipedOutputStream object
            System.out.println("Writing the following data: " + inputString);
            pipedOutputStream.write(inputString.getBytes());

            // reading the input that was written to the output stream
            System.out.print("Reading the following data: ");
            for (int i = 0; i < inputString.length(); i++) {
                System.out.print("" + (char) pipedInputStream.read());
            }

        } catch (IOException ex) {
            // close the stream
            pipedOutputStream.close();
            ex.printStackTrace();
        }
    }
}
```

In the above class, the PipedInputStream and the PipedOutputstream are connected to form a pipe. The output from the PipedOutputstream is fed to the PipedInputStream which further reads and prints the data.

The output is as follows:

Console | Problems | Javadoc | Declaration | Annotations

```
<terminated> PipedInputOutputStream [Java Application] C:\Program Files\javi
Writing the following data: Hello, How are you doing today?
Reading the following data: Hello, How are you doing today?
```

These classes are also used in the context of multithreading and will be discussed in Chapter 16.

PipedReader and PipedWriter

The PipedReader class is used to read piped character-input streams and the PipedWriter class is used to write piped character-output streams. Like the PipedInputStream and PipedOutputStream, these two classes are connected to one another where the PipedWriter class is the sender and the PipedInputStream is the receiver.

Output from the writer is sent as an input to the reader which reads the data.

PipedReaderWriterExample.java

```
package com.trial.java.fundamentals;

import java.io.IOException;
import java.io.PipedReader;
import java.io.PipedWriter;

public class PipedReaderWriterExample {

    public static void main(String[] args) throws IOException {

        // declare the input String
        String inputString = "Hello, How are you doing today?";

        // create a piped reader object
        PipedReader pipedReader = new PipedReader();

        // create a piped writer object
        PipedWriter pipedWriter = new PipedWriter();

        try {
            // connect the reader and the writer
            pipedWriter.connect(pipedReader);

            // write data to the writer object
            System.out.println("Writing the following data: " + inputString);
            pipedWriter.write(inputString);

            // reading the input that was written to the writer
            System.out.print("Reading the following data: ");
            for (int i = 0; i < inputString.length(); i++) {
                System.out.print("" + (char) pipedReader.read());
            }

        } catch (IOException ex) {
            // close the writer
            pipedWriter.close();
            ex.printStackTrace();
        }
    }
}
```

The output is:

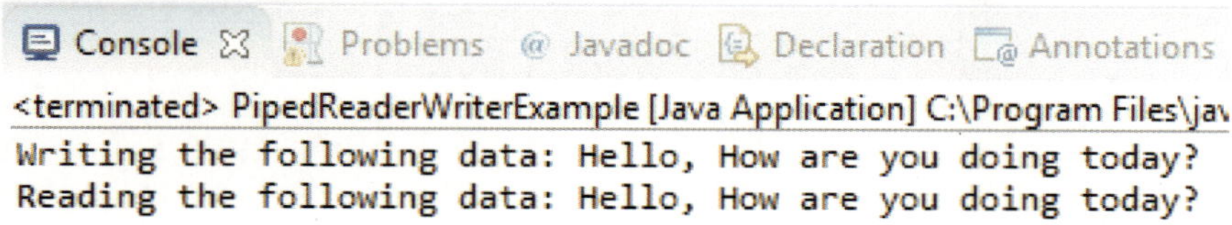

The PipedReader and the PipedWriter classes are also used in a multithreaded context which will be discussed in Chapter 16.

Additional information about the I/O package is provided at the following link:

https://docs.oracle.com/javase/7/docs/api/java/io/package-summary.html

The scope of this book does not cover all the classes that are part of the java I/O package.

CHAPTER 10

NEW I/O (NIO)

The java New I/O package is a library that was introduced starting from java version 4. It is an alternative to the existing traditional I/O package. This package NIO provides high-speed, block-oriented input output operations in our regular Java code. This NIO package makes use of low-level optimizations in a manner better than the traditional I/O without using native machine code. This means that the I/O operations are performed directly at the operating system level, which reduces the time spent on time consuming I/O operations (Friesen, 2015).

The NIO package is based on the concepts of Buffer, Channels, Selectors and Non-Blocking I/O.

We shall now discuss these concepts in brief.

CHANNELS AND BUFFERS

In traditional java I/O we make use of character and byte streams to perform I/O operations such as read and write.

But, in NIO, Channels and Buffers are at the heart of the I/O operations. In NIO, the data is written to a Buffer from a Channel and read vice versa.

A Channel is simply an object that permits you to read and write data to it. Here a channel is analogous to a Stream. Using NIO channels, we do not write data directly to the Channel but to Buffers, which provides decoupling of the data and the connection stream.

Channels are slightly different from streams as they are bi-directional. We can open a channel for reading, writing or both the operations.

A Buffer is an object in NIO that holds your data that can be read or data that has to be written to a particular destination. A buffer is very similar to an array in java. It is basically a simple array of bytes. But it provides many more additional features than a simple array such as structured access to the data, various methods to manipulate data, tracking of the read and write operations performed on the data and so on.

A channel reads and reads data from and to a buffer respectively. This is illustrated below:

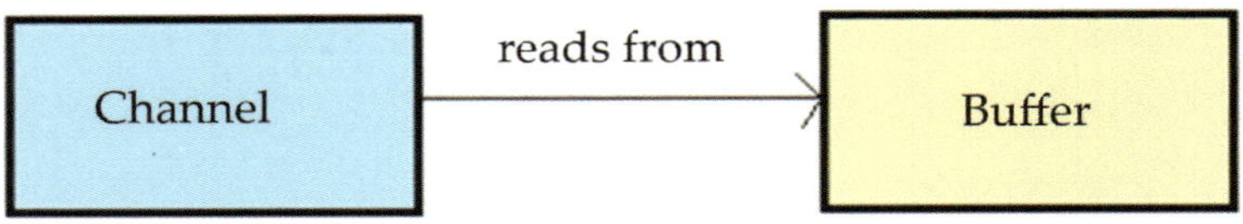

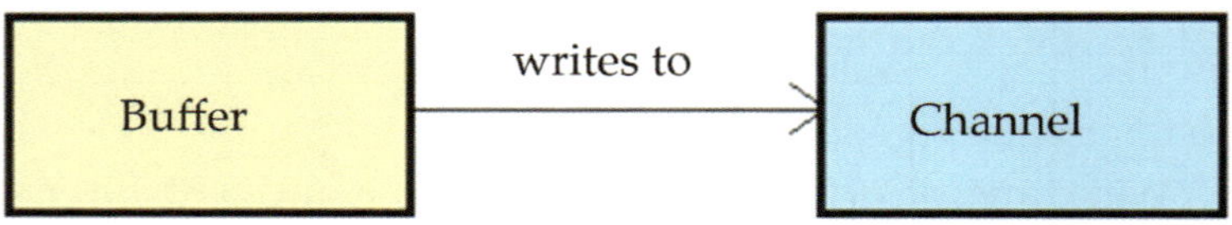

The NIO package consists of a Buffer class that holds primitive data types. This class has the following subclasses:

- IntBuffer : Buffer that operates on primitive type int
- ShortBuffer : Buffer that operates on primitive type short
- LongBuffer : Buffer that operates on primitive type long
- FloatBuffer : Buffer that operates on primitive type float
- DoubleBuffer : Buffer that operates on primitive type double
- CharBuffer : Buffer that operates on primitive type char
- ByteBuffer : Buffer that operates on primitive type byte

The Channels package consists of several types of channel classes and interfaces. Some of them have been described below.

Channel Classes (Friesen, 2015):

Table 8: Channel Classes (Friesen, 2015)

Class	**Description**
FileChannel	This channel helps read, write, map and manipulate files
DatagramChannel	This channel is used for datagram related sockets (selectable)
AsynchronousFileChannel	This channel is an asynchronous file channel
SocketChannel	This channel is used for connecting sockets (selectable)
Pipe	This channel consists of two unidirectional channels that implement a pipe

Channel Interfaces (Friesen, 2015):

Table 9: Channel Interfaces (Friesen, 2015)

Interface	**Description**
ByteChanel	A class implementing this channel interface can read/write bytes
AsynchronousByteChannel	A class implementing this channel interface supports asynchronous I/O operations
AsynchronousChannel	A class implementing this channel interface is an asynchronous file channel
NetworkChannel	A class implementing this channel interface implements a network socket
MulticastChannel	A class implementing this channel interface implements and supports IP multicasting operation
ReadableByteChannel	A class implementing this channel interface can perform read operations on bytes

The classes DatagramChannel and SocketChannel are marked as selectable classes which means that they can be selected by the Selector interface. This will be discussed in Section 10.4

The next section covers some examples demonstrating the use of Channels and Buffers

Examples of Channels and Buffers

Example 1: ByteBuffer put() method

```
NIOExample1.java

package com.java.nio;

import java.io.IOException;

public class NIOExample1 {

    public static void main(String[] args) throws IOException {

        // create a byteBuffer and allocate a size
        ByteBuffer byteBuffer = ByteBuffer.allocate(3);
        // use the put() method to add elements to it
        for (int i = 0; i < byteBuffer.capacity(); i++)
            byteBuffer.put((byte) 3);

        // display the contents of the Buffer
        System.out.println(Arrays.toString(byteBuffer.array()));
    }
}
```

The output is:

```
Console    Proble
<terminated> NIOExample1
[3, 3, 3]
```

Example 2: ByteBuffer get() method

NIOExample2.java

```
package com.java.nio;

import java.nio.ByteBuffer;

public class NIOExample2 {

    public static void main(String[] args) {

        // create a byteBuffer and allocate a size
        ByteBuffer byteBuffer = ByteBuffer.allocate(3);
        // use the put() method to add elements to it
        for (int i = 0; i < byteBuffer.capacity(); i++)
            byteBuffer.put((byte) (i+1));
        System.out.print("Contents of the ByteBuffer are:");
        // use the get() method to retrieve the elements from it
        for (int i = 0; i < byteBuffer.capacity(); i++) {
            System.out.print(byteBuffer.get(i) + " ");
        }
    }
}
```

The output is as follows:

```
Console  Problems  @ Javadoc
<terminated> NIOExample2 [Java Application] C:\
Contents of the ByteBuffer are:1 2 3
```

Example 3: Read a file using Channels and Buffers.

The following example shows the use of Channels and Buffers.

The example reads the following file:

```
myFile.txt
Hello, How are you today?
```

NIOExample3.java

```java
package com.java.nio;

import java.io.IOException;
import java.io.RandomAccessFile;
import java.nio.ByteBuffer;
import java.nio.channels.FileChannel;

public class NIOExample3 {
    public static void main(String args[]) throws IOException {

        // create a file and open it in read mode
        RandomAccessFile inputFile = new RandomAccessFile("myFile.txt", "rw");
        // create a FileChannel object
        FileChannel fileChannel = inputFile.getChannel();
        // create a ByteBuffer to store the file contents
        ByteBuffer byteBuffer = ByteBuffer.allocate(512);

        // read the file and display its contents
        while (fileChannel.read(byteBuffer) > 0) {
            // flip the buffer to prepare for get operation
            byteBuffer.flip();
            while (byteBuffer.hasRemaining()) {
                System.out.print((char) byteBuffer.get());
            }
            // clear the buffer to make it ready for next read operation
            byteBuffer.clear();
        }

        // close the file
        inputFile.close();
    }
}
```

The output is:

```
Console  Problems  Javadoc
<terminated> NIOExample3 [Java Application]
Hello, How are you today?
```

Example 4: Write to a File using Channels and Buffers

This example creates a new file named myFile1.txt and writes data to it.

NIOExample4.java

```
package com.java.nio;

import java.io.IOException;
import java.io.RandomAccessFile;
import java.nio.ByteBuffer;
import java.nio.channels.FileChannel;

public class NIOExample4 {

    public static void main(String args[]) throws IOException {

        // create a file and open it in read mode
        RandomAccessFile inputFile = new RandomAccessFile("myFile1.txt", "rw");

        // create a FileChannel object
        FileChannel fileChannel = inputFile.getChannel();
        //input string
        String data = "It is a good day today!";

        // create a ByteBuffer to store the data to write to the file
        ByteBuffer byteBuffer = ByteBuffer.wrap(data.getBytes());

        // write the data
        fileChannel.write(byteBuffer);

        // close the channel
        fileChannel.close();

        // close the file
        inputFile.close();
    }
}
```

The contents of the file myFile1 are as follows:

myFile1.txt

```
It is a good day today!
```

Example 5: Read and Write to a File using Channels and Buffers

This example writes data to a file and then reads the data written to the file.

```
NIOExample5.java
package com.java.nio;

import java.io.IOException;

public class NIOExample5 {

    public static void main(String[] args) throws IOException {

        // input String to write to the file
        String string = "It is a good day today";
        byte[] byteArray = string.getBytes();
        // create ByteBuffer to write the data to the file
        ByteBuffer byteBufferWrite = ByteBuffer.wrap(byteArray);

        // create a file and open it in read-write mode
        RandomAccessFile randomAccessFileWrite = new RandomAccessFile("myFile.txt", "rw");
        // create an object of type FileChannel for write() operation
        FileChannel outputFileChannel = randomAccessFileWrite.getChannel();

        // Write data to the file
        outputFileChannel.write(byteBufferWrite);

        // close the file and the channel
        outputFileChannel.close();
        randomAccessFileWrite.close();

        // create a file and open it in read mode
        RandomAccessFile randomAccessFileRead = new RandomAccessFile("myFile.txt", "r");
        // create an object of type FileChannel for read() operation
        FileChannel inputFileChannel = randomAccessFileRead.getChannel();

        // create a byteBuffer to store the contents of the file
        ByteBuffer byteBufferRead = ByteBuffer.allocate(1024);
        // create a charset to decode the contents of the buffer in acii format
        Charset charset = Charset.forName("US-ASCII");

        // read the file using the Channel
        while (inputFileChannel.read(byteBufferRead) > 0) {
            // use rewind() to bring the position of the buffer to beginning
            byteBufferRead.rewind();
            System.out.print(charset.decode(byteBufferRead));
            // flip the buffer to prepare it for the next read operation
            byteBufferRead.flip();
        }
        // close the file and channel
        inputFileChannel.close();
        randomAccessFileRead.close();
    }
}
```

The above example firsts writes data from a String to the file and then reads the data that was written in the file. If the file doesn't exist, a new file is created. If the file exists and is not empty, then the contents of the file are overwritten with the new contents.

The output generated by the above class is:

```
Console  Problems  Javadoc
<terminated> NIOExample5 [Java Application]
It is a good day today
```

The contents of the file 'myFile' are as follows:

myFile.txt

```
It is a good day today
```

Example 6: TransferFrom() method

This example transfers the contents of a file (myFile.txt) to another file (myFile1.txt) using channels.

Initially, the contents of the two files are as follows:

myFile.txt

```
It is a good day today
```

myFile1.txt

```
How are you?
```

The class is as follows:

NIOExample6.java

```
package com.java.nio;

import java.io.IOException;

public class NIOExample6 {

    public static void main(String[] args) throws IOException {

        // create a file to copy the contents from and open it in read-write
        // mode
        RandomAccessFile fromFile = new RandomAccessFile("myFile.txt", "rw");

        // create an object of type FileChannel
        FileChannel fromChannel = fromFile.getChannel();

        // create a file to write the contents to and open it in read-write mode
        RandomAccessFile toFile = new RandomAccessFile("myFile1.txt", "rw");

        // create an object of type FileChannel
        FileChannel toChannel = toFile.getChannel();

        // transfer contents from file 'myFile' to 'myFile1'
        toChannel.transferFrom(fromChannel, 0, fromChannel.size());

        // close the channels
        fromChannel.close();
        toChannel.close();

        // close the files
        fromFile.close();
        toFile.close();
    }
}
```

After execution of the program, the contents of myFile.txt have been updated as follows:

```
myFile1.txt

It is a good day today
```

Example 7: Transfer contents from one file to another using buffers

The contents of the two files 'inputFile.txt' and 'outputFile.txt' before the copy operation are as follows:

```
outputFile.txt

Hi!!!
```

```
inputFile.txt

Hello! How are you doing?
Have a good day!!!
```

The class NIOExample7 that performs the copy operation is shown below:

```java
NIOExample7.java

package com.java.nio;

import java.io.FileInputStream;

public class NIOExample7 {

    public static void main(String args[]) throws IOException {

        FileInputStream inputStream = new FileInputStream("inputFile.txt");
        // create an object of type ReadableByteChannel to read contents of
        // input file
        ReadableByteChannel sourceChannel = inputStream.getChannel();

        FileOutputStream outputStream = new FileOutputStream("outputFile.txt");
        // create an object of type WritableByteChannel to write to the output
        // file
        WritableByteChannel destinationChannel = outputStream.getChannel();

        // create ByteBuffer to store and manipulate data from the file
        ByteBuffer byteBuffer = ByteBuffer.allocate(1024);

        while (sourceChannel.read(byteBuffer) != -1) {
            // flip the buffer to prepare if for writing
            byteBuffer.flip();
            // write contents to destination file
            destinationChannel.write(byteBuffer);
            // clear the buffer
            byteBuffer.clear();
        }

        // close the channels
        sourceChannel.close();
        destinationChannel.close();

        // close the streams
        inputStream.close();
        outputStream.close();
    }
}
```

After execution of the class, the contents of the file 'outputFile' are updated as follows:

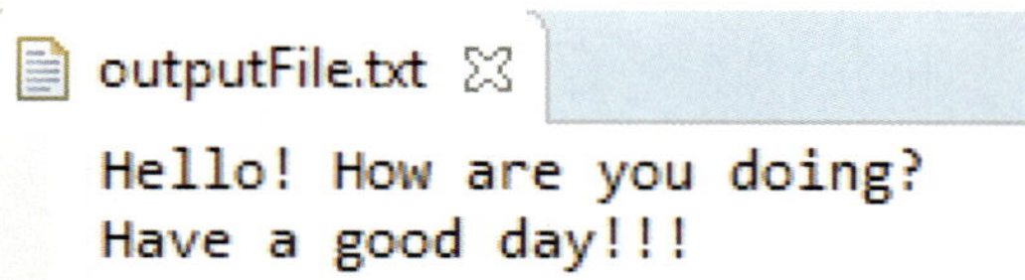

NIO PATH AND FILES CLASS

The NIO package in Java provides additional utility classes Path, Files and Paths that help in handling of files.

Path: This is an object that can be used to locate a files situated on a file system. It serves as an entrypoint for the java.nio.File class. Like its name, 'Path' represents the actual path of a file on the file system such 'C: \xyz.txt' for example. It represents a system dependant file path (docs. Oracle.com, 2017).

Files: This is a utility class that provides api that can be used to perform operations on files and different file types or directories. This class is composed of only static methods.

Paths: This class is another utility class that helps recover a **Path** object. It is made up entirely static methods that return a Path object from a string input or a URI.

The above classes are used in combination with one another. A Path object is a real representation of the underlying operating system. A path is dependent on the system; in Windows is shown as C:\mtfoler and a path in Linux is /home/myfolder. Path from two different Operating Systems cannot be compared.

A path object can be used to in many ways; by appending to it, extracting parts of the path from it, compare different paths and so on. Additionally, a Path object can be used in combination with the Files class to check if a file exists at the given path and manipulate files by performing different file operations such as file creation, opening, deletion, changing the owner and its permissions and so on.

The classes Files, Paths and Path provide several methods that help in file and directory manipulation.

Some important methods from these classes are described below.

Paths Class Methods

Table 10: Path class methods (docs.Oracle.com, 2017)

Method	Description
static Path get(String first, String otherStrings…)	This method takes the path as an input of multiple strings which when joined gives the entire path String and returns a Path object
static Path get(URI uri)	This method takes the given URI (uniform resource identifier) and returns a Path objects

Files Class Methods

Table 11: Files class methods (docs.Oracle.com, 2017)

Method	Description
static boolean deleteIfexists(Path path)	This method deletes a file if it exists at the given path and returns true if the file was deleted.
static boolean exists(Path path, LinkOption…options)	This method tests if a file exists and returns true if it does.
static byte[] readAllBytes(Path path)	This method reads all the bytes from a file and returns a byte array containing the bytes that were read
static List<String> readAllLines(Path path)	This method reads all the lines from a file and returns a list of Strings containing the contents of the file
static Path setOwner(Path path, UserPrincipal owner)	This method updates the owner of the file to the owner specified as a parameter.
static long size(Path path)	This method returns the size of a file in bytes
static Path write(Path path, byte[] bytes, OpenOption..options)	This method writes bytes to a file
static Path write(Path path, Iterable <? extends CharSequence, OpenOption..options)	This method writes lines of text input to a file.
static Path createDirectory(Path dir, FileAttribute>?> attributes)	This method creates a new directory and returns its path

Static path createFile(Path path, FileAttribute>?> attributes)	This method creates a new empty file and returns its path. This method fails if the file already exists.
Static BufferedReader new BufferedReader(Path path)	This methods opens a file at the specified path for reading and returns a BufferedReader object to read the file text
Static BufferedWriter new BufferedWriter(Path path, OpenOption…options)	This methods opens/creates a file at the specified path for writing and returns a BufferedReader object to write contents to the file

Path Class Methods

Table 12: Path class methods (docs.Oracle.com, 2017)

Method	**Description**
int compareTo(Path anotherPath)	This method compares two paths
boolean endsWith(Path otherPath)	This method returns true if the invoking path ends with the specified path
boolean startsWith(Path otherPath)	This method returns true if the invoking path starts with the specified path
Path toAbsolutePath()	This method returns a Path object with the absolute path
File toFile()	This method returns a File object that represents the Path
Path subpath(int beginIndex, int endIndex)	This method returns a relative path that is a sequence of the names of the elements in the path
URI toUri()	This methods returns a URI representing the path
Path normalize()	This method eliminates redundant elements and returns a path
boolean isAbsolute()	This method returns true if the given path is absolute
Path getFileName()	This method returns the name of the file or directory held by the path
Path getName(int index)	This method returns a name element as a Path object
Path getRoot()	This method returns the root directory/element of the path
Path getParent()	This method returns the path of the parent or null if no parent exists for the path
int getNameCount()	This method returns the number of elements present in the path

Examples

Example 1: ***Simple File creation***

NIOExample8.java

```java
package com.java.nio;

import java.io.File;

public class NIOExample8 {

    public static void main(String[] args) {

        // create a new file at a particluar location
        File file = new File("c:\\myFile.text");

        // prints true if the file exists at the specified location
        System.out.println(file.exists());

        // prints the absolute path of the file
        System.out.println("Absolute path is: " +file.getAbsoluteFile());
    }
}
```

The output is:

```
Console    Problems    @ Javadoc
<terminated> NIOExample8 [Java Application]
false
Absolute path is: c:\myFile.text
```

As seen from the output, as the file did not exist before creation, the method returns false. A new file named myFile.txt is created at the location specified by the path.

Example 2: Retrieve information about the path using static methods of the Paths and Path class

NIOExample9.java

```java
package com.java.nio;
import java.nio.file.Path;
import java.nio.file.Paths;
public class NIOExample9 {
    public static void main(String[] args) {
        //getting the path instance
        Path path = Paths.get("F:\\workspace\\Trial\\outputFile.txt");
        //this will print the complete path
        System.out.println("Path is; " +path);
        //get the file name
        path = path.getFileName();
        //print the file name
        System.out.println("File Name; " +path);
        //gets the Name at a particular index
        path = path.getName(0);
        //print the name
        System.out.println(path);
        //get the number of elements on the path
        int count = path.getNameCount();
        System.out.println("Number of elements: " +count);
        Path path2 = Paths.get("F:\\workspace\\Trial\\outputFile.txt");
        //get subpath
        path = path2.subpath(0, 2);
        System.out.println("Sub Path: " + path);
        //get parent path
        path = path.getParent();
        System.out.println("Parent path: " + path);
        Path path1 = Paths.get("F:\\workspace\\Trial\\outputFile.txt");
        //get root path. This will print the drive such as C:\
        path = path1.getRoot();
        System.out.println("Root Path: " + path);
        //get Current directory
        Path currentDir = Paths.get(".");
        System.out.println("Current Directory:" +currentDir.toAbsolutePath());
    }
}
```

The output is:

Console | @ Javadoc | Declaration | Problems

```
<terminated> NIOExample9 [Java Application] C:\Program Files\
Path is; F:\workspace\Trial\outputFile.txt
File Name; outputFile.txt
outputFile.txt
Number of elements: 1
Sub Path: workspace\Trial
Parent path: workspace
Root Path: F:\
Current Directory:F:\workspace\Trial\.
```

Example 3: equals(), startsWith() and endsWith() methods

NIOExample10.java

```
package com.java.nio;

import java.nio.file.Path;

public class NIOExample10 {

    public static void main(String[] args) {

        Path path = Paths.get("F:\\workspace\\Trial\\outputFile.txt");
        Path otherPath = Paths.get("F:\\workspace\\Trial\\outputFile1.txt");

        // get beginning
        Path beginningOfPath = Paths.get("F:\\");

        // get ending
        Path endingOfPath = Paths.get("outputFile.txt");

        // match the paths if they are equal
        if (path.equals(otherPath)) {
            System.out.println("Paths are equal");
        } // match the beginning of the file
        else if (path.startsWith(beginningOfPath)) {
            System.out.println("The beginnings of both the Paths match");
        } // match the endings of the file
        else if (path.endsWith(endingOfPath)) {
            System.out.println("The ends of both the Paths match");
        }
    }
}
```

The output is:

```
Console  Problems  Javadoc  De
<terminated> NIOExample10 [Java Application] C:\P
The beginnings of both the Paths match
```

Example 4: Iterate over the Name elements of a path

NIOExample11.java

```
package com.java.nio;

import java.nio.file.Path;

public class NIOExample11 {

    public static void main(String[] args) {

        Path path = Paths.get("F:\\workspace\\Trial\\outputFile.txt");
        System.out.println("Iterating over the elements of a Path");
        for (Path name: path) {
            System.out.println(name);
        }
    }
}
```

The output is as follows:

```
Console ⊠  Problems  @ Javadoc
<terminated> NIOExample11 [Java Application] C:
Iterating over the elements of a Path
workspace
Trial
outputFile.txt
```

The Path class implements the Comparable interface which means that two paths can be compared using the compareTo method (docs. Oracle.com, 2017).

Example 5: Read the contents of a file using the method readAllLines()

```java
NIOExample12.java ⊠
package com.java.nio;

import java.io.IOException;

public class NIOExample12 {

    public static void main(String[] args) throws IOException {

        // get path object for the file
        Path path = Paths.get("outputFile.txt");

        // read the contents of the file as lines
        List<String> contents = Files.readAllLines(path);
        // print the contents of the file
        for (String content : contents) {
            System.out.println(content);
        }
    }
}
```

The output is:

```
Console ⊠  Problems  @ Javadoc
<terminated> NIOExample12 [Java Application]
Hello! How are you doing?
Have a good day!!!
```

Example 6: Write to a file using the write() method

NIOExample13.java

```
package com.java.nio;

import java.io.IOException;
import java.nio.file.Files;
import java.nio.file.Path;
import java.nio.file.Paths;

public class NIOExample13 {

    public static void main(String[] args) throws IOException {

        // Get the path of the file
        Path path = Paths.get("output.txt");

        // declare the input to be written to the file
        String inputString = "How are you doing on this fine day?";
        try {
            // write to the file
            Files.write(path, inputString.getBytes());
        } catch (IOException e) {
            System.out.println(e);
        }
    }
}
```

The above class writes to the file output.txt. The contents of this file are:

output.txt

```
How are you doing on this fine day?
```

Example 7: Reading the contents of a file using a BufferedReader object

NIOExample14.java

```
package com.java.nio;

import java.io.BufferedReader;

public class NIOExample14 {

    public static void main(String[] args) {
        //get path of the file
        Path path = Paths.get("output.txt");
        //get a reader object using the newBufferedReader() method
        try (BufferedReader reader = Files.newBufferedReader(path, Charset.forName("UTF-8")))
        {
            String line = " ";
            //print the contents
            while((line = reader.readLine()) != null)
                System.out.println(line);
        }
        catch (IOException e)
        {
            System.out.println(e);
        }
    }
}
```

The output is as follows:

```
Console  Problems  Javadoc  De
<terminated> NIOExample14 [Java Application] C:\Pr
It is a beautiful day today, isn't it?
```

Example 8: Write to a file using a BufferedWriter object

```
NIOExample15.java
package com.java.nio;

import java.io.BufferedWriter;

public class NIOExample15 {

    public static void main(String[] args) {

        //get path of the file
        Path path = Paths.get("output.txt");

        //get a BufferedWriter object using the newBufferedWriter() method
        try (BufferedWriter writer = Files.newBufferedWriter(path, Charset.forName("UTF-8")))
        {
            //write to the file
            writer.write("It is a beautiful day today, isn't it?");
        }
        catch (IOException e)
        {
            System.out.println(e);
        }
    }
}
```

On execution of the above code, the file output.txt is updated with the contents specified. The contents of the file output.txt are:

```
output.txt
It is a beautiful day today, isn't it?
```

Example 9: Write to a file by providing options

Various options for opening a file are defined by the class StandardOpenOption. This class provides us with useful file operation constants such APPEND, CREATE, CREATE_NEW, READ etc. In this example, we make use of constants from this class to open the file in append mode. Additionally, we write a List of Strings to the file.

The initial contents of the file are:

```
output.txt
It is a beautiful day today, isn't it?
```

The class is as follows:

NIOExample16.java

```
package com.java.nio;

import java.io.IOException;
import java.nio.charset.StandardCharsets;
import java.nio.file.Files;
import java.nio.file.Path;
import java.nio.file.Paths;
import java.nio.file.StandardOpenOption;
import java.util.ArrayList;
import java.util.List;

public class NIOExample16 {

    public static void main(String[] args) {

        /// Get the path of the file
        Path path = Paths.get("output.txt");

        // declare the input to be written to the file
        String firstLine = "How are you doing on this fine day?";
        String secondLine = "Let us go out and explore the city!";
        //add the inputs to a list
        List<String> inputList = new ArrayList<String>();
        inputList.add(firstLine);
        inputList.add(secondLine);

        try {
            // write to the file using the write() method with options
            //provide the path, a list of input strings, the charset and the options for writing to the file
            Files.write(path, inputList, StandardCharsets.UTF_8, StandardOpenOption.CREATE, StandardOpenOption.APPEND);
        }
        catch (IOException e)
        {
            System.out.println(e);
        }
    }
}
```

The updated contents of the file output.txt are as follows:

output.txt

```
It is a beautiful day today, isn't it?
How are you doing on this fine day?
Let us go out and explore the city!
```

Example 10: File createFile(), isRegularFile(), isReadable() , isWritable() methods

NIOExample17.java

```
package com.java.nio;

import java.io.IOException;
import java.nio.file.Files;
import java.nio.file.LinkOption;
import java.nio.file.Path;
import java.nio.file.Paths;

public class NIOExample17 {

    public static void main(String[] args) throws IOException {
        // create a file by specifying only its path
        Path path = Files.createFile(Paths.get("myOutputFile1.txt"));

        // print its absolute path
        System.out.println("Path is:" + path.toAbsolutePath());

        // verify if the file is readable, writable and a regular file with opaque content
        if (Files.isReadable(path) && Files.isWritable(path) && Files.isRegularFile(path, LinkOption.NOFOLLOW_LINKS))
            System.out.println("File is readable and writable and is a regular file");
    }
}
```

The output is:

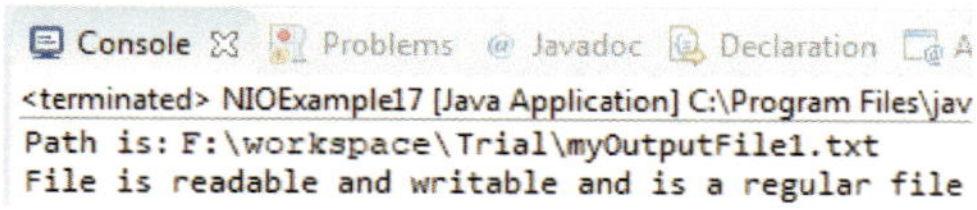

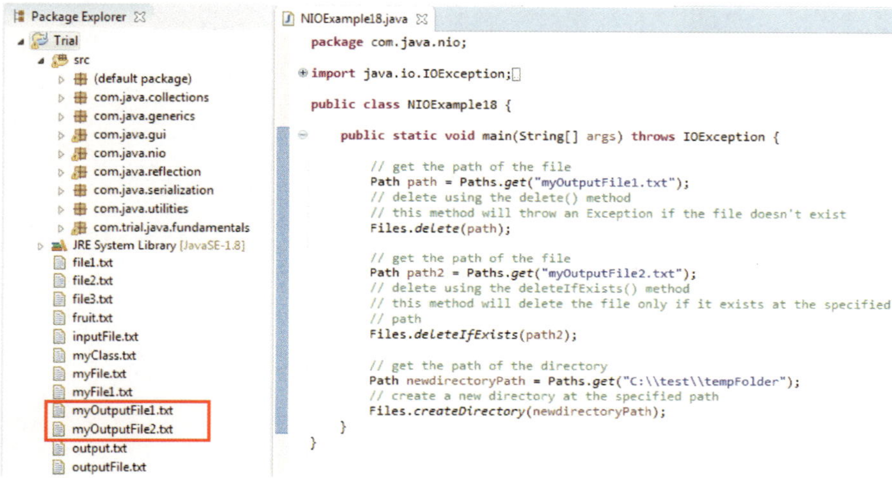

On execution of the code, the highlighted files are deleted and a new directory is created at the specified location.

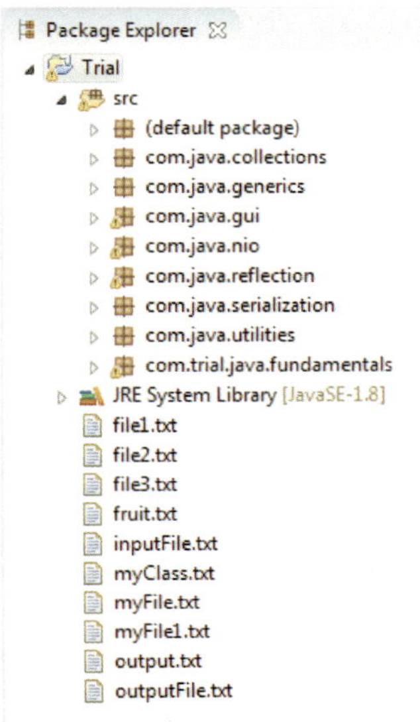

Example 10: FileSystem API

NIOExample19.java

```java
package com.java.nio;

import java.nio.file.FileSystem;
import java.nio.file.FileSystems;
import java.nio.file.Path;

public class NIOExample19 {

    public static void main(String[] args) {

        //get the default FileSystem
        FileSystem fileSystem = FileSystems.getDefault();

        //get Path of a file using the FileSystem object
        Path path = fileSystem.getPath("file1.txt");
        System.out.println("File Name:" + path.getFileName());

        //iterate and list all the system directories
        Iterable<Path> dirs = fileSystem.getRootDirectories();
        System.out.println("Listing all the system directories:");
        for (Path name : dirs) {
            System.out.println(name);
        }

        System.out.println("Checking if the File System is open");
        // will always print true as file systems on the system are open by
        // default
        System.out.println(fileSystem.isOpen());

        System.out.println("Checking if the File System is read-only:");
        System.out.println(fileSystem.isReadOnly());
    }
}
```

The output generated is as follows:

```
Console  Problems  Javadoc  Declaration
<terminated> NIOExample19 [Java Application] C:\Progr
File Name:file1.txt
Listing all the system directories:
C:\
F:\
Q:\
S:\
U:\
V:\
Checking if the File System is open
true
Checking if the File System is read-only:
false
```

NIO SCATTER AND GATHER

The Java NIO package provides an interesting functionality called as scatter and gather. This a very powerful technology provided by this package that permits you to write bytes of data from multiple buffers to a channel and read data into a channel from multiple buffers. This functionality is inbuilt within the NIO package, which is generally used to perform read() and write() operations on channels using multiple buffers.

Scattering Read: This operation reads data from a single channel into many buffers (Horstmann and Cornell, 2002).

This is depicted below:

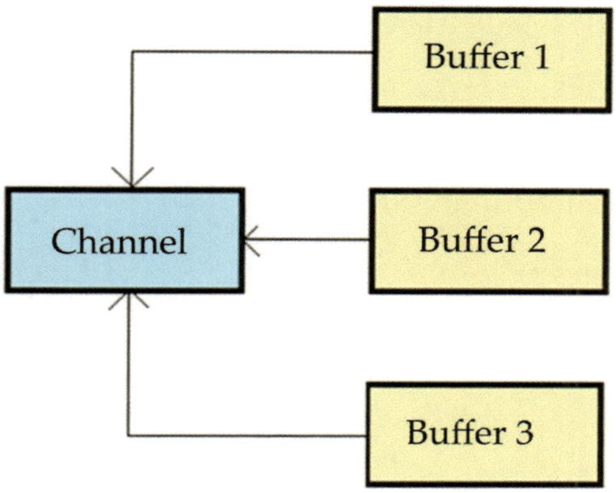

Programmatically the scattering read is done as follows:

```
ByteBuffer buffer1 = ByteBuffer.allocate(512);
ByteBuffer buffer2  = ByteBuffer.allocate(512);
ByteBuffer[] byteBufferArray = { buffer1, buffer2 };
//read data from multiple buffers
myChannel.read(byteBufferArray);
```

Gathering Write: This operation writes data from many buffers into a single channel ((Horstmann and Cornell, 2002). This is depicted below:

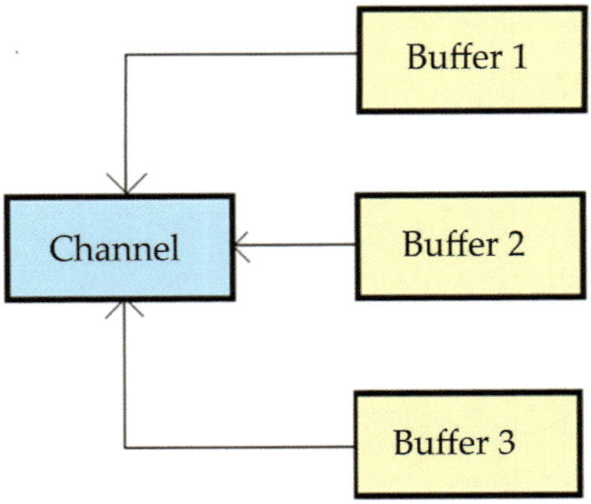

Programmatically the gathering write is done as follows:

```
ByteBuffer buffer1 = ByteBuffer.allocate(512);
ByteBuffer buffer2 = ByteBuffer.allocate(512);
//write data into multiple buffers
ByteBuffer[] bufferArray = { buffer1, buffer2 };
myChannel.write(bufferArray);
```

SELECTORS

In Java NIO a new concept called 'Selectors' has been introduced. This functionality basically provides a way to handle many sources of data. In java NIO, a Selector is basically a class that examines your channels and checks which channel is available for communication i.e. read and write operations.

This concept is very useful in a multithreaded context as by using Selectors, we now have the possibility to make use of a single thread to manipulate several data sources. This is efficient in terms of memory as context switching between threads is expensive for the underlying operating system. Additionally threads take up memory.

The abstract class Selector defined in the java.nio.channels package has been provided by NIO to provide this functionality. It is basically a multiplexor that takes in selectable channels. Selectable channels are those that can be used in non-blocking mode.

It is important to take note of the fact that in addition to providing read and write functionalities, Selectors are capable of listening for incoming connections and writing to several slow channels.

As the selector is capable of monitoring the streams of communication, it need less threads to handle the channels, thereby improving the efficiency.

NON-BLOCKING I/O

Java NIO permits us to perform Non-Blocking I/O operations.

For instance, imagine a thread asking a channel to read some data into a buffer. During the time the channel reads the buffer, the thread can be assigned to some other task. In this way, time is saved. Once the channel reads the data from the buffer, the thread can resume its previous task.

The exact same process is applicable in case of write() operations.

CHAPTER 11

ADVANCED JAVA CONCEPTS

NESTED CLASSES

Similar to nested loops, in java we have the possibility of writing and declaring nested classes in Java. These classes are called as inner classes. The syntax of a nested class is as follows:

```
    Class Outer {
        Class Inner {

        }
}
```

Nested classes are used as they help in logical grouping of classes that are used in a single place. Further they promote encapsulation and make the code more readable.

Nested class are of 2 types: Static/ Non-static or Inner classes

Static Nested classes

An inner class declared as static is called a static inner class. A static inner class has access to the static members of the class enclosing it, except for private members. It does not have the right to access the non-static members of the enclosing class. It can be declared as either public or default.

The syntax of such a class is as follows:

```
public class OuterClass {

        public static class InnerClass {


        }

}
```

A simple example of a static InnerClass is shown below:

OuterClass.java

```java
package com.trial.java.fundamentals;

public class OuterClass {

    int i = 10;
    static int j = 10;

    public static class InnerClass {

        int i = 20;

        private void method1() {
            // access outer class variable
            System.out.println("Outer class variable: " + i);
            // inner class variable
            System.out.println("Inner class variable: " + j);
        }

    }

    public static void main(String args[]) {

        OuterClass.InnerClass obj2 = new OuterClass.InnerClass();
        obj2.method1();

    }

}
```

The output generated by the class OuterClass is as follows:

```
Console  Problems  Javadoc
<terminated> OuterClass [Java Application]
Outer class variable: 20
Inner class variable: 10
```

An object of the inner class can be created using the syntax as shown in the above class OuterClass.

Inner/ Non-Static Classes

A non-static nested class, as its name suggests is an inner class that is not static. There are further divided into three types:

1. ***Basic Inner class:*** This is a class that is declared within another class. A simple example is shown below:

```java
NonStaticOuterClass.java
package com.trial.java.fundamentals;

public class NonStaticOuterClass {

    int i = 30;

    public class NestedNonStaticInnerClass {

        private void method1() {
            System.out.println("In inner class method");
            System.out.println("Accessing outer class variable i:" + i);
        }
    }

    public static void main(String args[]) {

        NonStaticOuterClass obj1 = new NonStaticOuterClass();

        NestedNonStaticInnerClass obj2 = obj1.new NestedNonStaticInnerClass();
        obj2.method1();

    }
}
```

As compared to the static inner class, we instantiate the non-static inner class with the object of the outer class. Non-static inner classes have access to all the members of the enclosing outer class, even their private members as shown in the class above.

The output generated is as follows:

```
Console ⊠  Problems  @ Javadoc  Dec
<terminated> NonStaticOuterClass [Java Application]
In inner class method
Accessing outer class variable i:30
```

2. ***Local Inner classes:*** These classes are nested classes that are declared within a method body or any block of code such methods, expressions and statements. We can declare these classes in an if loop, in an assignment statement, in a method, in a block of code and so on.

An example of a local class is as follows:

```java
LocalOuterClass.java ⊠
package com.trial.java.fundamentals;

public class LocalOuterClass {

    int i= 40;
    public void method1()
    {
        System.out.println("In local outer class method method1()");
        class LocalInnerClass
        {
            void method2()
            {
                System.out.println("In local inner class method method2()");
                System.out.println("Accessing outer class variable i from the inner class:" + i);
            }
        }
        LocalInnerClass obj1 = new LocalInnerClass();
        obj1.method2();
    }


    public static void main(String[] args) {

        LocalOuterClass obj1 = new LocalOuterClass();
        obj1.method1();

    }
}
```

In the above example, the inner class cannot be accessed from the main method of the outer class. Hence, its instance has been created and used within the outer/enclosing class method. The output generated is as shown below:

```
Console ⌧  Problems  @ Javadoc  Declaration  Annotation
<terminated> LocalOuterClass [Java Application] C:\Program Files\java\jdk1.8.
In local outer class method method1()
In local inner class method method2()
Accessing outer class variable i from the inner class:40
```

A key critical point to note is that the local class cannot be declared as public. It has to be declared as default.

3. ***Anonymous inner classes:*** These classes are nested classes that are declared within a method body and they do not have a name, which is why they are called as anonymous inner classes.

These classes are similar to local classes except that they do not have a name. They can be declared via two ways: class and interface. Both have been explained below:

Using a Class

In this case, a class is sub-classed in another class. The example AnaonymousClassDemo shows how to create and instantiate an anonymous class.

```
AnonymousClassDemo.java ⌧
package com.trial.java.fundamentals;
public class AnonymousClassDemo
{
  public static void main(String[] args)
  {
      //create anonymous class
    AnonymousClass obj1 = new AnonymousClass() {
      public void method1 ()
      {
        System.out.println("Anonymous class method1");
      }
    }; // anonymous class body closes here
    //the instance obj1 contains an object of the anonymous subclass of AnonymousClass.
    obj1.method1();
  }
}

class AnonymousClass
{
  public void method1()
  {
    System.out.println("Classic class ");
  }
}
```

As seen from the example, the class Anonymous class is a simple class like any other java class. The important part is in the class AnonymousClassDemo, where an anonymous class instance of class AnonymousClass has been created. As we can see, an object of class Anonymous class with a method body has been created along with the instantiation of the object. The body ends with a semicolon. This is not a normal class as we generally do not see method definitions when we instantiate a class. In reality, the above code is actually creating a subclass/child class of the class AnonymousClass. The instance object obj1 is an instance of the anonymous subclass declared within the class AnonymousClassDemo. So, it is a subclass.

When we execute this program, the output is as below:

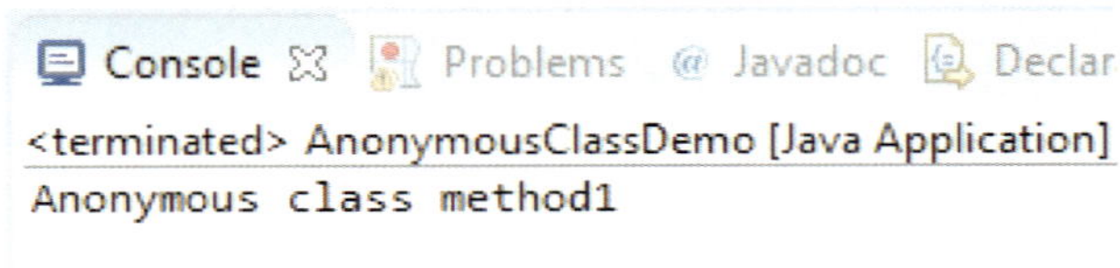

As noted from the output, the method1() of the anonymous class declared in the class AnonymousClassDemo has been invoked. The overridden method has been called. This class is called an anonymous class because it literally has no name. Its entire structure has been created within an instance object.

Using an Interface

In this case, an interface is instantiated and implemented at the same time by a class. This is shown by the class AnonymousImplementation below:

```
AnonymousImplementation.java

package com.trial.java.fundamentals;

public class AnonymousImplementation {

        public static void main(String[] args)
        {
            //create anonymous class and implement the interface method
            AnonymousInterface obj1 = new AnonymousInterface() {
            public void method1 ()
            {
              System.out.println("Anonymous class method1");
            }
          }; // anonymous class body closes here
          //the instance obj1 contains an object of the anonymous subclass of AnonymousInterface.
          obj1.method1();
        }
    }

    interface AnonymousInterface
    {
      public void method1();

    }
```

The figure above shows that this example is similar to the previous one; the only difference being that in this example, an interface has been instantiated and its method has been implemented by the class AnonymousImplmentation on instantiation.

The output of this class is the same as from the previous example.

```
Console    Problems  @ Javado
<terminated> AnonymousImplementation
Anonymous class method1
```

Why use these anonymous classes?

Anonymous inner classes help in overriding methods of a superclass. But this can be done in a separate class as well. Then why should we make use of an anonymous inner class? Well, this is helpful when you want to override a small part/function of code without creating a whole new class via inheritance and overriding. In short, the overhead of creating a new class can be avoided using such classes. Additionally, if the particular piece of code is going to be used only once, an anonymous class makes more sense.

In general, nested classes serve readability of code and allow us to view the classes conveniently package-wise. Additionally, local or non-static nested classes are used when you need to create several instances of the local class and get access to the members (both static and non-static), constructor and methods of the enclosing class. Static nested classed should be used when you want to access only the static members of the enclosing class.

WRAPPER CLASSES IN JAVA

As we have already seen, java has 8 primitive data types. Each one of these classes has a class dedicated to it. These classes are called as wrapper classes. They are named as such because they 'wrap' the primitive data type and it value and convert it into an object of its wrapper class.

Wrapper classes are used so that primitive data types can perform operations similar to that of objects. This is especially useful when using members of the Collections framework which will be discussed in the next chapter.

Additionally they provide the functionality to convert objects into primitive types as well.

Since the java se version 5 this is done automatically. It is called as autoboxing and unboxing where primitives are converted to objects and vice versa (Gosling, 2000).

Below is a table that shows the primitive types along with their respective wrapper classes:

Table 13: Wrapper classes

Primitive Data Type	**Wrapper Class**
Int	Integer
Long	Long
Float	Float
Double	Double
Byte	Byte
Short	Short
Char	Character
Boolean	Boolean

A sample java program making use of wrapper classes is shown below:

```
WrapperClasses.java

package com.trial.java.fundamentals;

public class WrapperClasses {

    public static void main(String[] args) {

        int int1=1;

        //auotboxing done by compiler automatically.
        //primitive type 'int' converted to object 'Integer'
        Integer int2 = int1;
        System.out.println("Autoboxing:" + int2);

        //converting a primitive type to Object using wrapper class
        Integer int3=Integer.valueOf(int1);
        System.out.println("Autoboxing:"+int3);

        //unboxing done automatically by compiler
        //Object 'Integer' converted to primitive type 'int'
        int int4 = int3;
        System.out.println("Unboxing:"+int4);

        //unboxing done using Wrapper class method
        int int5 = int3.intValue();
        System.out.println("Unboxing:"+int5);

    }

}
```

The output is as follows:

```
Console  Problems  @ Javadoc
<terminated> WrapperClasses [Java Application]
Autoboxing:1
Autoboxing:1
Unboxing:1
Unboxing:1
```

The wrapper class can take in String arguments in their constructor as well. The declaration

Integer i = “33”; is completely legal.

An important thing to know about wrapper classes is that their objects are immutable and hence thread safe.

Wrapper classes can also be used for binary, octal, hexadecimal conversions as well. A simple example is shown in the class

WrapperExample.

```
WrapperExample.java

package com.trial.java.fundamentals;

public class WrapperExample {

    public static void main(String[] args) {

        int i = 15;
        String bin = Integer.toString(i, 2);
        System.out.println("Binary reprsentation of 15 is:"+ bin);

        String dec = Integer.toString(i, 10);
        System.out.println("Decimal reprsentation of 15 is:"+ dec);

        String oct = Integer.toString(i, 8);
        System.out.println("Octal reprsentation of 15 is:"+ oct);

        String hex = Integer.toString(i, 16);
        System.out.println("Octal reprsentation of 15 is:" +hex);

    }

}
```

The output generated by the class WrapperExample is:

```
Problems  Servers  Properties  Cc
<terminated> WrapperExample [Java Application]
Binary reprsentation of 15 is:1111
Decimal reprsentation of 15 is:15
Octal reprsentation of 15 is:17
Octal reprsentation of 15 is:f
```

IMMUTABLE CLASSES AND OBJECTS

An immutable object is an object/instance whose state cannot be altered post creation. Once the object is initialized, no further changes in its state can be performed. Such objects are used in applications that are concurrent or multithreaded where there is a high possibility that the object is accessed by multiple threads. As their state cannot be changed/altered the possibility of data corruption is avoided.

An example of an Immutable class is the String class.

In java immutable classes can be created in the following way:

1. Declare the class as final
2. Declare all the variables and methods as private and final
3. Do not provide getters and setters for private variables
4. All fields should be initialized via a constructor
5. Clone the objects so that they return a copy and not the actual object
6. If the class uses Mutable objects make them final

An example of an immutable class is as shown below:

ImmutableClass.java

```
package com.trial.java.fundamentals;

public final class ImmutableClass {

    private final int[] arr;
    private final String myString;

    public ImmutableClass(int[] arr, String myString) {
        this.arr = arr.clone(); //  make a defensive copy
        this.myString = myString;
    }

    public String toString() {
        StringBuffer stringBuffer = new StringBuffer("Characters in array are: ");
        for (int i = 0; i < arr.length; i++) {
            stringBuffer.append(arr[i] + " ");
        }
        return "\nArray contents: " + stringBuffer.toString() +  " myString: "+ this.myString;
    }

    public static void main(String[] args) {

        int[] arr = { 1, 2 };
        ImmutableClass immutableClassObject = new ImmutableClass(arr, "Hello");
        System.out.println("Values of the object before construction:" + immutableClassObject);
        arr[1] = 3; // change (i.e. mutate) the element
        System.out.println("Values of the object after construction:" + immutableClassObject);
    }
}
```

As seen from the class ImmutableClass, the fields have been declared as private and final. Moreover, they have been initialized via the constructor and a clone has been provided at all times.

The values are not changed which is visible in the output shown below:

```
Console ☒  Problems  @ Javadoc  Declaration  Annotations
<terminated> ImmutableClass [Java Application] C:\Program Files\java\jdk1
Values of the object before construction:
Array contents: Characters in array are: 1 2  myString: Hello
Values of the object after construction:
Array contents: Characters in array are: 1 2  myString: Hello
```

SERIALIZATION AND DESERIALIZATION IN JAVA

In java, we have the possibility of saving the state of an object as a stream of bytes. This is known as serialization. The reverse process is called as deserialization.

Serialization is defined as the conversion of the state of an object to a byte stream so that the byte stream can later be reverted back to a working copy of the object (Eckel, 2003).

The serialized object contains the data stored in the object along with metadata of the object. In java, if a class or any of its parent classes/ superclasses implement the Serializable interface, the class is Serializable, which means that it can be stored in the form of bytes and recovered and transformed back into an object. The process of Deserialization is the reverse of Serialization. It converts the serialized java object back to its original object copy.

The Serialization interface is a part of the java.io package. As discussed in chapter 9, the java.io package provides us with several streams that help us read and write objects. The same methods can be used in the process of Serialization and Deserialization. An example demonstrating the process of serialization is shown below:

SerializationExample.java

```java
package com.java.serialization;

import java.io.FileOutputStream;
import java.io.IOException;
import java.io.ObjectOutputStream;
import java.io.Serializable;

public class SerializationExample {

    public static void main(String[] args) throws IOException {

        // create the object
        Fruits fruit = new Fruits("Orange", "Seeded");
        // create a file output stream to write the object state to a file
        FileOutputStream fout = new FileOutputStream("fruit.txt");

        // wrap it in an object of the ObjectOutputStream
        ObjectOutputStream out = new ObjectOutputStream(fout);

        // write the fruit object in the object output stream object
        out.writeObject(fruit);

        // flush and close the stream
        out.flush();
        out.close();
    }
}

class Fruits implements Serializable {

    /**
     *
     */
    private static final long serialVersionUID = 1L;
    String name;
    String fruitType;

    public Fruits(String name, String fruitType) {

        this.name = name;
        this.fruitType = fruitType;
    }
}
```

The above example makes use of the ObjectOutputStream that contains the functionality to write objects. The above class creates a file named fruit.txt in the workspace which stores the state of the object 'fruit' that we create in the program. The contents of this file are as follows:

SerializationExample.java   fruit.txt


```
¬í sr com.java.serialization.Fruits      L   fruitTypet Ljava/lang/String;L nameq ~ xpt Seededt Orange
```

The process of deserialization is exactly the reverse. This is demonstrated by the class Deserialization example that reads from the file 'fruit.txt' and creates an object of the type Fruit.

SerializationExample.java

```java
package com.java.serialization;

import java.io.FileInputStream;
import java.io.FileOutputStream;
import java.io.IOException;
import java.io.ObjectInputStream;
import java.io.ObjectOutputStream;
import java.io.Serializable;

public class SerializationExample {

    public static void main(String[] args) throws IOException, ClassNotFoundException {

        // create the object
        Fruits fruit = new Fruits("Orange", "Seeded");
        // create a file output stream to write the object state to a file
        FileOutputStream fout = new FileOutputStream("fruit.txt");

        // wrap it in an object of the ObjectOutputStream
        ObjectOutputStream out = new ObjectOutputStream(fout);

        // write the fruit object in the object output stream object
        out.writeObject(fruit);

        // flush and close the stream
        out.flush();
        out.close();

        // create an object input stream object that reads the file that stores
        // the serialized object
        ObjectInputStream in = new ObjectInputStream(new FileInputStream("fruit.txt"));

        // read the object
        Fruits deserialzedFruit = (Fruits) in.readObject();

        // display the contents of the object
        System.out.println("Fruit Name: " + deserialzedFruit.name + " Fruit Type:" + deserialzedFruit.fruitType);

        // close the input stream
        in.close();
    }
}

class Fruits implements Serializable {

    /**
     *
     */
    private static final long serialVersionUID = 1L;
    String name;
    String fruitType;

    public Fruits(String name, String fruitType) {

        this.name = name;
        this.fruitType = fruitType;
    }
}
```

The output generated is as follows:

```
Console   Problems
<terminated> SerializationExample [Java Application]
Fruit Name: Orange Fruit Type:Seeded
```

As seen from the output, the state of the object has been restored correctly. An important and noteworthy advantage of this process is that it is transversal, meaning that an object is serializable across platforms. It is independent of the JVM and hence we have the possibility to serialize an object on one platform and deserialize it on another platform.

Serialization and the Transient Keyword

In case you do not wish to serialize a class member variable, it can be declared as transient. The use of this keyword has been described by the same example as above, but the field 'fruitType' has been declared as transient.

SerializationExample.java

```
package com.java.serialization;

import java.io.FileInputStream;
import java.io.FileOutputStream;
import java.io.IOException;
import java.io.ObjectInputStream;
import java.io.ObjectOutputStream;
import java.io.Serializable;

public class SerializationExample {

    public static void main(String[] args) throws IOException, ClassNotFoundException {

        // create the object
        Fruits fruit = new Fruits("Orange", "Seeded");
        // create a file output stream to write the object state to a file
        FileOutputStream fout = new FileOutputStream("fruit.txt");

        // wrap it in an object of the ObjectOutputStream
        ObjectOutputStream out = new ObjectOutputStream(fout);

        // write the fruit object in the object output stream object
        out.writeObject(fruit);

        // flush and close the stream
        out.flush();
        out.close();

        // create an object input stream object that reads the file that stores
        // the serialized object
        ObjectInputStream in = new ObjectInputStream(new FileInputStream("fruit.txt"));

        // read the object
        Fruits deserialzedFruit = (Fruits) in.readObject();

        // display the contents of the object
        System.out.println("Fruit Name: " + deserialzedFruit.name + " Fruit Type:" + deserialzedFruit.fruitType);

        // close the input stream
        in.close();
    }
}

class Fruits implements Serializable {

    /**
     *
     */
    private static final long serialVersionUID = 1L;
    String name;
    transient String fruitType;

    public Fruits(String name, String fruitType) {

        this.name = name;
        this.fruitType = fruitType;
    }
}
```

As seen from the class SerializationExample, the rest of the code remains unchanged. The only difference is the addition of the transient keyword. But the output changes as now the variable is not serialized and hence its state is not preserved as shown below:

```
Console ⌘  Problems
<terminated> SerializationExample [Java Application]
Fruit Name: Orange Fruit Type:null
```

CHAPTER 12

THE COLLECTIONS FRAMEWORK

The Java Collections Framework is an architecture that manipulates a collection of objects independent of the implementation details (Collins, 2011). This framework is nothing but a collection of classes and interfaces that help manipulate objects. Additionally, many useful classes that implement data structures are provided by this framework. The principal advantage of this framework is that general operations such as deletion, insertion etc. can be rapidly performed using the classes and API's provided by this framework.

The Collections framework hierarchy is shown below:

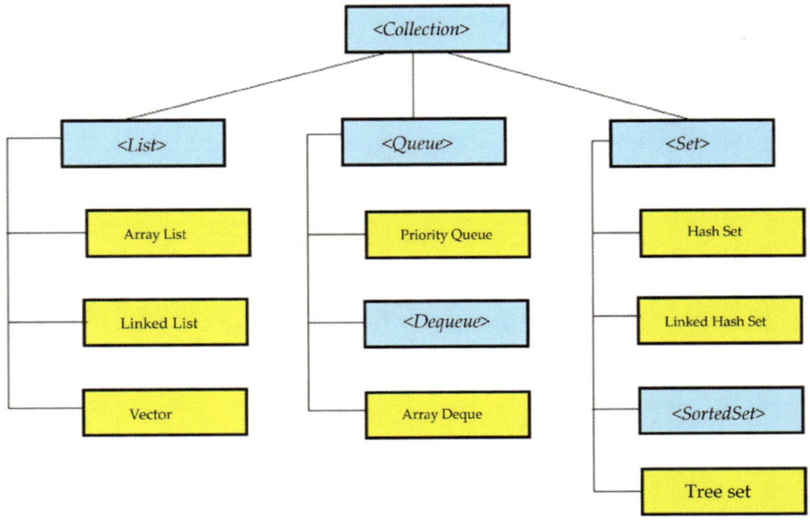

The interfaces are shown in blue and the classes are shown in yellow.

Additionally, another interface called the Map interface is provided by this framework. It ia not a part of the collection interface hierarchy. Its separate hierarchy is shown as follows:

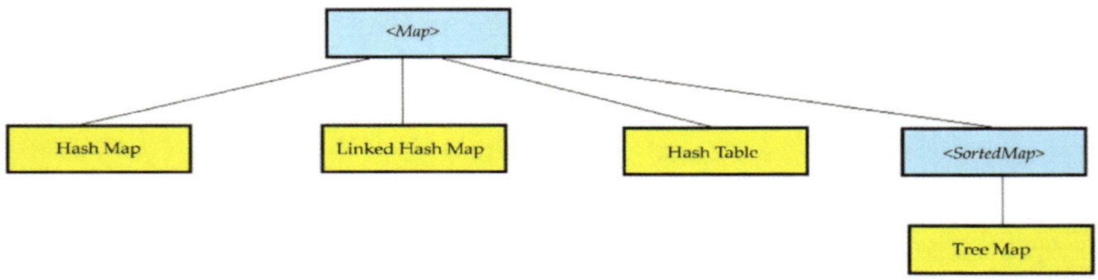

The Collection interface serves as the backbone of the framework. All collections implement this interface and hence inherit and implement all its methods. Each of the classes implementing their respective interfaces of this framework will now be discussed briefly.

LIST INTERFACE AND ITS IMPLEMENTATIONS

A list like its names suggests is a list of items or a sequence of items. Similar to an array, its index starts at 0 and any element in a list can be accessed via its index. A list can contain duplicate elements and accepts null values as well.

This interface has three implementations: ArrayList, LinkedList and Vector

ArrayList: This is a resizable implementation of an array. The ArrayList grows dynamically in size and can hold null values.

```
ArrayListExample.java

package com.java.collections;

import java.util.ArrayList;

public class ArrayListExample {

    public static void main(String[] args) {

        ArrayList arrayList = new ArrayList();
        arrayList.add(1);
        arrayList.add(2);
        arrayList.add(null);
        System.out.println(arrayList);

        int i = (int) arrayList.get(0);
        System.out.println("Value at index 0:" + i);
    }
}
```

The ArrayList class overrides the toString() method and hence can be printed as a string directly as shown above. The output is:

```
Console   Problems
<terminated> ArrayListExample
[1, 2, null]
```

In java version 7 and above, a concept called generics has been introduced. Many classes, called as generic classes have type parameters in their declarations such as the letter E in ArrayList<E>. This is a random generic type. So, when we create an instance/object of this class, we have the possibility to provide the type of the input parameter. This helps in stronger checks at compile time. The example shown above can be re-written as follows:

ArrayListExample.java

```
package com.java.collections;

import java.util.ArrayList;

public class ArrayListExample {

    public static void main(String[] args) {

        ArrayList<Integer> arrayList = new ArrayList<Integer>();
        arrayList.add(1);
        arrayList.add(2);
        arrayList.add(null);
        System.out.println(arrayList);

        int i = arrayList.get(0);
        System.out.println("Value at index 0:" + i);
    }
}
```

As we can see in the class above, the ArrayList has been declared to contain only Integer values. Additionally, we now do not need to cast the variable i to int. The output is the same as before. Generics have been discussed in chapter 13.

LinkedList: LinkList is a doubly-linked linked list data structure implementation. Apart from its constructors, it inherits all its methods from its parent. It permits duplicate and null values.

A simple example demonstrating the use of a LinkedList is shown by the class LinkedListExample.

LinkedListExample.java

```
package com.java.collections;

import java.util.LinkedList;

public class LinkedListExample {

    public static void main(String[] args) {

        LinkedList<Integer> linkedList = new LinkedList<Integer>();
        linkedList.add(1);
        linkedList.add(2);
        linkedList.add(3);
        linkedList.add(null);
        System.out.println("Contents of the LinkedList are:" +linkedList);
        linkedList.remove(3);
        System.out.println("Contents of the LinkedList after removal of an element are:" +linkedList);
    }
}
```

The output generated is as follows:

```
Console ⊠ Problems
<terminated> LinkedListExample [Java Application] C:\Program Files\java\jdk1
Contents of the LinkedList are:[1, 2, 3, null]
Contents of the LinkedList after removal of an element are:[1, 2, 3]
```

Vector: This class is similar to the ArrayList class and implements an array that grows and shrinks dynamically. It accepts null values and duplicates. The elements of a vector can be obtained by their indexes. The size expands and shrinks on a need-basis. This class is very much like the ArrayList class, the only difference being that it is thread-safe making it a suitable choice for multithreaded applications. But, if your application does not work in a concurrent context that requires synchronization, then ArrayList should be preferred over vector as it is faster and hence performs better.

A simple example of the Vector class is shown below:

```java
VectorExample.java ⊠
package com.java.collections;

import java.util.Vector;

public class VectorExample {

    public static void main(String[] args) {

        Vector<Integer> vector = new Vector<Integer>();
        vector.add(1);
        vector.add(2);
        vector.add(3);
        System.out.println(vector);
    }
}
```

The output is:

```
Console ⊠ Problem
<terminated> VectorExample
[1, 2, 3]
```

Stack: This class is a subclass of the Vector class and it implements a standard LIFO (last in first out) stack. This class contains all the methods of the vector class and implements some standard stack data structure methods if its own such as pop() to remove and return the top element or the head, peek() to return the top, push() to add a new element, empty() to check if the stack is empty or not and search() that returns the position of the element that is searched.

An illustration demonstrating the use of this class is shown below:

StackExample.java

```
package com.java.collections;

import java.util.Stack;

public class StackExample {

    public static void main(String[] args) {

        // declare a stack of integers
        Stack<Integer> stack = new Stack<Integer>();
        // add elements to the stack
        stack.add(3);
        stack.add(10);
        stack.add(2);
        stack.add(24);

        // display the elements of the stack
        System.out.println("Elements of the stack are:" + stack);

        // display the head/top of the stack
        System.out.println("Head element of the stack:" + stack.peek());

        // pop an element from the stack
        int pop = stack.pop();
        System.out.println("Element " + pop + " was removed from the stack");
        // display the stack after deletion of an element
        System.out.println("Elements of the stack after deletion are:" + stack);

        // add an element to the stack using the push() method
        stack.push(5);
        // display the stack after adding an element
        System.out.println("Elements of the stack after pushing an element are:" + stack);

        // display the first and last element of the stack
        System.out.println("First element:" + stack.firstElement());
        System.out.println("Last element/Top of the stack:" + stack.lastElement());

        // remove all items of the stack
        stack.removeAllElements();

        // display the stack after deleting all of its contents
        System.out.println("Elements of the stack after deleting all of its contents are:" + stack);

    }
}
```

The output generated by the class StackExample is as follows:

```
Console ⌧ Problems
<terminated> StackExample [Java Application]
Elements of the stack are:[3, 10, 2, 24]
Head element of the stack:24
Element 24 was removed from the stack
Elements of the stack after deletion are:[3, 10, 2]
Elements of the stack after pushing an element are:[3, 10, 2, 5]
First element:3
Last element/Top of the stack:5
Elements of the stack after deleting all of its contents are:[]
```

QUEUE INTERFACE AND ITS IMPLEMENTATIONS

A queue is a list of elements that are ordered, similar to the list interface. But, the intended use if somewhat different in case of queues. Here a simple First-In-First-Out algorithm has been implemented where the elements that are inserted first and removed first (Collins, 2011). This interface is implemented by the class PriorityQueue and the Deque Interface.

PriorityQueue: This class implements the queue interface and extends the AbstractQueue class and hence is composed of a combination of implemented methods from the interface Queue and inherited methods from the AbstractQueue class. This class does not permit null values and is implemented as a priority heap. The elements are ordered as per natural ordering or by a comparator at construction time of objects. Similar to a queue in data structures, this class provides default queue-related methods such as add(), remove(), poll() and peek().

A simple example of a PriorityQueue is shown below:

PriorityQueueExample.java

```
package com.java.collections;

import java.util.PriorityQueue;

public class PriorityQueueExample {

    public static void main(String[] args) {

        //create a PriorityQueue
        PriorityQueue<Integer> priorityQueue=new PriorityQueue<Integer>();
        //add elements to it
        priorityQueue.add(1);
        priorityQueue.add(2);
        priorityQueue.add(3);
        priorityQueue.add(4);

        //print the head using element() and peek() methods
        System.out.println("Head of the queue:"+priorityQueue.element());
        System.out.println("Head of the queue::"+priorityQueue.peek());
        //display the elements of the queue
        System.out.println("Elements of the Queue: " + priorityQueue);
        //remove an element
        priorityQueue.remove();
        //display the elements of the queue
        System.out.println("Elements of the Queue after deletion of one element: " +priorityQueue);

        //remove another element
        priorityQueue.poll();
        //display the elements of the queue
        System.out.println("Elements of the Queue after deletion of another element: " +priorityQueue);
    }
}
```

The output generated is:

Console Problems

```
<terminated> PriorityQueueExample [Java Application] C:\Program Files\java\jdk1.8.
Head of the queue:1
Head of the queue::1
Elements of the Queue: [1, 2, 3, 4]
Elements of the Queue after deletion of one element: [2, 4, 3]
Elements of the Queue after deletion of another element: [3, 4]
```

Dequeue Interface: This interface implements the queue interface is called as the double ended queue and pronounced as deck. It is a simple double ended queue that allows insertion and removal of objects at both ends (Collins, 2011). Similar to the PriorityQueue standard methods for insertion, deletion and retrieval of elements have been provided. Two classes implement the deque interface, namely LinkedList and ArrayDeque. The class LinkedList has already been discussed in the previous section. We shall now discuss the ArrayDeque class.

ArrayDeque: This class provides yet another array implementation that can be resized dynamically. They do not permit null values as elements and are not restricted in terms of capacity. It is faster as compared to LinkedList and Stack implementations.

A simple example demonstrating the use of this class is shown below:

ArrayDequeExample.java

```java
package com.java.collections;

import java.util.ArrayDeque;

public class ArrayDequeExample {

    public static void main(String[] args) {

        // create an ArrayDeque
        ArrayDeque<Integer> arrayDeque = new ArrayDeque<Integer>();
        // add elements
        arrayDeque.add(1);
        arrayDeque.add(2);
        arrayDeque.add(3);
        arrayDeque.add(4);
        // display the elements of the queue
        System.out.println("Elements of the queue:" + arrayDeque);
        System.out.println("Head of the queue:" + arrayDeque.peek());
        System.out.println("First Element of the queue:" + arrayDeque.peekFirst());
        // display last element of the queue
        System.out.println("Last Element of the queue:" + arrayDeque.peekLast());
        System.out.println("First Element of the queue:" + arrayDeque.getLast());
        // delete an element using the remove method
        // this method removes the head of the queue
        arrayDeque.remove();
        // display the elements of the queue
        System.out.println("Elements of the queue:" + arrayDeque);

        // delete the first element using the removeFirst() method
        arrayDeque.removeFirst();
        // display the elements of the queue
        System.out.println("Elements of the queue:" + arrayDeque);

        // delete the last element using the removeLast() method
        arrayDeque.removeLast();
        // display the elements of the queue
        System.out.println("Elements of the queue:" + arrayDeque);

        // delete all the elements using the removeAll() method
        arrayDeque.removeAll(arrayDeque);
        // display the elements of the queue
        System.out.println("Elements of the queue:" + arrayDeque);
    }

}
```

The output generated is as follows:

Console | Problems

```
<terminated> ArrayDequeExample [Java Appl
Elements of the queue:[1, 2, 3, 4]
Head of the queue:1
First Element of the queue:1
Last Element of the queue:4
First Element of the queue:4
Elements of the queue:[2, 3, 4]
Elements of the queue:[3, 4]
Elements of the queue:[3]
Elements of the queue:[]
```

SET INTERFACE AND ITS IMPLEMENTATIONS

This interface implements only the Collection Interface and does not permit duplicate elements. This Set is analogous to its mathematical equivalent Set and they do not maintain order of the elements. This interface has the following implementations: HashSet, LinkedHashSet and SortedSet interface. The SortedMap interface is further implemented by the TreeSet class.

HashSet: This is an implementation class that stores the elements in a hashtable, doesn't allow duplicate values but permits null elements. The order of the elements is not maintained and objects of this type are not synchronized. General methods to manipulate objects have been provided such as add(), remove(), etc.

A simple example describing a hashset is as follows:

HashSetExample.java

```
package com.java.collections;

import java.util.HashSet;

public class HashSetExample {

    public static void main(String[] args) {

        HashSet<Integer> hashset = new HashSet<Integer>();
        hashset.add(5);
        hashset.add(2);
        hashset.add(3);
        hashset.add(4);

        System.out.println("Elements of the hashset are:"+ hashset);
        //add a duplicate element
        //this element will be ignored as duplicates are not allowed.
        hashset.add(2);
        //display the contents of the set
        System.out.println("Elements of the hashset are:"+ hashset);
    }
}
```

The output is:

Console | Problems

```
<terminated> HashSetExample [Java Application] C:\Pr
Elements of the hashset are:[2, 3, 4, 5]
Elements of the hashset are:[2, 3, 4, 5]
```

As shown by the output, the elements are oredered in ascending order/natural order.

LinkedHashSet: This implementation of the Set interface implements a hashtable with a LinkedList that runs overs all its elements. Elements belonging to this class are maintained in the order of insertion (insertion order) and null values are permitted.

The following class LinkedHashSetExample demonstrates the use of this class:

LinkedHashSetExample.java

```
package com.java.collections;
import java.util.LinkedHashSet;

public class LinkedHashSetExample {

    public static void main(String[] args) {

        LinkedHashSet<Integer> linkedHashSet = new LinkedHashSet<Integer>();
        linkedHashSet.add(5);
        linkedHashSet.add(2);
        linkedHashSet.add(3);
        linkedHashSet.add(4);
        //display the contents of the linked hashset
        //insertion order is maintained
        System.out.println("Elements of the linked hashset are:"+ linkedHashSet);
        //add a duplicate element
        //this element will be ignored as duplicates are not allowed.
        linkedHashSet.add(2);
        //display the contents of the linked hashset
        System.out.println("Elements of the linked hashset are:"+ linkedHashSet);
    }
}
```

The output is:

```
Console  Problems
<terminated> LinkedHashSetExample [Java Application] C:\Pro
Elements of the linked hashset are:[5, 2, 3, 4]
Elements of the linked hashset are:[5, 2, 3, 4]
```

As shown by the output, the order of insertion of the elements has been maintained and duplicate values are not permitted.

SortedSet Inerface: This interface implements the Set interface and provides a complete ordering of elements. Ordering is done on the basis of natural ordering or with the help of the Comparable Interface. All elements inserted into a class implementing this set must implement the comparable interface as well. The class implementing this interface is the TreeSet class.

- ***TreeSet:*** The elements in a TreeSet are stored in a red black tree and are ordered based on their respective values. Null values are allowed. It is quite similar in its structure to the HashSet. The only variation is that the elements are ordered in an ascending manner.

A simple class implementing the TreeSet is shown below:

```
TreeSetExample.java

package com.java.collections;

import java.util.TreeSet;

public class TreeSetExample {

    public static void main(String[] args) {

        TreeSet<Integer> treeSet = new TreeSet<Integer>();
        treeSet.add(1);
        treeSet.add(4);
        treeSet.add(2);
        treeSet.add(3);
        // display the elements of the TreeSet
        System.out.println("Elements of the TreeSet: " + treeSet);

        // add a duplicate element
        // this element will be ignored as duplicates are not allowed
        treeSet.add(2);
        // display the elements of the TreeSet
        System.out.println("Elements of the TreeSet: " + treeSet);

    }
}
```

The output is:

```
Console  Problems
<terminated> TreeSetExample [Java Application]
Elements of the TreeSet: [1, 2, 3, 4]
Elements of the TreeSet: [1, 2, 3, 4]
```

As shown by the output, the order of insertion of the elements has in the TreeSet been maintained and duplicate values are not permitted.

MAP INTERFACE AND ITS IMPLEMENTATIONS

A map is an object that holds key-value pairs. Each key maps exactly one value and it generally doesn't permit null values for keys. This interface doesn't inherit from the Collection interface but has properties similar to that of the collection objects.

This interface has three implementations: HashMap, LinkedHashMap and TreeMap

- **HashMap:** This is a collection class based on the Map interface and it stores key-value pairs. HashMap is similar to the HashTable class of the Set Interface and does not maintain the elements in order. It is basically a hashTable based implementation of the Map Interface. It is not synchronized and also permits null values for keys and values.

A simple example of the use of HaspMap is shown below:

```
HashMapExample.java

package com.java.collections;

import java.util.HashMap;

public class HashMapExample {

    public static void main(String[] args) {

        HashMap<String, Integer> hashMap = new HashMap<String, Integer>();

        // Add elements to the the HashMap
        hashMap.put("X", 1);
        hashMap.put("Y", 2);
        hashMap.put("Z", 3);
        //display the elements of the HashMap
        System.out.println("Contents of the HashMap: " +hashMap);
    }
}
```

The output is:

```
Console  Problems
<terminated> HashMapExample [Java Application] C:\
Contents of the HashMap: {X=1, Y=2, Z=3}
```

- **LinkedHashMap:** Similar to the LinkedHashSet, the LinkedHashSet class implements a hashtable with a linked list that runs over all of its elements. The linked HashMap maintains the order of insertion like the LinkedHashSet and permits null values.

A simple example of this class is shown below:

LinkedHashMapExample.java

```
package com.java.collections;

import java.util.LinkedHashMap;

public class LinkedHashMapExample {

    public static void main(String[] args) {

        LinkedHashMap<String, Integer> linkedHashMap = new LinkedHashMap<String, Integer>();
        // Add elements to the the linked HashMap
        linkedHashMap.put("X", 4);
        linkedHashMap.put("Y", 2);
        linkedHashMap.put("Z", 3);

        // display the elements of the Linked HashMap
        System.out.println("Contents of the HashMap: " + linkedHashMap);
        // retrieve an element using its key
        int x = linkedHashMap.get("X");
        System.out.println("Value of element with the key X is:" + x);
    }

}
```

The output is as follows:

Console Problems

<terminated> LinkedHashMapExample [Java Application]

```
Contents of the HashMap: {X=4, Y=2, Z=3}
Value of element with the key X is:4
```

- **TreeMap:** This class extends the NavigableMap interface and implements a Red-Black tree. The treeMap class maintains the natural order, the elements being sorted in the ascending order. This class is similar to the HashMap class except that it is ordered and the hashmap isn't. Additionally treeMap is not synchronized and hence should be avoided in case of multithreaded applications. The treeMap permits null values for a corresponding key but does not permit duplicate keys. If the same key is added again with a new value, its value is updated.

A simple example demonstrating the use of this class is shown below:

TreeMapExample.java

```
package com.java.collections;

import java.util.TreeMap;

public class TreeMapExample {

    public static void main(String[] args) {

        TreeMap<String, Integer> treeMap = new TreeMap<String, Integer>();

        // add elements to the TreeMap
        treeMap.put("X", 5);
        treeMap.put("Y", 2);
        treeMap.put("Z", null);

        // display the elements of the TreeMap
        System.out.println("Contents of the TreeMap are: " + treeMap);

        //add a duplicate key
        //this updates the value corresponding to the key
        treeMap.put("Z", 4);
        // display the elements of the TreeMap
        System.out.println("Contents of the TreeMap are: " + treeMap);
    }
}
```

The output is:

Console Problems

```
<terminated> TreeMapExample [Java Application] C:\Program
Contents of the TreeMap are: {X=5, Y=2, Z=null}
Contents of the TreeMap are: {X=5, Y=2, Z=4}
```

ITERATOR

An iterator helps you go through each element in a collection. All the classes in the collections framework implement the Iterator Interface. The Iterator helps you navigate your collection, retrieve elements, delete elements and perform operations on all the elements of the collection. Each class in the collections framework has an Iterator() method that returns an iterator object, with the help of which we can iterate over the elements of the collection. The iterator has the following methods that help in iteration:

next(): returns the succeeding element in the collection

hasNext(): this returns true if the collection has another element

set(): this assigns the value of the object to the element.

previous(): returns the previous element in the collection

hasPrevious(): this returns true if at the current point, the collection has a previous element

Additionally, it has common methods such as add() and remove() that are used to add and remove objects from the collection object.

An example depicting the use of the iterator is shown below:

IteratorExample.java

```
package com.java.collections;

import java.util.ArrayList;
import java.util.Iterator;

public class IteratorExample {

    public static void main(String[] args) {

        // create an ArrayList
        ArrayList<Integer> arrayList = new ArrayList<Integer>();
        // add elements to it
        arrayList.add(3);
        arrayList.add(5);
        arrayList.add(1);
        // obtain the Iterator object
        Iterator<Integer> iterator = arrayList.iterator();

        // loop through the list
        while (iterator.hasNext()) {
            // get next element
            int element = iterator.next();
            //print the element
            System.out.println(element);
        }
    }
}
```

Although the above example uses an ArrayList and iterates over it using an iterator, this is applicable to all the classes in the collections framework that implement the interface Iterator.

The output generated the class IteratorExample is as follows:

```
Console ✕ Problem
<terminated> IteratorExample
3
5
1
```

ListIterator

This is just like the iterator interface but it can iterate over the elements of a collection in both directions: forward and backward.

A simple example using a ListIterator is shown below:

```
ListIterartorExample.java ✕
package com.java.collections;

import java.util.LinkedList;
import java.util.ListIterator;

public class ListIterartorExample {

    public static void main(String[] args) {

        LinkedList<Integer> linkedList = new LinkedList<Integer>();
        linkedList.add(1);
        linkedList.add(2);
        linkedList.add(3);

        ListIterator<Integer> listIterator = linkedList.listIterator();
        System.out.println("Traversing the LinkedList in a forward manner:");
        // loop through the linked list in a forward fashion
        while (listIterator.hasNext()) {
            // get next element
            int element = listIterator.next();
            // print the element
            System.out.println(element);
        }
        System.out.println("Traversing the LinkedList in a backward manner:");
        // loop through the linked list in a backward fashion
        while (listIterator.hasPrevious()) {
            // get next element
            int element = listIterator.previous();
            // print the element
            System.out.println(element);
        }

    }

}
```

```
Console ⊠   Problems
<terminated> ListIterartorExample [Java Application] C:\Program
Traversing the LinkedList in a forward manner:
1
2
3
Traversing the LinkedList in a backward manner:
3
2
1
```

In addition to the iterator, the Map interface has some methods that help to iterate over each key-value set. This iteration is done with the help of the entrySet() method as shown in the example below:

```java
MapEntryExample.java ⊠
package com.java.collections;

import java.util.Map;
import java.util.TreeMap;

public class MapEntryExample {

    public static void main(String[] args) {

        TreeMap<String, Integer> treeMap = new TreeMap<String, Integer>();

        // add elements to the TreeMap
        treeMap.put("X", 5);
        treeMap.put("Y", 2);
        treeMap.put("Z", 4);

        // display each entry in the Map using entrySet() api
        for (Map.Entry<String, Integer> entry : treeMap.entrySet()) {
            System.out.println("Key:"+ entry.getKey() + " Value:" + entry.getValue());
        }

    }
}
```

As we can see, each complete entry comprising of key and value pairs can be retrieved together. The entrySet() returns a set which contains the key and value pair.

The output is as follows:

```
Console ⊠   Problems
<terminated> MapEntryExample
Key:X Value:5
Key:Y Value:2
Key:Z Value:4
```

The entry set can also be used in combination with the Iterator. This is shown below:

```
MapEntryExample1.java

package com.java.collections;

import java.util.Iterator;
import java.util.Map.Entry;
import java.util.TreeMap;

public class MapEntryExample1 {

    public static void main(String[] args) {

        TreeMap<String, Integer> treeMap = new TreeMap<String, Integer>();

        // add elements to the TreeMap
        treeMap.put("X", 5);
        treeMap.put("Y", 2);
        treeMap.put("Z", 4);

        // obtain iterator for the entrySet
        Iterator<Entry<String, Integer>> iterator = treeMap.entrySet().iterator();

        // iterate over the entries and display each entry
        while (iterator.hasNext()) {
            Entry<String, Integer> entry = iterator.next();
            System.out.println("Key:" + entry.getKey() + " Value:" + entry.getValue());
        }

    }

}
```

The output generated is the same as the output from the previous example.

LEGACY COLLECTION CLASSES

Before the collections framework was introduced in Java version 2, there existed some classes and interfaces that provided support of storing objects similar to those defined in the framework now. They had behavior similar to those of the new collection classes. When the collections framework was introduced, these existing classes were reengineered so that they support the new framework. Hence, these classes are named or called as legacy classes. For these legacy classes, before the Iterator interface came into place, the Enumeration interface was provided to list through the elements of these classes.

The legacy classes are as follows:

- Vector
- Properties

- Stack
- Dictionary
- HashTable

Some of these classes such as Vector, Stack and HashTable have already been discussed. The Properties and Dictionary class will not be discussed in the scope of this book.

Enumeration: This is another interface that helps iterate over collection objects. Similar to the hasNext() method of the iterator, it has a hasMoreElements() method that checks if elements are present in the collection. This is used by Legacy classes such as Vector and Properties class.

A simple example using enumeration for iteration is shown below:

```
EnumerationExample.java
package com.java.collections;

import java.util.Enumeration;
import java.util.Vector;

public class EnumerationExample {

    public static void main(String[] args) {

        Vector<Integer> vector = new Vector<Integer>();
        vector.add(1);
        vector.add(2);
        vector.add(3);

        // Get the enumeration object
        Enumeration<Integer> enumeration = vector.elements();

        // iterate through the Vector
        while (enumeration.hasMoreElements()) {
            // get next element
            int element = enumeration.nextElement();
            // print the element
            System.out.println(element);
        }
    }
}
```

The output obtained is as follows:

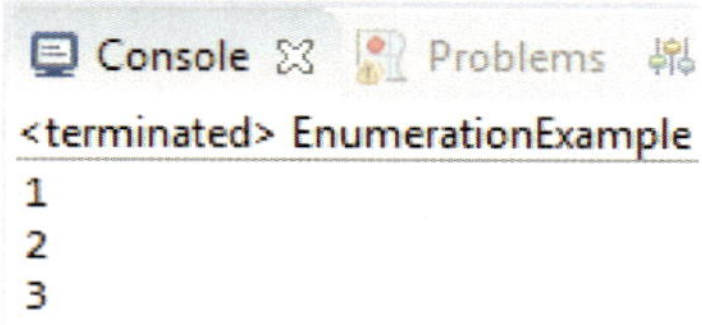

COLLECTIONS CLASS

This class of consists exclusively static methods that operate on or return collections (Collins, 2011). Some useful methods of this class are as follows:

Table 14: Methods of the Collections class

Method	Description
emptyList()	Returns an empty list that is unmodifiable
emptyMap()	Returns an empty Map that is unmodifiable
emptySet()	Returns an empty Set that is unmodifiable
synchronizedList()	Returns a synchronized/thread-safe List
synchronizedMap()	Returns a synchronized/thread-safe Map
synchronizedSet()	Returns a synchronized/thread-safe Set
Sort(List<T> l)	Sorts the list in ascending order of its elements
synchronizedSortedList()	Returns a synchronized/thread-safe and sorted List
synchronizedSortedMap()	Returns a synchronized/thread-safe and sorted Map
synchronizedSortedSet()	Returns a synchronized/thread-safe and sorted Set
replaceAll(List<T> T oldVal, T newVal)	Replaces all occurrences of a value in one list by another
T max(Collection<T> c)	Returns the maximum element of a collection based on natural ordering
T min(Collection<T> c)	Returns the minimum element of a collection based on natural ordering
T binarySearch(List<T> l, T key)	Performs a binary search on a list for the given key
shuffle(List<T> l)	Shuffles the elements of the list in a random order
fill(List<T> l, T obj)	Fills the list with specified objects

The uses of some of these methods have been demonstrated by the following class:

CollectionsExample.java

```java
package com.java.collections;

import java.util.List;

public class CollectionsExample {

    public static void main(String[] args) {

        List<Integer> arrayList = new ArrayList<Integer>();
        arrayList.add(4);
        arrayList.add(2);
        arrayList.add(7);
        System.out.println("Unsorted ArrayList:" +arrayList);
        //sort the ArrayList
        Collections.sort(arrayList);
        System.out.println("Sorted ArrayList:" + arrayList);
        //Get the maximum element as per natural ordering
        int max = Collections.max(arrayList);
        System.out.println("Maximum element:" +max);
        //Get the maximum element as per natural ordering
        int min = Collections.min(arrayList);
        System.out.println("Minimum Element:" +min);

        //create an unmodifiable list
        List<Integer> arrayList2 = Collections.unmodifiableList(arrayList);
        System.out.println(arrayList2);
        //try adding elements
        //this throws an exception
        arrayList2.add(3);
        System.out.println(arrayList2);
    }
}
```

The above class shows the use of the max(),min(), sort() and unmodifableList() methods.

The output is:

Console | Problems | Servers | Properties

<terminated> CollectionsExample [Java Application]

```
Unsorted ArrayList:[4, 2, 7]
Sorted ArrayList:[2, 4, 7]
Maximum element:7
Minimum Element:2
[2, 4, 7]
Exception in thread "main" java.lang.UnsupportedOperationException
	at java.util.Collections$UnmodifiableCollection.add(Collections.java:1055)
	at com.java.collections.CollectionsExample.main(CollectionsExample.java:31)
```

As seen clearly from the above output, when we try to insert an element into the newly returned unmodifiable list, we get an exception.

Another example that makes use of some the methods of this class are as follows:

```
CollectionsExample2.java
package com.java.collections;

import java.util.ArrayList;
import java.util.Collections;
import java.util.List;

public class CollectionsExample2 {

    public static void main(String[] args) {

        List<Integer> arrayList = new ArrayList<Integer>();
        arrayList.add(4);
        arrayList.add(2);
        arrayList.add(7);
        arrayList.add(120);
        System.out.println("Contents of the ArrayList:" + arrayList);

        // Search for a particular value from the list
        // if the element is found, the method returns the index of the element
        // if the element is not found it returns a negative value
        int searchIndex = Collections.binarySearch(arrayList, 7);
        if (searchIndex >= 0) {
            System.out.println("Element found");
        } else {
            System.out.println("Element not found");
        }

        // shuffle the list
        Collections.shuffle(arrayList);
        // display the contents of the shuffled list
        System.out.println("Contents of the ArrayList after shuffling" + arrayList);

        // Fill the list with a value
        Collections.fill(arrayList, 100);
        // display the contents of the shuffled list
        System.out.println("Contents of the ArrayList after fill() operation:" + arrayList);

    }

}
```

The output of the program CollectionsExample2 is as follows:

```
Console  Problems
<terminated> CollectionsExample2 [Java Application] C:\Program Files\java\jdk1.8
Contents of the ArrayList:[4, 2, 7, 120]
Element not found
Contents of the ArrayList after shuffling[4, 2, 7, 120]
Contents of the ArrayList after fill() operation:[100, 100, 100, 100]
```

COMPARABLE INTERFACE

This is an interface provided by java in the java.lang package and is used to order/sort the objects of a class defined by the user. It is made up of a single method namely compareTo(Object obj) that is used to compare the object invoking this method (current object) and the object provided as a parameter to the method.

The objects can be sorted based on a single element only. This means that if a class has three properties such as Age, Id and phoneNumber, only one of these three attributes can be used to sort the objects.

This method can be used to order elements of the following types: Strings, Wrapper Classes and objects of User-Defined classes.

The String class and the Wrapper classes that exist for primitive data types implement the comparable interface by default.

ComparableExample.java

```
package com.java.collections;

import java.util.ArrayList;
import java.util.Collections;
import java.util.List;

public class ComparableExample implements Comparable<ComparableExample> {

    Integer age;
    Integer id;

    public ComparableExample(int age, int id) {
        this.age = age;
        this.id = id;
    }

    public static void main(String[] args) {

        List<ComparableExample> list = new ArrayList<ComparableExample>();
        list.add(new ComparableExample(22, 94));
        list.add(new ComparableExample(12, 44));
        list.add(new ComparableExample(35, 76));

        Collections.sort(list);
        System.out.println("Contents of the list before sorting are:");
        for (ComparableExample obj : list) {
            System.out.println("Age:" + obj.age + " Id:" + obj.id);
        }
        System.out.println("Contents of the list after sorting are:");
        for (ComparableExample obj : list) {
            System.out.println("Id:" + obj.id + " Age:" + obj.age);
        }

    }

    @Override
    public int compareTo(ComparableExample obj) {
        // compare and sort on the basis of 'id'
        return (this.id).compareTo(obj.id);
    }

}
```

In case of user defined classes, this interface needs to be implemented. To implement the compareTo() method, it is necessary that the class implements the comparable interface and overrides the compareTo() method.

In addition to these classes, some classes in the CollectionsFramework such as List, TreeMap etc implement this interface by default. Hence, if the sort() method is called on them, the default compareTo() implementation method of this interface is called. In natural conditions, this method sort the elements in their natural order.

A simple example demonstrating the use of the comparable interface is shown below:

The output generated is as follows:

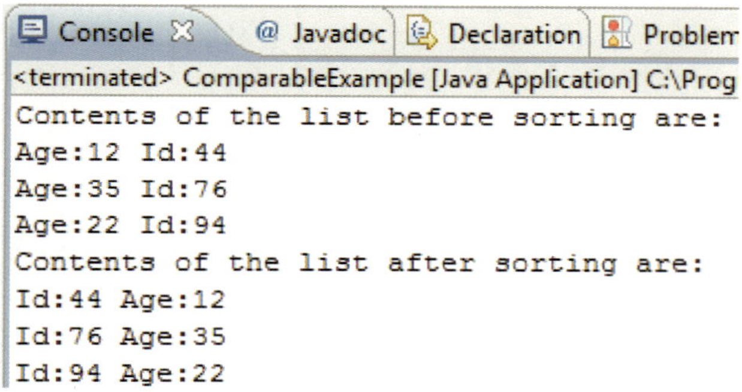

COMPARATOR INTERFACE

This is another interface found in the java.util package that helps order data of objects of user-defined classes. It is made up of a single method called as int compare(Object obj1, Object obj2).

It compares and orderes the objects provided as method arguments on the basis of 1 or more attributes/properties of the class. This means that different comparators based on different attributes of the object can be used to sort the collection.

This method returns a negative/less than zero value if the value of the first parameter is less than the second, 0 if they are equal and a positive integer/greater than zero value if the value of the first parameter is greater than the value of the second parameter.

To implement the compare() method, the class must implement the Comparator interface and provide an implementation for the compare method.

A simple example explaining the use of the compare() method is shown below:

ComparatorExample.java

```
package com.java.collections;

import java.util.ArrayList;
import java.util.Collections;
import java.util.Comparator;

public class ComparatorExample {

    Integer age;
    Integer id;

    public ComparatorExample(int age, int id) {
        this.age = age;
        this.id = id;
    }

    // create a comparator as an anonymous class
    public static Comparator<ComparatorExample> AgeComparator = new Comparator<ComparatorExample>() {

        @Override
        // override the compare method and compare on the basis of the field 'age'
        public int compare(ComparatorExample o1, ComparatorExample o2) {
            return (int) (o1.age - o2.age);
        }
    };

    public static void main(String[] args) {

        ArrayList<ComparatorExample> list = new ArrayList<ComparatorExample>();
        list.add(new ComparatorExample(22, 94));
        list.add(new ComparatorExample(12, 44));
        list.add(new ComparatorExample(35, 76));

        System.out.println("Contents of the list before sorting are:");
        for (ComparatorExample obj : list) {
            System.out.println("Age:" + obj.age + " Id:" + obj.id);
        }
        // call the sort method with the comparator as a parameter
        Collections.sort(list, ComparatorExample.AgeComparator);

        System.out.println("\nContents of the list after sorting are:");
        for (ComparatorExample obj : list) {
            System.out.println("Age:" + obj.age + " Id:" + obj.id);
        }
    }
}
```

As we can see, this class implements the comparator as an anonymous class and compares the objects on the basis of age.

The output generated is as follows:

```
Console ⊠  Problems
<terminated> ComparatorExample [Java Application]
Contents of the list before sorting are:
Age:22 Id:94
Age:12 Id:44
Age:35 Id:76

Contents of the list after sorting are:
Age:12 Id:44
Age:22 Id:94
Age:35 Id:76
```

The output clearly shows that the list has been sorted on the basis of age. A comparator can defined in another class separately. Additionally the logic of the compare method can be varied which is shown in the example below.

```java
ComparatorExample2.java ⊠
package com.java.collections;

import java.util.ArrayList;
import java.util.Collections;
import java.util.Comparator;

public class ComparatorExample2 {

    Integer age;
    Integer id;

    public ComparatorExample2(int age, int id) {
        this.age = age;
        this.id = id;
    }

    public static void main(String[] args) {

        ArrayList<ComparatorExample2> list = new ArrayList<ComparatorExample2>();
        list.add(new ComparatorExample2(22, 94));
        list.add(new ComparatorExample2(12, 44));
        list.add(new ComparatorExample2(35, 76));

        System.out.println("Contents of the list before sorting are:");
        for (ComparatorExample2 obj : list) {
            System.out.println("Age:" + obj.age + " Id:" + obj.id);
        }
        // call the sort method with the comparator as a parameter
        Collections.sort(list, new IdComparator());

        System.out.println("\nContents of the list after sorting are:");
        for (ComparatorExample2 obj : list) {
            System.out.println("Age:" + obj.age + " Id:" + obj.id);
        }
    }
}

// create a new class that implements the comparator interface
class IdComparator implements Comparator<ComparatorExample2> {

    @Override
    // override the compare method and compare the objects on the basis of the
    // field 'id'
    public int compare(ComparatorExample2 o1, ComparatorExample2 o2) {
        if (o1.id == o2.id)
            return 0;
        else if (o1.id > o2.id)
            return 1;
        else
            return -1;
    }
}
```

As shown in the above example, a new class that implements the comparator interface has been added to the class. This class implements the compare method in a slightly different way than the previous example. But the base logic is the same. If the objects under consideration are equal return 0, if the first is greater than the second, return a positive value and if the second is greater than the first return a negative value. The output generated is as follows:

```
Console ⊠  Problems
<terminated> ComparatorExample2 [Java Application]
Contents of the list before sorting are:
Age:22 Id:94
Age:12 Id:44
Age:35 Id:76

Contents of the list after sorting are:
Age:12 Id:44
Age:35 Id:76
Age:22 Id:94
```

As we can notice from the above output, the list of objects has been sorted on the basis of the parameter 'Id'.

Another way to implement the comparator method is by calling the compareTo() method on the parameter to be compared. This can be done only on objects of the Wrapper classes and Strings.

The same class with the changed method is shown below:

ComparatorExample2.java

```java
package com.java.collections;

import java.util.ArrayList;
import java.util.Collections;
import java.util.Comparator;

public class ComparatorExample2 {

    Integer age;
    Integer id;

    public ComparatorExample2(int age, int id) {
        this.age = age;
        this.id = id;
    }

    public static void main(String[] args) {

        ArrayList<ComparatorExample2> list = new ArrayList<ComparatorExample2>();
        list.add(new ComparatorExample2(22, 94));
        list.add(new ComparatorExample2(12, 44));
        list.add(new ComparatorExample2(35, 76));

        System.out.println("Contents of the list before sorting are:");
        for (ComparatorExample2 obj : list) {
            System.out.println("Age:" + obj.age + " Id:" + obj.id);
        }
        // call the sort method with the comparator as a parameter
        Collections.sort(list, new IdComparator());

        System.out.println("\nContents of the list after sorting are:");
        for (ComparatorExample2 obj : list) {
            System.out.println("Age:" + obj.age + " Id:" + obj.id);
        }
    }
}

// create a new class that implements the comparator interface
class IdComparator implements Comparator<ComparatorExample2> {

    @Override
    // override the compare method and compare the objects on the basis of the
    // field 'id'
    public int compare(ComparatorExample2 o1, ComparatorExample2 o2) {

        return o1.id.compareTo(o2.id);
    }
}
```

This returns the same output as shown in previously.

CHAPTER 13

GENERICS IN JAVA

In java, generics are a way to generalize classes, interfaces and methods. For example, when we write a method to add two numbers, we need to specify the type such as integer, double, float etc. But, what if we can write a generic method that works on all data types? This functionality simplifies the programming efforts significantly.

DEFINING GENERIC TYPES

A particular type can be made generic with the use of delimiters '<>' with an enclosing parameter.

Consider the following simple class:

```
public class Addition {
}
```

This class can be converted into a generic class as follows:

```
public class Addition<T> {
}
```

As seen from the class Addition, all occurrences of any ‘type’ have been replaced by the parameter ‘T’. It is called a Type variable and it can hold any non-primitive object type such as String, Integer, Array types, interfaces, classes and so on.

As per the conventions of the java programming language, the type variable is usually an uppercase letter. Some frequently used parameter types are as follows:

Table 15: Parameter Types in generics

Parameter Name	Description
T	Type
K	Key
N	Number
V	Value
E	Element

The type <E> is largely used by the Collections framework that was discussed in Chapter 12.

The above generic class Addition can be instantiated as follows:

Addition.java

```
package com.java.generics;

public class Addition<T> {

    T a;
    T b;

    public static void main(String args[]) {
        Addition<Integer> a = new Addition<Integer>();

    }

}
```

Generic Methods: Like generic classes, we can have generic methods as well. The method parameters take one of the parameters as their input. This is shown by the class below:

Addition.java

```
package com.java.generics;

public class Addition<T> {

    T a;

    public void setA(T obj) {
        this.a = obj;

    }

    public T getA() {
        return this.a;
    }

    public static void main(String args[]) {

        Addition<Integer> object1 = new Addition<Integer>();
        object1.setA(5);
        System.out.println("Value is: " + object1.getA());

        Addition<Double> object2 = new Addition<Double>();
        object2.setA(5.5);
        System.out.println("Value is: " + object2.getA());

    }
}
```

The class Addition has been modified to include a field, a setter and a getter that are generic.

As this class is generic, it can be instantiated in several ways with different types as shown by the class Addition.

The output generated is as follows:

```
Console
<terminated> Addition
Value is: 5
Value is: 5.5
```

If you want to display elements of a group of objects, you can simply write a generic method that can display the elements of all classes. An example using the parameter E for elements is shown blow:

GenericsExample1.java

```
package com.java.generics;

public class GenericsExample1 {

    public static <E> void displayElements(E[] elements) {
        for (E element : elements) {
            System.out.println(element);
        }
    }

    public static void main(String args[]) {

        Integer[] integerArray = { 1, 2, 3, 4, 5 };
        Double[] doubleArray = { 1.5, 2.5, 3.5, 4.5, 5.5 };

        System.out.println("Displaying Elements of Integer array");
        displayElements(integerArray);

        System.out.println("Displaying Elements of Double array");
        displayElements(doubleArray);

    }
}
```

The output is as follows:

Console Problems @ Javadoc

```
<terminated> GenericsExample1 [Java Application]
Displaying Elements of Integer array
1
2
3
4
5
Displaying Elements of Double array
1.5
2.5
3.5
4.5
5.5
```

Generic methods can be used on objects from the collections framework as well. To display elements a collection, a method similar to the displayElements() method can be used. An example that demonstrates the use of generics for displaying the elements of a class belonging to the collections framework is shown below:

GenericsExample2.java

```java
package com.java.generics;

import java.util.ArrayList;
import java.util.Collection;
import java.util.LinkedList;

public class GenericsExample2 {

    static <T> void displayCollection(Collection<T> c) {
        for (T element : c) {
            System.out.println(element);
        }
    }

    public static void main(String[] args) {

        ArrayList<Integer> arrayList = new ArrayList<>();

        arrayList.add(3);
        arrayList.add(4);
        System.out.println("Displaying Elements of the ArrayList");
        displayCollection(arrayList);

        LinkedList<String> linkedList = new LinkedList<>();
        linkedList.add("A");
        linkedList.add("B");
        linkedList.add("C");
        linkedList.add("D");

        System.out.println("Displaying Elements of the LinkedList");
        displayCollection(linkedList);

    }

}
```

The output generated is as follows:

Console Problems @ Javadoc

```
<terminated> GenericsExample2 [Java Application
Displaying Elements of the ArrayList
3
4
Displaying Elements of the LinkedList
A
B
C
D
```

BOUNDED TYPE PARAMETERS

As a programmer, you may face situations where you would want to have restrictions on the types that can be used as parameters. For instance, you may want to limit the type to a descendant of the class Number. All the wrapper classes descend from this class.

Bounded parameters are specified by the use of 'extends' keyword within the <> delimiters as shown below:

public class Addition<T extends Number> {

}

The declaration 'T extends number' specifies that this class can accept types that descend from the Number class. This is called as the upper bound of the parameter.

Similarly, a method can be declared to have bounded parameters as follows:

```
GenericsExample3.java

package com.java.generics;

public class GenericsExample3 {

    public <T extends Number> void get(T t) {
        System.out.println("T: " + t.getClass().getName());

    }

    public static void main(String[] args) {

        GenericsExample3 object1 = new GenericsExample3();
        object1.get(new Integer(4));
        object1.get(new Double(4.5));

    }
}
```

The output generated is as follows:

```
Console   Problems
<terminated> GenericsExample3
T: java.lang.Integer
T: java.lang.Double
```

In the above class, if we try to pass a type that is not a descendant of the Number class, we get a compile time error as shown below:

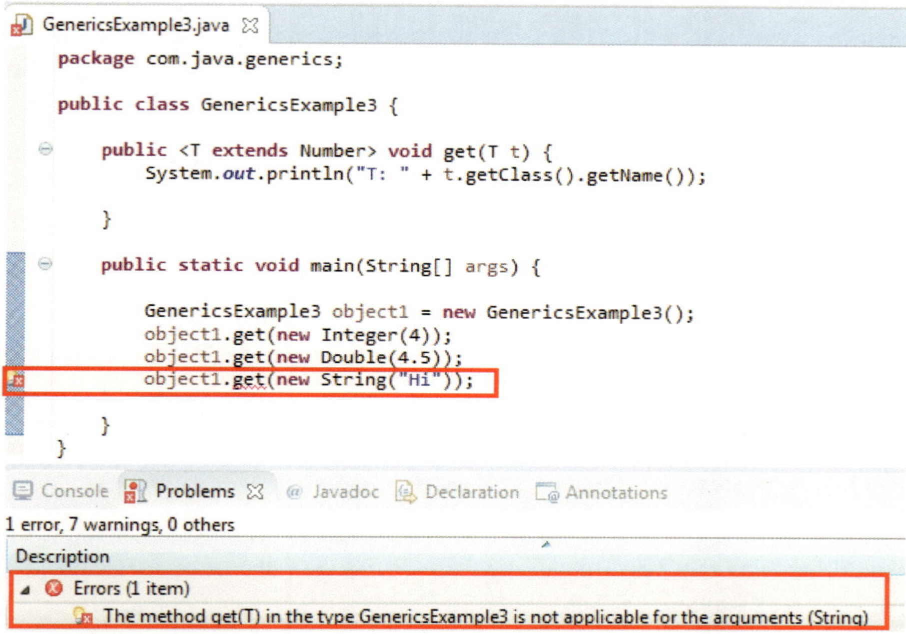

Another thing to note is that a type parameter can have multiple bounds. The syntax is as follows:

T extends A & B

A simple example is:

class A{}

interface B{}

public class GenericsExample4<T extends A & B> {

}

Note that the 2nd parameter always has to be an interface as a class cannot extend more than one class.

If one the parameter is a class then it should be mentioned first.

The following declaration is not valid and will give a compile time error.

public class GenericsExample4<T extends B & A> {

}

WILDCARDS

In case of generics, we use the symbol '?' (question mark) which stands for a wildcard element. It is used to represent a type that is unknown. This can be used in many scenarios such as in case of fields, variables etc.

There exist 3 types of wildcards in Java: Upper, Lower and Unbounded wildcards

Upper Bounded Wildcards

Wildcards with an upper bound can be used to add restrictions to your variables. Such wildcards are analogous to the bounded type parameters as explained in the previous section.

Upper Bounded Wildcards are declared as follows:

Class className <? extends UpperBound>

So, if we want to declare a method or a class that accepts all descendants of the Number class, we would declare an upper bounded wildcard as follows:

class MyClass <? Extends Number> {}

or

public void method1(List<? Extends Number> list1) {}

It is crucial to note that there is a difference between List<Number> and List<? Extends Number>.

The former matches only a list of type Number whereas the latter matches a list of Numbers or any of its child classes.

A simple example demonstrating the use of upper bounded wildcards is shown below:

GenericsExample4.java

```
package com.java.generics;

import java.util.ArrayList;
import java.util.List;

public class GenericsExample4 {
    // less restrictive method
    //this method will accept Number and its sub-types
    static void addNumberTypes(List<? extends Number> list) {
        double number, result = 0;
        for (Number num : list) {
            number = num.doubleValue();
            result = result + number;
        }
        System.out.println(result);
    }
    // more restrictive method
    //this method will accept all Number types only
    static void addNumberType(List<Number> list) {
        double number, result = 0;
        for (Number num : list) {
            number = num.doubleValue();
            result = result + number;
        }
        System.out.println(result);
    }

    public static void main(String[] args) {
        // create arraylist of Number type
        List list1 = new ArrayList();
        list1.add(1);
        list1.add(2);
        list1.add(3);
        // create arraylist of Double type
        List<Double> list2 = new ArrayList<Double>();
        list2.add(1.3);
        list2.add(2.5);
        list2.add(3.8);
        //accepts only the type Number
        System.out.println("Sum of all the numbers in the list");
        addNumberType(list1);
        // Accept Number and any of its sub types.
        System.out.println("Sum of all the numbers in the list");
        addNumberTypes(list2);
    }
}
```

The output is as follows:

Console | Javadoc | Declaration

```
<terminated> GenericsExample4 [Java Application]
Sum of all the numbers in the list
6.0
Sum of all the numbers in the list
7.6
```

Lower Bounder Wildcards

A lower bounded wildcard is the exact opposite of an upper bounded wildcard. A wildcard is said to be lower bounded if we restrict the lower bound of the type parameter to a specific type or a super class/super type of that type.

The syntax is as follows:

Class className <? Super lowerBound> or

To declare a class that accepts Integer values and all values that belong to the superclass of Integer we add a lower bounded parameter as follows:

class MyClass <? super Number> {}

or

public void method1(List<? super Number> list1) {}

A simple example demonstrating the use of lower bounded wildcards is as follows:

GenericsExample5.java

```
package com.java.generics;

import java.util.ArrayList;
import java.util.List;

public class GenericsExample5 {

    // less restrictive method
    //this method will accept Number and its sub-types
    static void displayNum(List<? super Integer> list) {
        for (Object num : list) {
            System.out.println(num);
        }
    }
    public static void main(String[] args) {
        // create ArrayList of Integer type
        List<Integer> list1 = new ArrayList<Integer>();
        list1.add(1);
        list1.add(2);
        list1.add(3);
        // create ArrayList of Number type which is a supertype of Integer
        List<Number> list2 = new ArrayList<Number>();
        list2.add(1.5);
        list2.add(2.5);
        list2.add(3.5);
        //accepts type Integer and its supertypes
        System.out.println("The numbers in the list");
        displayNum(list1);
        System.out.println("The elements in the list");
        displayNum(list2);
    }
}
```

The output generated is as follows:

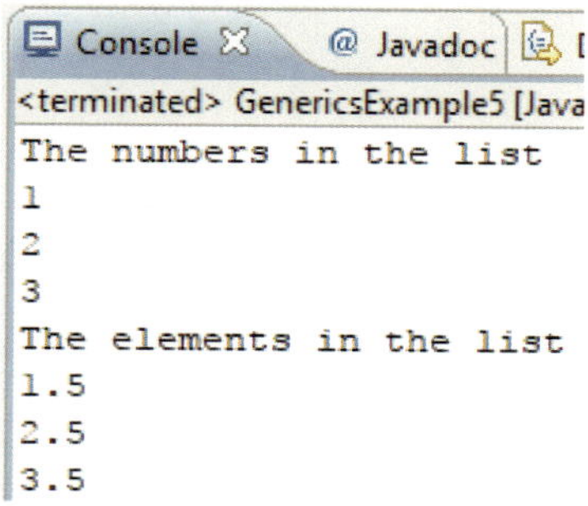

A key point to note is that we can specify either an upper bounded wildcard or a lower bounded wildcard but not both.

Unbounded Wildcards

This wildcard is specified just by the question mark (?) within the delimiter <>. It specifies that the type of the parameter is unknown. An example is List<?>. This wildcard is used when the method implementing an unbounded wildcard can be implemented by using the functions provided by the object class. Secondly, this unbounded wildcard is used when the class/method doesn't depend on the the type Parameter T. A wildcard should never be used as a type argument for a generic class or as an argument passed during instantiation of a generic class. This is because if any object is allowed to pass, there may arise many issues related to the implementation.

Consider a method that displays a list of objects:

```
public static void displayList(List<object> list) {
   for (Object object : list)
      System.out.println(object);
}
```

What if we want to display a list of Strings or a list of Doubles or a list of Integers using the same method? The above method doesn't allow this as these classes aren't sub types of the object class.

Unbounded Wildcards can be used in this case. The above method can be re-written as follows:

```
public static void displayList(List<?> list) {
    for (Object object : list)
        System.out.println(object);
}
```

A simple example demonstrating the use of unbounded wildcards is shown below:

GenericsExample6.java

```
package com.java.generics;
import java.util.ArrayList;
import java.util.List;
public class GenericsExample6 {
    //Only works for a list of objects and its subtypes
    //restrictive method
    static void displayItems(List<Object> list){
        for (Object listItem : list){
            System.out.println(listItem);
        }
    }
    //Work for a list of any type of object
    //less restrictive method
    static void displayListItems(List<?> list){
        for (Object listItem : list){
            System.out.println(listItem);
        }
    }

    public static void main(String args[]){
        //create an ArrayList of type Object
        List<Object> list1 = new ArrayList<Object>();
        list1.add(1.2);
        list1.add(1.3);
        //create an ArrayList of type String
        List<String> list2 = new ArrayList<String>();
        list2.add("A");
        list2.add("B");
        list2.add("C");
        //use the restrictive method that only accepts a list of objects
        System.out.println("The elements in list1 are:");
        displayItems(list1);
        //use the less restrictive method that accepts a list of any type of objects
        System.out.println("The elements in list1 are:");
        displayListItems(list1);
        System.out.println("The elements in list2 are:");
        displayListItems(list2);
    }
}
```

The output is as follows:

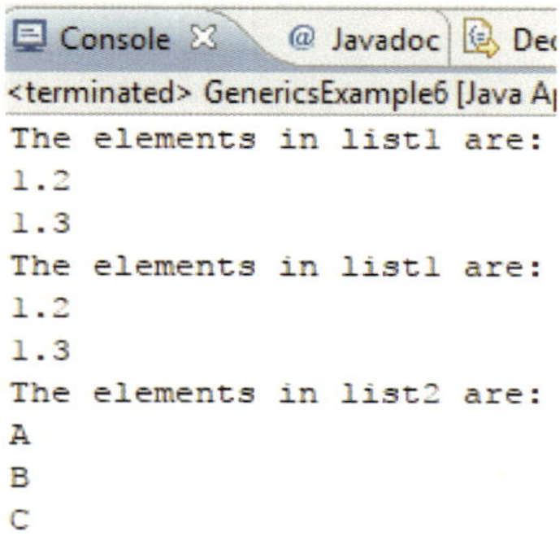
Console @ Javadoc Dec
<terminated> GenericsExample6 [Java A

```
The elements in list1 are:
1.2
1.3
The elements in list1 are:
1.2
1.3
The elements in list2 are:
A
B
C
```

Another significant point to remember is that one shouldn't get confused between generic declarations such as List<Number> and List<? extends Number>

When we consider a method such as void method1(MyClass<Number> list) {} , we can see that it accepts a list of MyClass objects with an argument Number. This means that we can pass a Number value as follows:

MyClass<Number>

But we are not allowed to pass the following parameters:

MyClass<Double>

MyClass<Float>

MyClass<Integer>

Why, one may ask. This is because a list of MyClass<Double>, MyClass<Float> is not a subtype of Number.

The relationship is shown as follows:

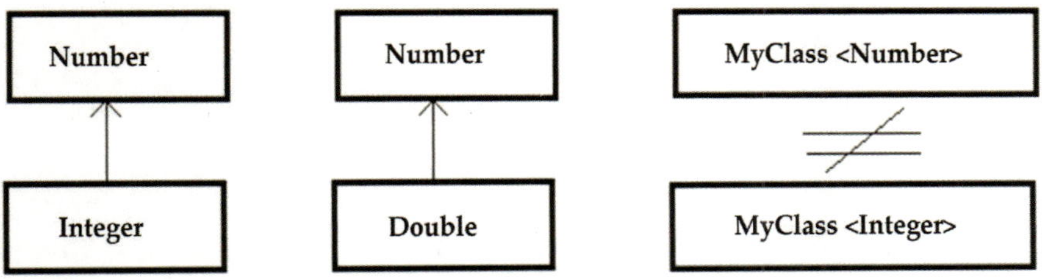

The integer class is a subclass of the type Number and so it the class Double.

But, MyClass<Integer>, a list of MyClass objects that accept an Integer is not a subclass of MyClass<Number> which is a list of MyClass objects that accept a Number parameter.

This because if we have two concrete classes A and B, and B extends A; this has no relation to the following declarations MyClass<A> and MyClass<B>.

So, if we want to have a relationship between the declarations MyClass<A> and MyClass<B> we make use of the wildcard with an upper or lower bound.

CHAPTER 14

REGULAR EXPRESSIONS

Regular expressions or Regex is a sequence of characters that depict or represent a string/pattern to be searched within some text. In java, there is an api called regex api that provides the pattern matching functionality for search and enables easy manipulation of strings. This is provided by the java.util.regex package.

It is made up of the following 3 classes:

1. Matcher class
2. Pattern class
3. PatternSyntaxException class

It additionally defines a MatchResult interface that is implemented by the Matcher class.

Objects of the Pattern class represent a regular expression. This is the pattern that we look for in a string. This class does not provide constructors and hence to create and use a pattern one of its static methods needs to invoked. These methods return a Pattern object. This will become clear once we see a few examples.

Some methods of the Pattern class are as follows:

- static Pattern compile(String regex): This method takes a pattern as an input, compiles it and returns a pattern object.
- Matcher matcher(CharSequence input): This method takes a sequence of charcters as input and matches the input against a pattern.
- static boolean matches(String regex, CharSequence input): This method takes the regex pattern and the string to test it against as inputs. It serves 2 purposes: compilation of the pattern and matching the input against the pattern.
- String[] split(CharSequence input): This method is similar to split method of Object class. This method splits the input string into string arrays.
- String pattern(): this method returns the pattern

Objects of the matcher class perform the matching operations on strings. It is an engine that interprets the pattern object and matches it against the given string. Similar to the pattern class, no public constructors have been provided. The class Matcher implements a matcher() method (MatchResult Interface) that takes a string as input (the string against which the pattern is matched) and this method must be invoked by a pattern object.

Some important methods of the Matcher class are as follows:

- boolean matches(): This method checks whether the given input matches the pattern
- Boolean find(): this method looks for successive expression/part of the string that matches the pattern
- boolean find(int start): This method looks for the successive expression in the string that matches the pattern from the given start index number
- String group(): This method returns the matched subsequence based on the mattern

- int start(): This method returns the start index/first index of the subsequence that matches
- int end(): This method returns the start last index of the subsequence that matches
- int groupCount(): This method returns the count of total number of substrings matched against the pattern

This class has some replacement methods that manipulate strings and help in replacement operations that will be discussed further in this chapter.

A PatternSyntaxException is the exception thrown when there is some syntax error in the pattern provided. It is an unchecked exception and is thrown in such cases.

Some methods of this class are as follows:

- String getPattern(): This method returns the pattern that throws the exception
- String getMessage(): This message gives the description of the syntax error and its index, the pattern which caused the error and a visual indicator of the index where the error is present
- int getIndex(): returns the index of the error
- String getDescription(): returns the description of the syntax error

EXAMPLES OF REGULAR EXPRESSIONS IN JAVA

Example1: This example shows a very simple pattern matching.

JavaRegexExample1.java

```
package com.trial.java.fundamentals;

import java.util.regex.*;

class JavaRegexExample1 {
    public static void main(String args[]) {

        String inputString = "aabb";
        String regexPattern = ".*ab*";

        // match the pattern against the input string. It returns true if the
        // input string containd the pattern
        boolean isMatched = Pattern.matches(regexPattern, inputString);

        if (isMatched == true)
            System.out.println("The input text contains the letters ab ");
        else
            System.out.println("The input text does not contain the letters ab");
    }
}
```

In the above class we check if the input string contains the letters ab with 1 character preceding and 0 or more characters succeeding them. The dot (.) operator here represents one character.

The output is as follows:

```
Problems  Servers  Properties  Cons
<terminated> JavaRegexExample1 [Java Application]
The input text contains the letters ab
```

Example 2: This example shows different ways to use the Pattern and Matcher classes.

```
JavaRegexExample2.java
package com.trial.java.fundamentals;

import java.util.regex.*;

public class JavaRegexExample2 {

    public static void main(String args[]) {

        // Way 1: Using instances of Pattern and Matcher class
        Pattern p = Pattern.compile(".*ab");
        Matcher m = p.matcher("cab");
        boolean isMatched = m.matches();
        if (isMatched == true)
            System.out.println("The input text contains the letters ab");
        else
            System.out.println("The input text does not contain the letters ab");

        // Way 2: Use the static method compile() of the Pattern class
        // and invoke the matcher method on it directly
        isMatched = Pattern.compile(".*ab").matcher("cab").matches();
        if (isMatched == true)
            System.out.println("The input text contains the letters ab");
        else
            System.out.println("The input text does not contain the letters ab");

        // Way 3: Use the static method matches() from the Pattern class
        // directly and provide it with the pattern and the input string
        isMatched = Pattern.matches(".*ab", "cab");
        if (isMatched == true)
            System.out.println("The input text contains the letters ab");
        else
            System.out.println("The input text does not contain the letters ab");

    }
}
```

This example checks if the input string contains the substring 'ab' that has one character before the letters 'ab' and ends with ab. The output is as follows:

```
Problems  Servers  Properties  Cons
<terminated> JavaRegexExample2 [Java Application]
The input text contains the letters ab
The input text contains the letters ab
The input text contains the letters ab
```

Example 3: Dot operator

JavaRegexExample3.java

```java
package com.trial.java.fundamentals;

import java.util.regex.Pattern;

public class JavaRegexExample3 {

    public static void main(String[] args) {

        boolean isMatched = Pattern.matches(".a", "aa");// match one character
        if (isMatched == true)
            System.out.println("The input text contains the letter a");
        else
            System.out.println("The input text does not contain the letter a");

        isMatched = Pattern.matches("..a", "baa");// match 2 characters
        if (isMatched == true)
            System.out.println("The input text contains the letter a");
        else
            System.out.println("The input text does not contain the letter a");

        isMatched = Pattern.matches(".a", "bca");// does not match so it will
                                                  // return false
        if (isMatched == true)
            System.out.println("The input text contains the letter a");
        else
            System.out.println("The input text does not contain the letter a");

    }

}
```

The output is as follows:

```
Problems  Servers  Properties  Console
<terminated> JavaRegexExample3 [Java Application] C:\Prog
The input text contains the letter a
The input text contains the letter a
The input text does not contain the letter a
```

CHARACTER CLASSES IN PATTERN CLASS

The pattern class consists of several regular expression constructs that can be used. The following table represents some of these patterns. The first column represents the construct and the second column describes under which conditions it will match the input.

Table 16: Character classes (docs.Oracle.com, 2017)

Construct	Description
[abc]	a, b, or c (simple class)

[^abc]	Any character except a, b, or c (negation)
[a-zA-Z]	a through z, or A through Z, inclusive (range)
[a-d[m-p]]	a through d, or m through p: [a-dm-p] (union)
[a-z&&[def]]	d, e, or f (intersection)
[a-z&&[^bc]]	a through z, except for b and c: [ad-z] (subtraction)
[a-z&&[^m-p]]	a through z, and not m through p: [a-lq-z] (subtraction)

The above constructs can be better understood with the following example shown in RegexExample4.

```
JavaRegexExample4.java

package com.trial.java.fundamentals;

import java.util.regex.Pattern;

public class JavaRegexExample4 {

    public static void main(String[] args) {

        // 1.match one character: a or b or c
        // returns true
        System.out.println(Pattern.matches("[abc]", "c"));
        // returns false
        System.out.println(Pattern.matches("[abc]", "d"));

        // 2.negation: match any character other than a,b,c
        // returns true
        System.out.println(Pattern.matches("[^abc]a", "xa"));
        // returns false as only one character must be present before a
        System.out.println(Pattern.matches("[^abc]a", "xba"));

        // 3.range: match characters in a particular range
        // returns true as the input is within the range
        System.out.println(Pattern.matches("[a-zA-L]", "G"));

        // 4.intersection: forms a union
        // returns true as c is a letter between a-z and is a/b/c
        System.out.println(Pattern.matches("[a-z&&[abc]]", "c"));
        // returns false as e is not a part of both patterns
        System.out.println(Pattern.matches("[a-z&&[abc]]", "e"));

        // 5.negation within a range
        // returns true as r is a letter between a-z and isn't a/b/c
        System.out.println(Pattern.matches("[a-z&&[^abc]]", "r"));
        // returns false as d is a part of the 2nd pattern
        System.out.println(Pattern.matches("[a-z&&[^abc]]", "c"));

        // 6.negation of a range
        // returns true as r is a letter between a-z and isn't in the range a-g
        System.out.println(Pattern.matches("[a-z&&[^a-g]]", "r"));
        // returns false as d is a part of the 2nd pattern
        System.out.println(Pattern.matches("[a-z&&[^a-d]]", "d"));

    }
}
```

The output is as follows:

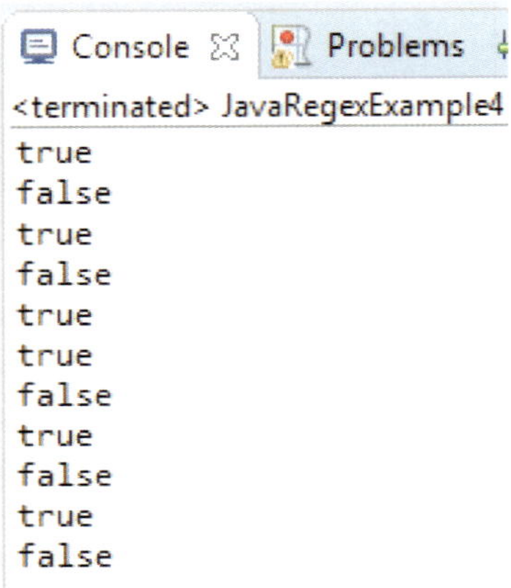

JAVA REGEX QUANTIFIERS

In java, the regex package allows you to provide quantifiers that specify the number of occurrences of a character that you want to match against.

The following table describes the quantifiers and their meaning:

The quantifiers state the number of occurrences of a character.

Table 17: Quantifiers

Quantifier	**Description**
X?	X must occur once or not at all
X+	X must occur once or more times
X*	X must occur 0 or more times
X{n}	X must occur exactly n times
X{n,}	X must occur n or more times
X{y,z}	X must occur at least y times but less than z times

The following class RegexExample5 demonstrates the use of these quantifiers.

JavaRegexExample5.java

```
package com.trial.java.fundamentals;

import java.util.regex.Pattern;

public class JavaRegexExample5 {

    public static void main(String[] args) {

        System.out.println("Using the quantifier X?");
        // match a/b/c 0 or more times : returns true
        System.out.println(Pattern.matches("[abc]?", "a"));

        // match a/b/c 0 or more times : returns true as 0 occurrences are
        // considered
        System.out.println(Pattern.matches("[abc]?", ""));

        System.out.println("Using the quantifier X+");
        // match a/b/c once or more times : returns true
        System.out.println(Pattern.matches("[abc]+", "a"));

        // match a/b/c once or more times : returns false
        System.out.println(Pattern.matches("[abc]+", "d"));

        System.out.println("Using the quantifier X*");
        // match a/b/c 0 or more times : returns true
        System.out.println(Pattern.matches("[abc]*", "a"));

        System.out.println("Using the quantifier X{n}");
        // match exactly 3 occurrences of 'a' : returns true
        System.out.println(Pattern.matches("a{3}", "aaa"));

        // match a/b/c once or more times : returns false as 'a' doesn't occur
        // exactly 3 times
        System.out.println(Pattern.matches("a{3}", "aaaa"));

        System.out.println("Using the quantifier X {n,}");
        // match n or more occurences of 'a' : returns true
        System.out.println(Pattern.matches("a{3,}", "aaaa"));

        System.out.println("Using the quantifier X {y,z}");
        // match between 3 and 6 occurrences of 'a' : returns true
        System.out.println(Pattern.matches("a{3,6}", "aaaa"));

        // match between 3 and 6 occurrences of 'a' : returns false as 'a'
        // occurs outside the range
        System.out.println(Pattern.matches("a{3,6}", "aa"));

    }

}
```

The output is as follows:

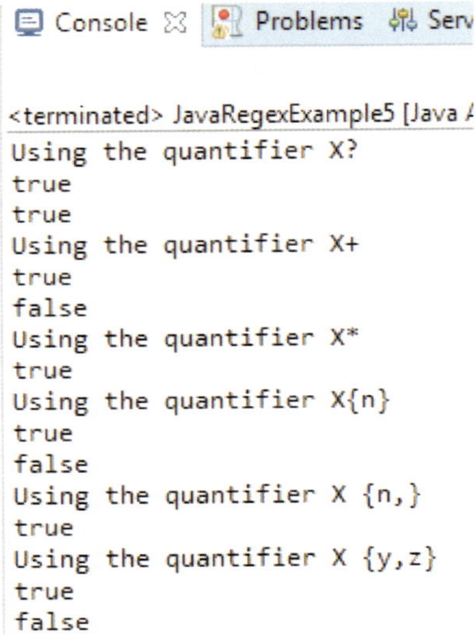

PREDEFINED CHARACTER CLASSES

Similar to the character class, the java regex package provides us with some predefined character classes that offer small codes for expressions that are used on a regular basis such as words, digits etc.

These constructs are defined in the following Table:

Table 18: Predefined character classes (docs.Oracle.com, 2017)

Character Construct	**Description**
\d	Matches a range of digits [0-9]
\D	Doesn't match any digits [^0-9]
\s	Matches whitespace character [\t\n\x0B\f\r]
\S	Doesn't match any whitespace characters [^\s]
\w	Matches any word [a-zA-Z_0-9]
\W	Doesn't match any word character [^\w]
.	Matches Any character (may/may not match line terminators)

These constructs have been explained by the class RegexExample6 as shown below:

```
JavaRegexExample6.java

package com.trial.java.fundamentals;
import java.util.regex.Pattern;

public class JavaRegexExample6 {

    public static void main(String[] args) {

        System.out.println("Using \\d");
        // match only digits : returns true
        System.out.println(Pattern.matches("\\d", "1"));

        // match only digits : returns false as no digit present
        System.out.println(Pattern.matches("\\d", "a"));

        // match 2 digits : returns true as 2 digits are present
        System.out.println(Pattern.matches("\\d\\d", "12"));

        System.out.println("Using \\D");
        // match non-digits : returns true
        System.out.println(Pattern.matches("\\D", "a"));

        // match non-digits : returns false
        System.out.println(Pattern.matches("\\D", "1"));

        // match non-digits : returns false as more than 1 non-digit is present
        System.out.println(Pattern.matches("\\D", "abc"));

        // match non-digits combined with quantifiers : returns true as more than 1 non-digit is present
        System.out.println(Pattern.matches("\\D*", "abc"));

        System.out.println("Using \\s");
        // match whitespace characters : returns true
        System.out.println(Pattern.matches("\\s", " "));

        // match whitespace characters : returns false
        System.out.println(Pattern.matches("\\s", "d"));

        System.out.println("Using \\S ");
        // match non-whitespace characters: returns false
        System.out.println(Pattern.matches("\\S", " "));

        System.out.println("Using \\w");
        // match a word : returns true
        System.out.println(Pattern.matches("\\w+", "a"));

        // match a word : returns false as the exclamation mark is not a word
        System.out.println(Pattern.matches("\\w", "!"));

        // match a word combined with a quantifier: returns true as we have two occurrences
        System.out.println(Pattern.matches("\\w+", "aa"));

        System.out.println("Using \\W");
        // match a non-word : returns true
        System.out.println(Pattern.matches("\\W", "!"));

        // match a non-word : returns false
        System.out.println(Pattern.matches("\\W", "x"));

        // match a non-word combined with a quantifier: returns true
        System.out.println(Pattern.matches("\\W*", "!%*"));

    }
```

The output generated by the program is as follows:

```
Console ⊠ Problems
<terminated> JavaRegexExample6
Using \d
true
false
true
Using \D
true
false
false
true
Using \s
true
false
Using \S
false
Using \w
true
false
true
Using \W
true
false
true
```

REGEX BOUNDARY MATCHERS

The java regex package provides us with boundary matchers that help determine where exactly the match occurred in the given input string. These matches help in making the matching operation extremely precise as the precise location of the match can be determined by use of boundary matchers.

The regex package is composed of the following boundary matchers:

Table 19: Boundary Constructs (docs.Oracle.com, 2017)

Boundary Construct	**Description**
^	Matches a word the beginning of the input line
$	Matches a word at the end of the input line
\b	Matches a word boundary
\B	Matches a non-word boundary
\A	Matches the beginning of the input line
\G	Matches after the end of the previous match
\z	Matches the end of the input

\Z	Matches the end of the input line except for the final terminator (if any present)

The boundary constructs have been explained by the following examples.

Example1: ^and $

```
JavaRegexExample7.java

package com.trial.java.fundamentals;

import java.util.regex.Pattern;

public class JavaRegexExample7 {

    public static void main(String[] args) {

        System.out.println("Using construct ^");
        // match a word at the beginning of a line : returns true
        System.out.println(Pattern.matches("^hi", "hi"));

        // match a word at the beginning of a line : returns false
        System.out.println(Pattern.matches("^hi", "hello hi"));

        System.out.println("Using construct $");
        // match a word at the end of a line: returns true
        System.out.println(Pattern.matches("hi$", "hi"));

        // match a word at the end of a line: returns false
        System.out.println(Pattern.matches("hi$", "hi there"));

    }

}
```

The output generated by the class JavaRegexExample7 is as follows:

```
Console  Problems
<terminated> JavaRegexExample7
Using construct ^
true
false
Using construct $
true
false
```

Example 2: \b

JavaRegexExample8.java

```
package com.trial.java.fundamentals;

import java.util.regex.Matcher;

public class JavaRegexExample8 {

    public static void main(String[] args) {
        String data1 = "Hello, How are you today? Are you ready for Java?";

        String regex = "\\byou\\b";

        Pattern pattern = Pattern.compile(regex, Pattern.CASE_INSENSITIVE);
        Matcher matcher = pattern.matcher(data1);
        while (matcher.find()) {
            System.out.print("Start index: " + matcher.start());
            System.out.print(" End index: " + matcher.end() + " ");
            System.out.println("Regex group: " + matcher.group());
        }

    }

}
```

The output of the class JavaRegexExample8 generates is as follows:

```
Console   Problems
<terminated> JavaRegexExample8 [Java Application] C:\Progra
Start index: 15 End index: 18 Regex group: you
Start index: 30 End index: 33 Regex group: you
```

Example3: \B or non-word boundary

This construct helps you match a non-word boundary as well. For instance, if you want to find the word 'you' in longer words such as 'yourself' this construct can be used. In this case the constructs \Byou or the construct you\B is is used separated by an or as the word 'you' can occur in the start or the end of another word.

JavaRegexExample9.java

```java
package com.trial.java.fundamentals;

import java.util.regex.Matcher;
import java.util.regex.Pattern;

public class JavaRegexExample9 {

    public static void main(String[] args) {
        String data1 = "Hello, Ready to learn Java yourself on this joyous occasion?";

        String regex = "\\Byou|you\\B";

        Pattern pattern = Pattern.compile(regex, Pattern.CASE_INSENSITIVE);
        Matcher matcher = pattern.matcher(data1);
        while (matcher.find()) {
            System.out.print("Start index: " + matcher.start());
            System.out.print(" End index: " + matcher.end() + " ");
            System.out.println("Regex group: " + matcher.group());
        }

    }

}
```

The output generated is as follows:

Console Problems Servers Properties

```
<terminated> JavaRegexExample9 [Java Application] C:\Progra
Start index: 27 End index: 30 Regex group: you
Start index: 46 End index: 49 Regex group: you
```

Example 4: \G

This construct matches the pattern only if found at the end of the previous match.

JavaRegexExample10.java

```java
package com.trial.java.fundamentals;

import java.util.regex.Matcher;
import java.util.regex.Pattern;

public class JavaRegexExample10 {

    public static void main(String[] args) {
        String inputText = "YouYou  You";

        String regex = "\\GYou";
        Pattern pattern = Pattern.compile(regex, Pattern.CASE_INSENSITIVE);
        Matcher matcher = pattern.matcher(inputText);
        while (matcher.find()) {
            System.out.print("Start index: " + matcher.start());
            System.out.print(" End index: " + matcher.end() + " ");
            System.out.println("Regex group: " + matcher.group());
        }
    }

}
```

The output generates is:

```
Console ⊠  Problems  Servers  Properties
<terminated> JavaRegexExample10 [Java Application] C:\Pro
Start index: 0 End index: 3 Regex group: You
Start index: 3 End index: 6 Regex group: You
```

As we can clearly see from the output, only the first two occurrences are matched since they follow one another.

Example 5: \A

This construct is used to match the beginning of a line.

```java
JavaRegexExample11.java
package com.trial.java.fundamentals;

import java.util.regex.Matcher;
import java.util.regex.Pattern;

public class JavaRegexExample11 {

    public static void main(String[] args) {
        String inputText = "You are learning Java You";

        String regex = "\\Ayou";
        Pattern pattern = Pattern.compile(regex, Pattern.CASE_INSENSITIVE);
        Matcher matcher = pattern.matcher(inputText);
        while (matcher.find()) {
            System.out.print("Start index: " + matcher.start());
            System.out.print(" End index: " + matcher.end() + " ");
            System.out.println("Regex group: " + matcher.group());
        }
    }
}
```

The output generated is as follows:

```
Console ⊠  Problems  Servers  Properties
<terminated> JavaRegexExample11 [Java Application] C:\Pr
Start index: 0 End index: 3 Regex group: You
```

This construct is similar to the ^ construct we studied earlier. It serves as an alternative.

Example 6: \z or \Z

This construct is used to match the end of the line. It can be used to match a pattern at the end of the line as well.

JavaRegexExample12.java

```
package com.trial.java.fundamentals;

import java.util.regex.Matcher;
import java.util.regex.Pattern;

public class JavaRegexExample12 {

    public static void main(String[] args) {
        String inputText = "You are learning Java You";

        String regex = "you\\z";
        Pattern pattern = Pattern.compile(regex, Pattern.CASE_INSENSITIVE);
        Matcher matcher = pattern.matcher(inputText);
        while (matcher.find()) {
            System.out.print("Start index: " + matcher.start());
            System.out.print(" End index: " + matcher.end() + " ");
            System.out.println("Regex group: " + matcher.group());
        }
    }

}
```

As we see in the output shown below, the pattern is found at the end.

```
Console   Problems
<terminated> JavaRegexExample12 [Java Application] C:\Prog
Start index: 22 End index: 25 Regex group: You
```

This construct is similar to the $ construct that we studied earlier.

GROUPS IN REGEX

In java, using the regex package, we have the possibility to group multiple characters together and check for matches against a group of characters as well. The group construct is used to group characters together. As a result of using groups a collection of characters can be treated as a single unit (Gosling, 2000).

Defining Groups

As simple example is the following pattern: (ab).

Every group that we provide in the pattern has a group number. The numbering of the groups starts at 1. The group starts from 1 as the group 0 refers to complete regular expression and is not counted as an occurrence. An important method: the groupCount() method in the class

Matcher returns the count (number of groups matching the pattern).

For example, if we want to match a group of digits or a set of characters in a particular order we can write them with the help of groups.

A simple example is shown below:

```
JavaRegexExample13.java
package com.trial.java.fundamentals;

import java.util.regex.Matcher;
import java.util.regex.Pattern;

public class JavaRegexExample13 {

    public static void main(String[] args) {
        String inputText = "123 how are you";

        String regex = "(\\d+)";
        Pattern pattern = Pattern.compile(regex, Pattern.CASE_INSENSITIVE);
        Matcher matcher = pattern.matcher(inputText);
        while (matcher.find()) {
            System.out.print("Start index: " + matcher.start());
            System.out.print(" End index: " + matcher.end() + " ");
            System.out.println("Regex group: " + matcher.group());
            System.out.println(matcher.group(1));
        }
    }

}
```

In the above class, we match only digits as shown in the output below:

```
Console  Problems  Servers  Propertie
<terminated> JavaRegexExample13 [Java Application] C:\Pr
Start index: 0 End index: 3 Regex group: 123
123
```

If we want to match a particular group of digits followed by digits we use multiple groups.

This is shown in the following example:

```
JavaRegexExample14.java

package com.trial.java.fundamentals;

import java.util.regex.Matcher;
import java.util.regex.Pattern;

public class JavaRegexExample14 {

    public static void main(String[] args) {

        String inputText = "123 1234 how are you";

        String regex = "(\\d{3})(\\s*)(\\d{4})";
        Pattern pattern = Pattern.compile(regex, Pattern.CASE_INSENSITIVE);
        Matcher matcher = pattern.matcher(inputText);
        while (matcher.find()) {
            System.out.println(matcher.group(1));
            System.out.println(matcher.group(2));
            System.out.println(matcher.group(3));
        }

    }

}
```

The output is as follows:

```
Console    Problems
<terminated> JavaRegexExample14
123

1234
```

As we can see from the output above, the group (1) matches the first pattern and gives us 123.

The group(2) matches the second pattern and gives us whitespace. The group(3) matches the 3rd pattern and gives us 1234.

Another complex example with characters and digits is shown in the class RegexExample15.

```
JavaRegexExample15.java

package com.trial.java.fundamentals;

import java.util.regex.Matcher;
import java.util.regex.Pattern;

public class JavaRegexExample15 {

    public static void main(String[] args) {

        String inputText = "How1234 How1234";
        // multiple nested groups
        // will return group (ow), (How) and (1234)
        String regex = "(H(ow))(1234)+";
        Pattern pattern = Pattern.compile(regex, Pattern.CASE_INSENSITIVE);
        Matcher matcher = pattern.matcher(inputText);
        while (matcher.find()) {
            System.out.println(matcher.group(1));
            System.out.println(matcher.group(2));
            System.out.println(matcher.group(3));
        }
    }
}
```

The output is:

```
Console  Problems
<terminated> JavaRegexExample15
How
ow
1234
How
ow
1234
```

As we can notice from the output, the example makes use of 3 groups, 1 of which is a nested group.

Backreferences in Groups

While using regex, an important concept that is used is backreferencing. A backreference can be specified using a backslash. Its main purpose is to avoid repeating expressions or patterns. A part of the group is saved in memory and can be recalled with the help of backreferencing. A backslash followed by the number/index of the group is used. For instance consider the expression (\d\d) which defines two digits that match. Now, if we want to match a string with the same group of digits repeating again, we can write the regex pattern as (\d\d)\1. This means that match a group of 2 digits that has been repeated once.

This is shown by the following class:

```
JavaRegexExample16.java

package com.trial.java.fundamentals;

import java.util.regex.Matcher;
import java.util.regex.Pattern;

public class JavaRegexExample16 {

    public static void main(String[] args) {

        String inputText = "3434";
        // back-referencing
        String regex = "(\\d\\d)\\1";
        Pattern pattern = Pattern.compile(regex);
        Matcher matcher = pattern.matcher(inputText);
        while (matcher.find()) {
            System.out.print("Start index: " + matcher.start());
            System.out.print(" End index: " + matcher.end() + " ");
            System.out.println("Regex group: " + matcher.group(1));
        }
    }
}
```

The output generated by the class JavaRegaxExample is as follows:

```
Console   Problems
<terminated> JavaRegexExample16 [Java Application] C:\P
Start index: 0 End index: 4 Regex group: 34
```

For groups that are nested, the concept of backreferencing works in the exact same way as shown above.

Regex Replacement Methods

The pattern class has some useful replacement methods, similar to the String class as follows:

String replaceAll (String s) – replaces all occurrences of a string similar to the replacaAll method of String class

String replaceFirst (String s) – replaces first occurrence of a string similar to the replaceFirst() method of String class

StringBuffer appendTail (StringBuffer sb) – appends the tail of the input at the end of the input string after the occurrences have been found.

String appendReplcement (StringBuffer sb, String replacement) – Replaces the string with a replacement string like replaceAll() method

A simple example using replaceFirst and replaceAll methods is shown below:

JavaRegexExample17.java

```
package com.trial.java.fundamentals;

import java.util.regex.Matcher;
import java.util.regex.Pattern;

public class JavaRegexExample17 {

    public static void main(String[] args) {

        String inputText = "34123456";
        String regex = "34";
        Pattern pattern = Pattern.compile(regex);
        Matcher matcher = pattern.matcher(inputText);
        //replaceFirst occurence
        inputText= matcher.replaceFirst("a");
        System.out.println(inputText);
        //replaceAll occurences
        inputText= matcher.replaceAll("a");
        System.out.println(inputText);
    }
}
```

The output is as shown below:

```
Console  Problems
<terminated> JavaRegexExample17
a123456
a12a56
```

The same example with the help of the appendTail and appendReplcement method is shown below:

JavaRegexExample17.java

```
package com.trial.java.fundamentals;

import java.util.regex.Matcher;
import java.util.regex.Pattern;

public class JavaRegexExample17 {

    public static void main(String[] args) {

        String inputText = "34123456";
        String regex = "34";
        Pattern pattern = Pattern.compile(regex);
        Matcher matcher = pattern.matcher(inputText);
        StringBuffer sb = new StringBuffer();
        while (matcher.find()) {
            matcher.appendReplacement(sb, "a");
        }
        // StringBuffer after replacing all occurrences
        System.out.println(sb);

        // StringBuffer after appending the tail
        matcher.appendTail(sb);
        System.out.println(sb);

    }
}
```

Console Problems

```
<terminated> JavaRegexExample17
a12a
a12a56
```

As we can see from the output in the above figure which is the same one we got before, the appendReplacement method replaces all occurrences of the pattern and the appendTail method appends the rest of the input string to the StringBuffer.

CHAPTER 15

GRAPHICAL USER INTERFACE (GUI)

Java provides us with a platform for developing applications with a rich graphical User Interface (GUI) called as AWT which stands for Abstract Window Tooklit (Chan and Lee, 1998). AWT is an api that provides us with various components to create applications with a User interface. The components provided the AWT api are platform dependent which means that the look and feel of the various components vary based on the view provided by the underlying OS. Hence, these components are called as heavyweight components as they make use of resources of the operating system.

AWT provides us with several ui components such as Window, Button, Label etc. that are native to the OS, layout and managers to manage the layout of the ui, graphics tools and event handling mechanisms. These components are provided by the java.awt package.

The hierarchy of the AWT package is as shown below:

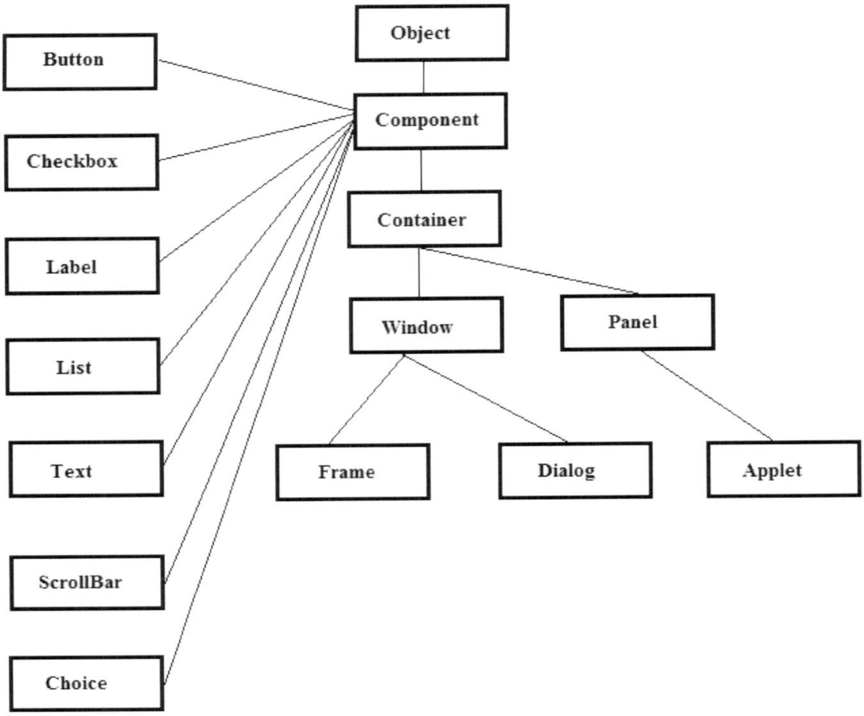

COMPONENTS OF AWT

Each one of the components in the AWT hierarchy has been described below.

Component: This is the superclass of all the awt components which is abstract. All the gui controls and components inherit from this component. All the ui controls are built on top of this base class.

Container: This is a component that is capable of holding other components such as button, labels and so on. Other types of containers that are capable of holding other components are: Window, Dialog, Panel and Frame. As visible in the hierarchy diagram, Window extends from the Container class, Frame and dialog inherit from the Window class whereas Panel inherits directly from the Container class.

We shall now see these containers.

Window: Window is a component that has no borders and menu bars. This component must be used with a Frame or a dialog class which are its subclasses or another window to create and display a window.

Frame: This component has a title and menu bar and other components can be added to it. It is made up of a maximize and minimize button.

Panel: Panel is a component like the frame but it doesn't have a title and menu bar. It is used for holding other components such as buttons, label, text fields and areas and so on.

Applet: It is a high level container for a component called as applet itself. It is a type of program that runs a java program within a browser.

Dialog: This component is a top level window that is made up of a border and title, inheriting from the window class. It is mainly used to take an input from the user.

The commonly used components are described in the following table:

Table 20: AWT components

Component	**Description**
Button	Class that creates a button with a label
Label	Class that helps place a text label
Checkbox	Class that helps add a component with two states : true/false
List	Class that helps create a scrollable list
TextField	Class that allows editing a single line text
TextArea	Class that allows editing a text of multiple lines
ScrollBar	Class that permits adding a scrollbar to scroll through a range of inputs/values
Choice	Class that provides a drop down menu with choices

Some important methods of the component class that are used very frequently are the following:

public void setSize(int width, int height): set/fix size of the container component

public void add(Component c): Add a component on the component invoking this method

public void setBackground(Color c): Set the given color as the background of the component

public void setVisible(boolean status) : Set the visibility of the component. The visibility is false by default.

public void setLayout(LayoutManager m): Set the layout for the component using the Layout Manager

LAYOUT MANAGER

In AWT, it is an object that is in charge of controlling the position of the components within a container and the size of the container. The various components inside a window or a frame can be arranged in a particular way with the help of a layout. For example, a simple Frame may consist of several buttons and labels. A layout Manager helps in better organizing these components by determining where they will be placed within the frame.

The AWT package in Java has the following layouts:

FlowLayout: This layout is used to arrange the component in a single row and if one row is not enough a new row is started.

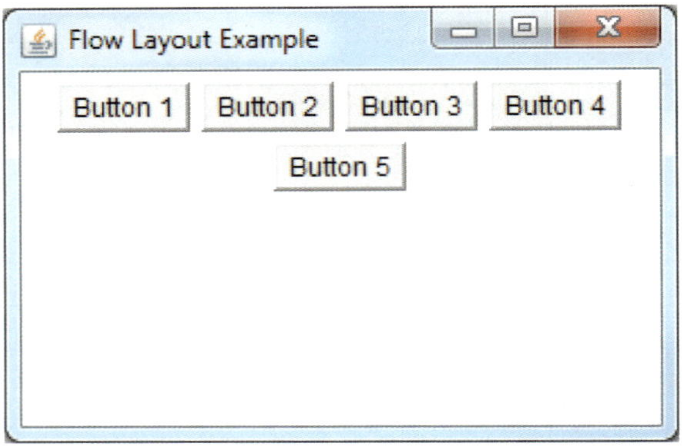

BorderLayout: This layout has 5 regions namely north, south, center, east and west. Each region can have only one component. So this layout must be used if you have limited number of components.

Visually, the border layout looks as shown below:

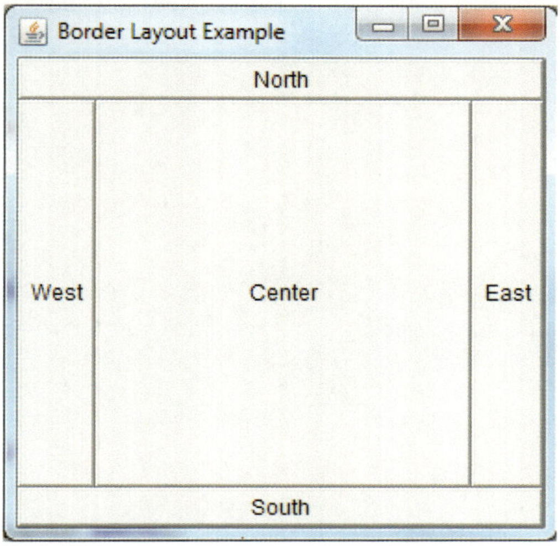

GridLayout: This layout is used to arrange the components in the form of a grid of rows and columns. All the components have equal size.

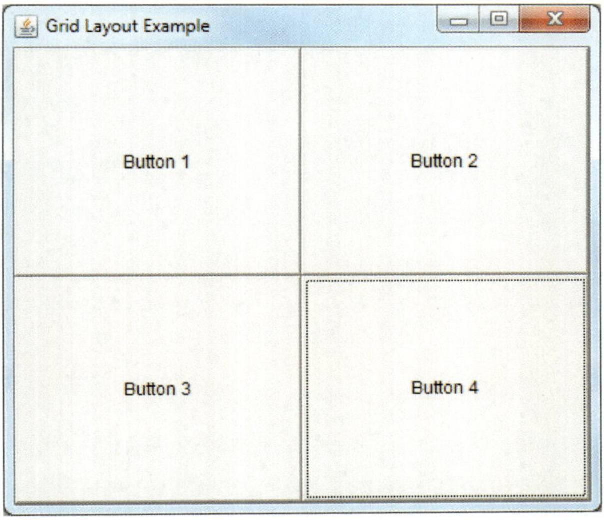

GridBagLayout: This layout is an advanced and flexible version of the GridLayout. It places the components in a grid of cells like GridLayout, but allows a component to occupy several cells. The height and/or width of a rows and/or column can be adjusted.

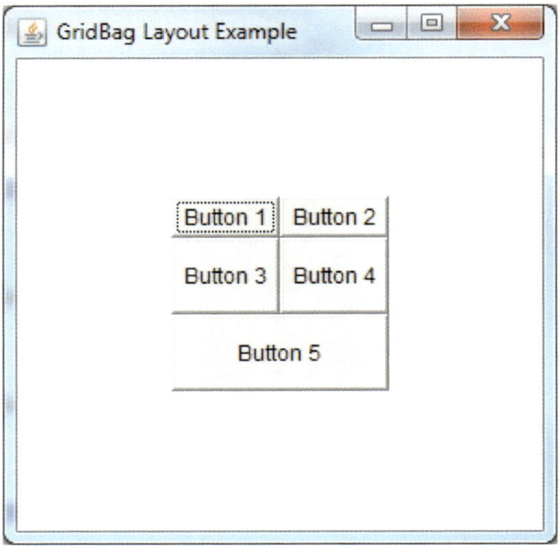

CardLayout: This layout makes use of a container in such a way that only one sub-component is visible at a time. Each component is treated as a card and based on the selected option; different components are shown to the user.

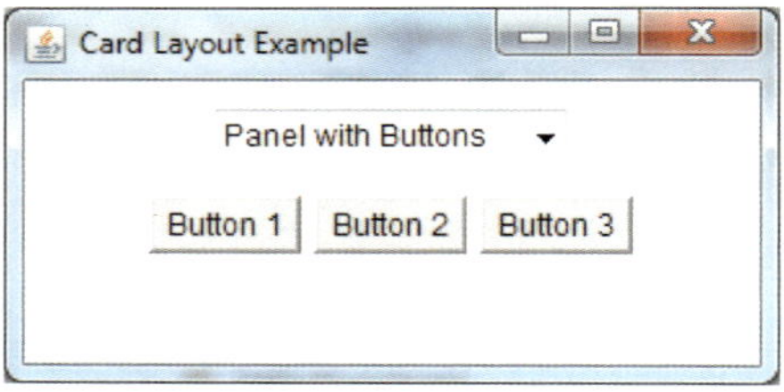

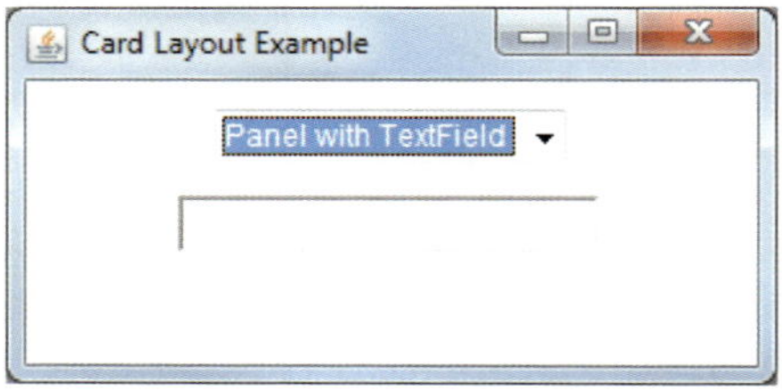

EXAMPLES

In java, the graphical UI can be created using awt via the Frame class. The basic necessity for creation of a graphical component is a frame. One approach is to inherit from the Frame class (using the extends keyword) and the second approach is to create an instance of the Frame class directly in your class. Both these approaches have been shown below:

Example 1: This example shows a simple frame with a button, label, text field, checkbox, title and a list.

AWTExample1.java

```
package com.java.gui;

import java.awt.Button;

public class AWTExample1 extends Frame {

    private static final long serialVersionUID = 1L;

    AWTExample1() {
        // create a label
        Label label = new Label("AWT Label");
        // add the label on the frame
        add(label);
        // create a button
        Button button = new Button("AWT Button");
        // add the button on to the frame
        add(button);
        // create a list
        List list = new List();
        list.add("1");
        list.add("2");
        list.add("3");
        list.setBounds(400, 100, 250, 240);
        // add the list on to the frame
        add(list);
        //create checkboxes
        Checkbox boxA = new Checkbox("A");
        Checkbox boxB = new Checkbox("B");
        Checkbox boxC = new Checkbox("C");
        //add them on to the frame
        add(boxA);
        add(boxB);
        add(boxC);
        //create a textField
        TextField text = new TextField("Hello! How are you?");
        //add it on to the frame
        add(text);
        // set the dimensions of the Frame
        setSize(500, 500);
        // set the title of Frame
        setTitle("AWT Example");
        // set the layout for the Frame
        setLayout(new FlowLayout());
        //make frame visible as it is not visible by default
        setVisible(true);
    }

    public static void main(String args[]) {
        AWTExample1 example1 = new AWTExample1();
    }
}
```

The output is as follows:

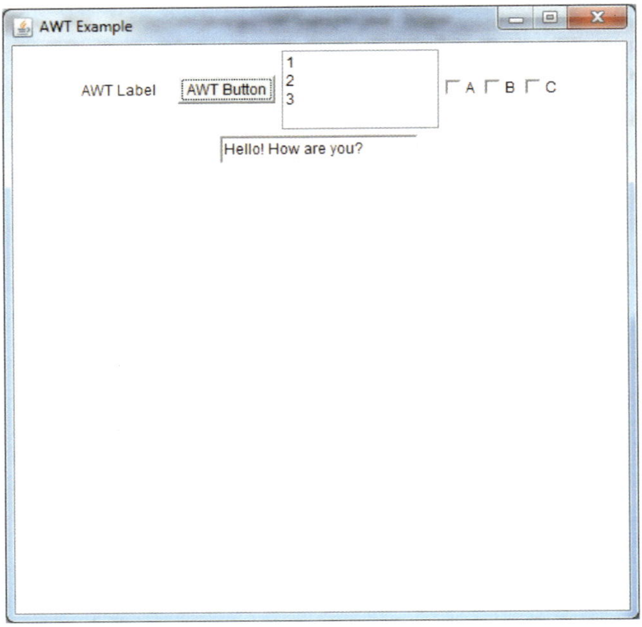

As seen from the output in figure, the gui has been created with a title, label, button, list, checkboxes and a text field.

Example 2: The second way of creating a frame is to create an instance of the Frame class. This is done as follows:

AwtExample.java

```
package com.java.gui;

import java.awt.Frame;

public class AwtExample {

    public AwtExample() {

        Frame frame = new Frame();
        frame.setTitle("Hello");
        frame.setSize(200, 150);
        frame.setVisible(true);
    }

    public static void main(String[] args) {

        AwtExample example1 = new AwtExample();

    }
}
```

The output is as follows:

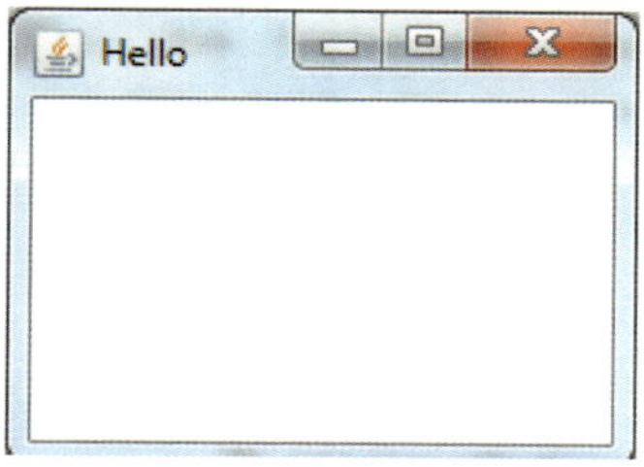

Example 3: Applets

Applets are a type of java programs that can be run in the browser. A simple Java applet is shown below:

AppletExample.java

```
package com.java.gui;

import java.applet.Applet;
import java.awt.Graphics;

public class AppletExample extends Applet {

    public void paint(Graphics g) {
        // write a simple text using the drawString() method of the Graphics class
        g.drawString("Applet Example!", 120, 100);
    }
}
```

Applets do not posess a main method, but to execute an applet we need to override the paint method from the Graphics class. As an applet is a type of a program, it needs to be executed as an applet. This option is available when you right click anywhere on the source file as follows:

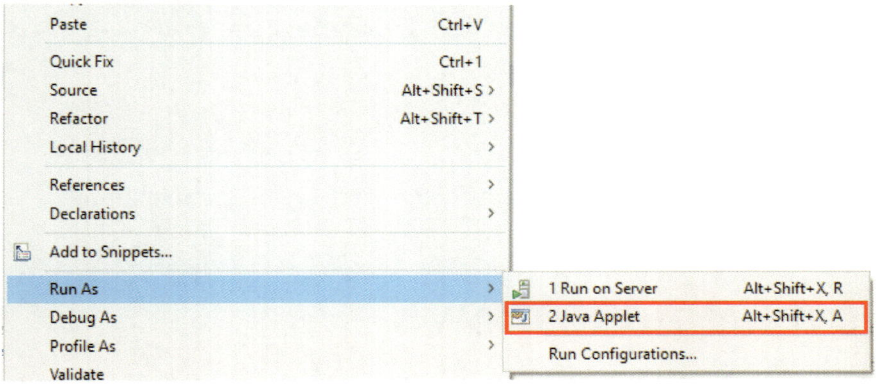

The output generated on execution is the following:

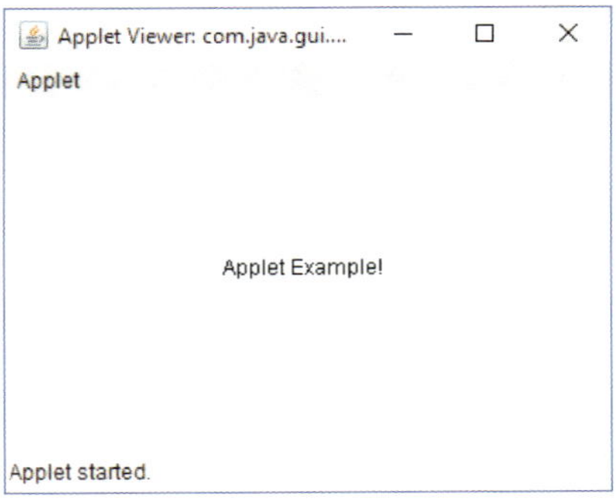

The above applet can be run in a browser as follows:

1. Create an html file with the applet code in the same directory as the class file AppletExample.class. This is shown below:

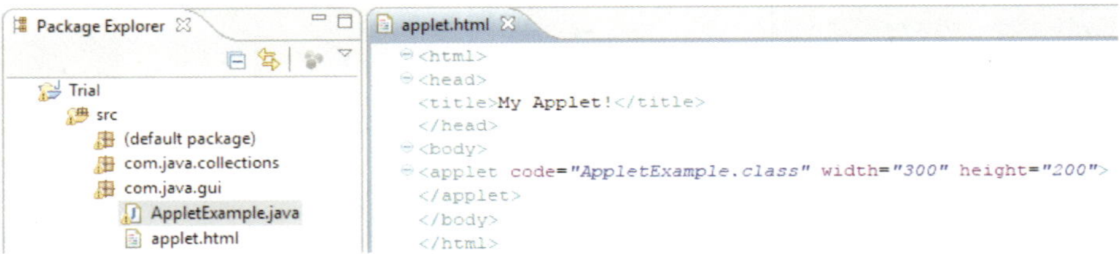

2. Make sure the java is enabled on your browser and load the html file on the browser. For example, if the path of the file is C:/workspace/applet.html then the url to be typed in the browser should be:

file:///C:/workspace/applet.html

The browser loads the applet and displays the same output as shown previously, but inside a browser.

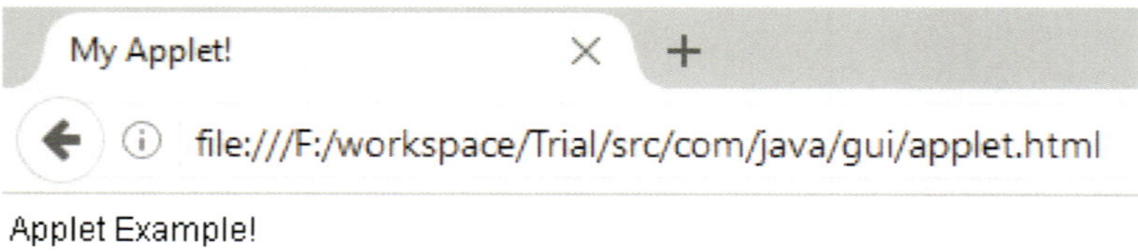

EVENT HANDLING IN AWT

An event in awt is described as the change in the state of an object. When a user interacts with the user interface, events are generated based on the user actions. A simple example is the clicking of a button. We may want something to happen on the click of a button such as present the user with a YES/NO dialog, or simply give an alert to the user or update the value of another field such as a text field and so on. There are a lot of possibilities. Such events are handled by the AWT framework with the help of Event Listeners. Each event has two components namely a source and listener. The source is the object that invoked the event and the listener is the component that provides a response for the generated event. AWT package has a wide range of event classes that help handling of events such as WindowEvent, ContainerEvent, MouseEvent and do on. The scope of this book does not describe all the AWT events. But a few simple examples demonstrating event handling are provided below:

AWTExample2.java

```
package com.java.gui;

import java.awt.Button;
import java.awt.FlowLayout;
import java.awt.Frame;
import java.awt.TextField;
import java.awt.event.ActionEvent;
import java.awt.event.ActionListener;

public class AWTExample2 extends Frame implements ActionListener {

    TextField text;

    public AWTExample2() {

        // create and add components on the frame
        text = new TextField("Hello! How are you?");
        add(text);
        text.setBounds(60, 50, 170, 20);
        Button button = new Button("Click here please!");
        button.setBounds(100, 120, 80, 30);

        // register the button with the listener and pass the current instance
        button.addActionListener(this);

        // add the components on the frame
        add(button);
        add(text);
        // set the dimensions of the Frame
        setSize(200, 300);
        // set title of the frame
        setTitle("AWT Listener example");
        setLayout(new FlowLayout());
        // make the frame visible
        setVisible(true);
    }

    public void actionPerformed(ActionEvent e) {
        text.setText("I am good. How are You?");
    }

    public static void main(String[] args) {

        AWTExample2 example = new AWTExample2();
    }
}
```

As seen from the class AWTExample2, an event is registered on the button which changes the message displayed in the text field. This is shown from the output. On execution of the program, the frame with the button and text field is displayed as follows:

When we click on the button, the text inside the text field is updated as shown:

The next example shows the use of Event Listeners along with the use of a dialog.

Similar to the previous example, in this example we use a button performs an action when it is clicked. In class AWTExample3 shown below, we create a simple frame along with a button and a text field. On clicking the button, a new Dialog appears that takes input from the user. This input is taken and the text field present is updated with this value.

AWTExample3.java

```
package com.java.gui;
import java.awt.*;
import java.awt.event.*;
//class that extends dialog class
class DialogExample extends Dialog implements ActionListener {
    private static final long serialVersionUID = 1L;
    TextField dialogTextField;
    public DialogExample(Frame frame) {
        super(frame, "Dialog Box Example", true);
        setLayout(new FlowLayout());
        Button button = new Button("OK");
        dialogTextField = new TextField(8);
        // register the button with the listener
        button.addActionListener(this);
        add(new Label("Enter Your name and click on OK please: "));
        add(dialogTextField);
        add(button);
        setSize(270, 100);
    }
    public void actionPerformed(ActionEvent e) {
        // retrieve value from the dialog and update the current frame
        AWTExample3.setText(dialogTextField.getText());
        // make the dialog invisible
        setVisible(false);
    }
}
public class AWTExample3 extends Frame implements ActionListener {
    private static final long serialVersionUID = 1L;
    DialogExample dialog;
    static TextField textField;

    public AWTExample3() {
        // create and add components on your frame
        setLayout(new FlowLayout());
        Button button = new Button("Click me");
        textField = new TextField(8);
        // register the button with the listener
        button.addActionListener(this);
        add(button);
        add(textField);
        dialog = new DialogExample(this);
        setSize(250, 100);
        setTitle("AWTExample3");
        setVisible(true);
    }

    public void actionPerformed(ActionEvent e) {
        // on button click display a new dialog
        // make the dialog visible
        dialog.setVisible(true);
    }
    public static void setText(String string) {
        textField.setText(string);
    }
    public static void main(String args[]) {
        new AWTExample3();
    }
}
```

The output generated is as follows:

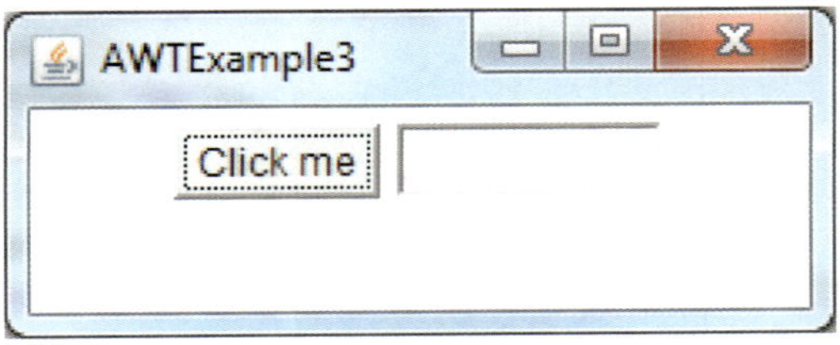

When we click on the button, a new dialog pops up.

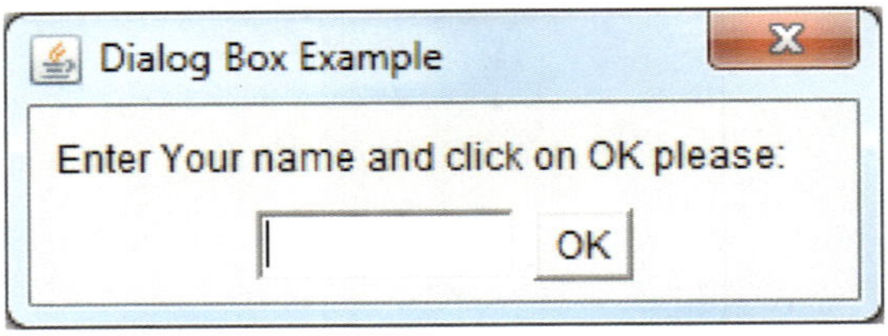

We enter the data as follows:

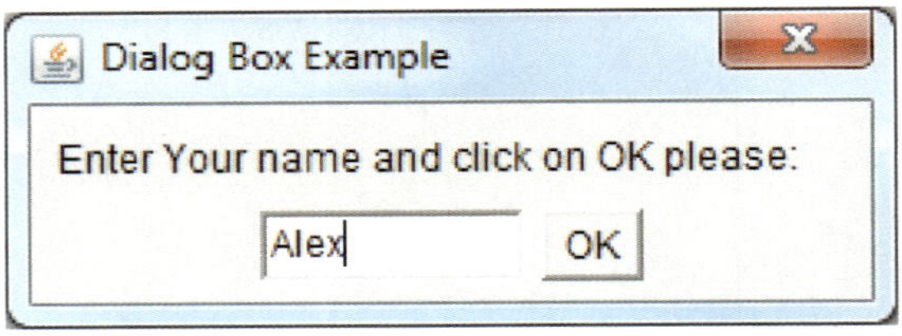

On clicking the OK button, the previous screen is updated with the value we entered as shown below:

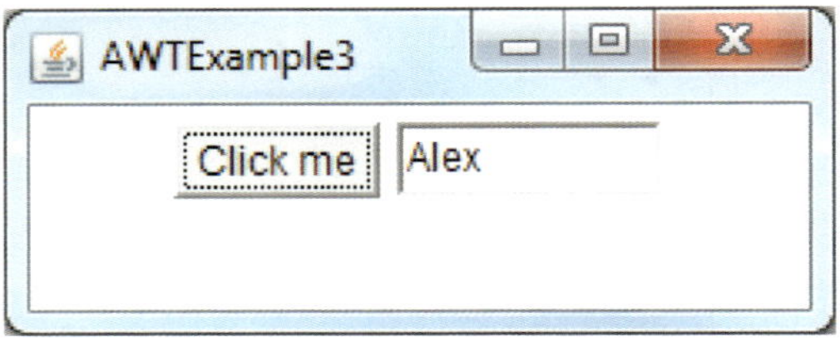

JAVA SWING API

Java has provided us with an improved gui api called Swing. This was developed to overcome the shortcomings of java AWT API and give more advanced API's to build GUI applications. This API is part of the Java Foundation Classes (Oracle) and has the added functionality of providing the 'look and feel' of the underlying OS. The swing components are built on the AWT components and provide many additional components such as panes, tables, trees and so on. Further, these components are lightweight which serves as a great advantage in terms of large applications is and they support the pluggable look and feel as well. This means that the application using these components can have a look and feel that is different from that of its underlying platform. Hence, this API is preferred over the traditional AWT api.

The hierarchy of the components in swing is the same as that of AWT as this api is built upon the existing AWT API. All the components are derived from the AWT components. All the components are derived from a parent class called as JComponent class which is built upon the existing AWT containers and is a child class of the Component class. The only difference is that instead of the abstract superclass Component, all the components such as Button, List etc. extend the class JComponent. For every AWT component there is an equivalent swing component which has the prefix 'J'. All the components are named with a label J before them such as Button class is now JButton. Additionally many miscellaneous components such as trees, color choosers, panes, sliders, toolbars, image buttons, radio buttons, etc. have been provided.

The hierarchy is as shown below:

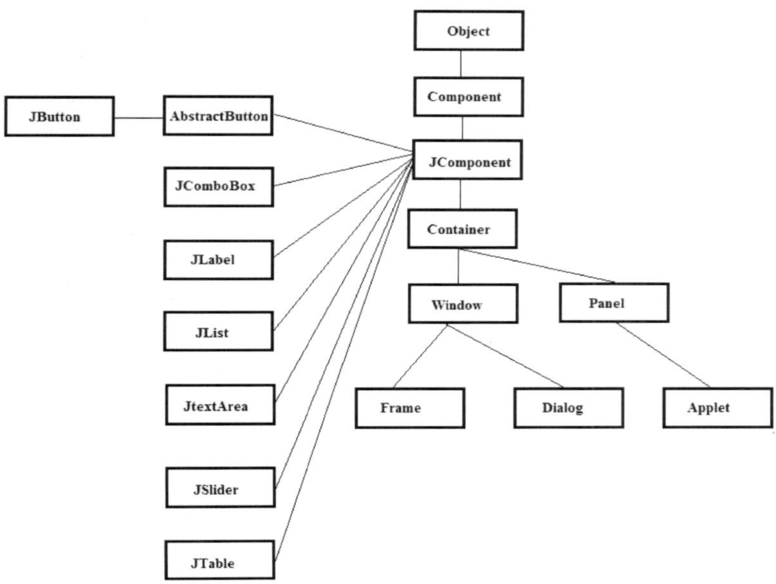

Let us now look at a few examples using the Swing components.

Example 1: A simple user interface with a button and a text field using swing components

SwingExample1.java

```
package com.java.gui;
import javax.swing.JButton;
import javax.swing.JFrame;
import javax.swing.JTextField;

public class SwingExample1{

    public static void main(String[] args) {

        JFrame jFrame=new JFrame();
        //create a JButton
        JButton button=new JButton("Click Me");
        button.setBounds(100,100,100, 30);
        //create a JtextField
        JTextField textfield = new JTextField("Hello!");
        textfield.setBounds(100,170,100, 30);
        //add the components on JFrame
        jFrame.add(button);
        jFrame.add(textfield);

        jFrame.setSize(350,300);
        jFrame.setLayout(null);
        jFrame.setVisible(true);
    }
}
```

The output generated is as follows:

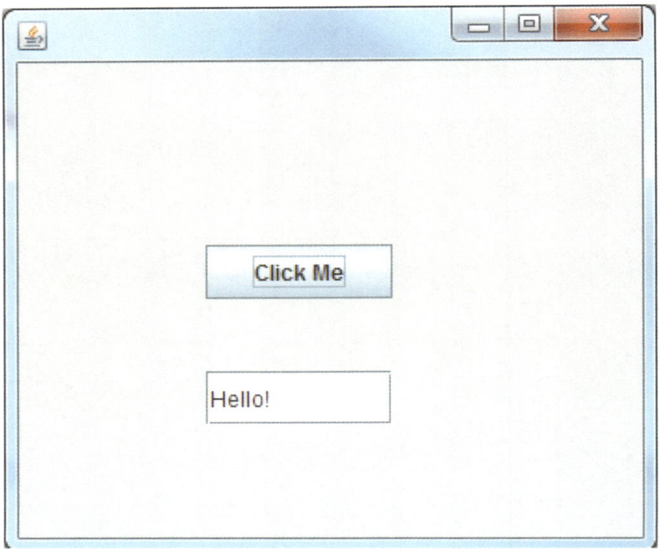

Example 2: Menus and Submenus in swing

SwingExample3.java

```
package com.java.gui;

import javax.swing.JFrame;

public class SwingExample3 {

    public static void main(final String args[]) {

        //create a frame
        JFrame frame = new JFrame("Menu and SubMenu Example");
        frame.setDefaultCloseOperation(JFrame.EXIT_ON_CLOSE);

        //create a MenuBar
        JMenuBar menuBar = new JMenuBar();

        //add a Menu
        JMenu simpleFileMenu = new JMenu("File");
        menuBar.add(simpleFileMenu);

        //add items to the menu
        JMenuItem newOption = new JMenuItem("New");
        simpleFileMenu.add(newOption);

        JMenuItem closeOption = new JMenuItem("Close");
        simpleFileMenu.add(closeOption);

        //create another menu
        JMenu saveOption = new JMenu("Save");
        //add the menu as a sub-menu
        simpleFileMenu.add(saveOption);

        //add items to the sub-menu
        JMenuItem saveOptionText = new JMenuItem("Save as Text");
        saveOption.add(saveOptionText);

        JMenuItem saveOptionPDF = new JMenuItem("Save as PDF");
        saveOption.add(saveOptionPDF);

        JMenuItem saveOptionWord = new JMenuItem("Save as Word");
        saveOption.add(saveOptionWord);
        //configure the frame
        frame.setJMenuBar(menuBar);
        frame.setSize(350, 250);
        frame.setVisible(true);
    }
}
```

The above class creates a frame containing a menu and a submenu as shown by the output below:

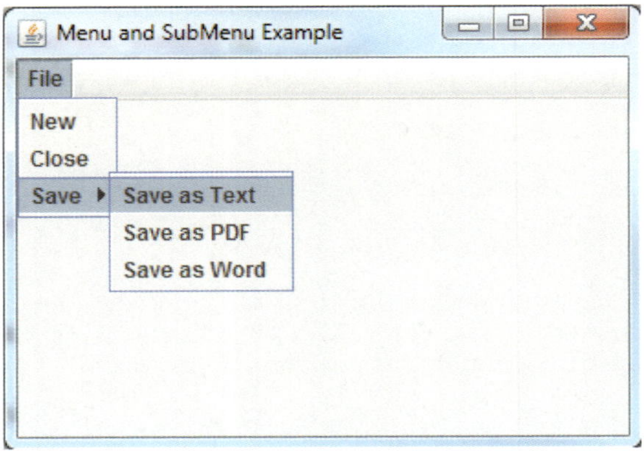

Example 3: Event Handling in Swing

SwingExample4.java

```
package com.java.gui;

import javax.swing.*;
import java.awt.*;
import java.awt.event.*;

class SwingExample4 extends JFrame implements ActionListener {

    private static final long serialVersionUID = 1L;
    JTextField textField;

    SwingExample4() {
        // set Layout
        setLayout(new FlowLayout());
        // add components
        JButton button = new JButton("Click Me");
        textField = new JTextField(10);
        add(button);
        add(textField);
        // register the button with a listener
        button.addActionListener(this);
    }

    public void actionPerformed(ActionEvent e) {
        textField.setText("How are you?");
    }

    public static void main(String args[]) {
        // create a Frame
        SwingExample4 frame = new SwingExample4();
        // configure the frame
        frame.setTitle("Swing Listener Example");
        frame.setBounds(250, 150, 280, 150);
        frame.setDefaultCloseOperation(JFrame.EXIT_ON_CLOSE);
        frame.setVisible(true);
    }
}
```

The output generated is as follows:

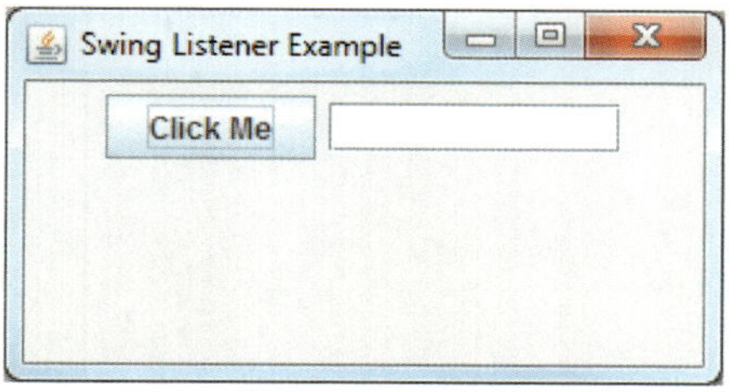

On clicking the buton, the text field is updated.

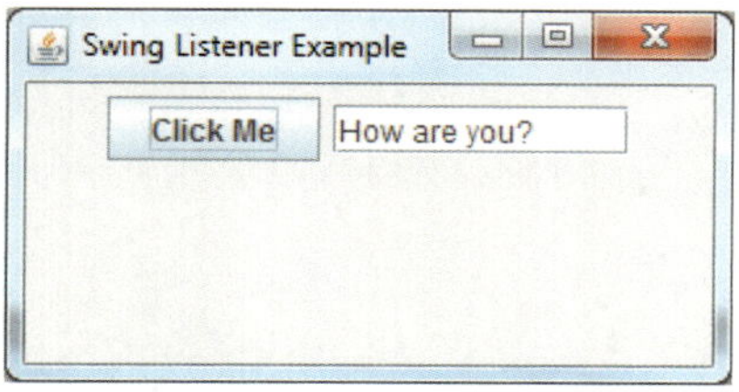

The class SwingExample4 gives us the same output as given by the AWTExample2. This is because AWT and Swing both use the same event handler.

Example 4: Event Handling in Swing using a yes/no dialog option

SwingExample5.java

```
package com.java.gui;

import java.awt.FlowLayout;
import java.awt.event.ActionEvent;
import java.awt.event.ActionListener;
import javax.swing.JButton;
import javax.swing.JFrame;
import javax.swing.JOptionPane;

public class SwingExample5 extends JFrame implements ActionListener {

    private static final long serialVersionUID = 1L;

    public static void main(String[] args) {

        // create a Frame
        SwingExample5 frame = new SwingExample5();
        // configure the frame
        frame.setTitle("Swing Dialog Example");
        frame.setBounds(250, 150, 290, 150);
        frame.setDefaultCloseOperation(JFrame.EXIT_ON_CLOSE);
        frame.setVisible(true);
    }

    SwingExample5() {
        // set Layout
        setLayout(new FlowLayout());
        // add components
        JButton button = new JButton("Click Me");
        add(button);
        // register the button with a listener
        button.addActionListener(this);
    }

    public void actionPerformed(ActionEvent e) {

        // on button click display a dialog with a yes/no option
        JOptionPane.showConfirmDialog(null, "Are you sure you want to proceed?", "Please select an Option!",
                JOptionPane.YES_NO_OPTION);
    }
}
```

On execution, the following window appears:

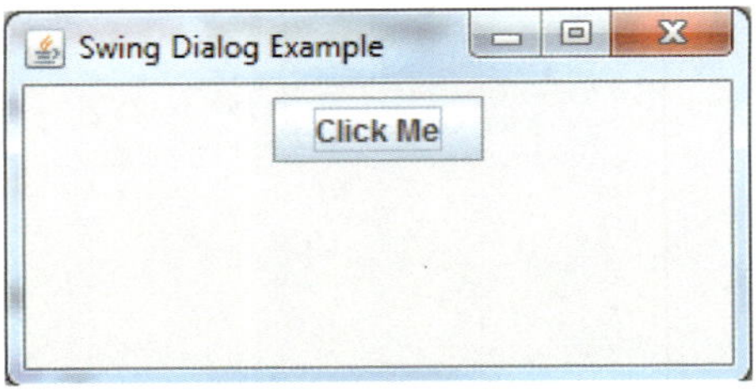

When the user clicks on it, a confirmation dialog is displayed.

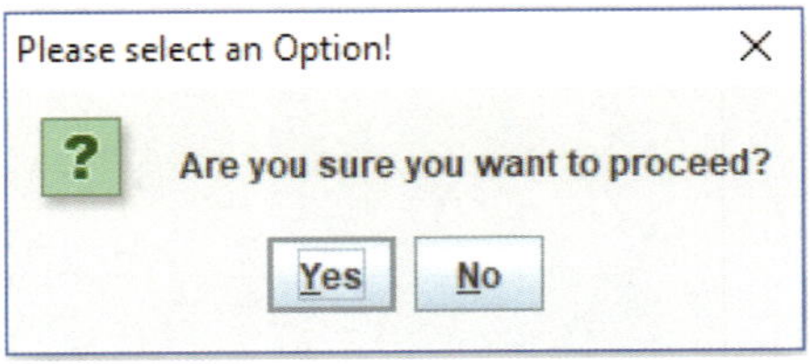

Based on the choice of the user, the flow of the program can be decided.

The AWT package is a large package and hence it has not been covered in detail in this book. For detailed information about the AWT API, consult the book YYYY. This book does not cover the Swing API but the book x can be referred if you want to look into the details.

CHAPTER 16

MULTITHREADING

As explained in chapter 1, multithreading is supported by Java. In java, a program can be logically divided in parts called as threads and each part can be executed simultaneously.

THREADS

A thread is simply a light weight process that runs parallely with other threads. They work independently of one another as each thread executes a different part of the application, but share memory. If some error occurs in one thread, the working of the other threads is not affected. All threads that belong to a single process share the common memory. This process of execution of many threads at the same time is defined as multithreading. Multithreading is a simple solution to achieve multi-tasking the program by executing parts of it simultaneously.

A very simple example of multithreading is the GUI that we discussed in chapter 15. All the GUI packages make use of threads to handle and manage various event generated by the application.

This is a very interesting feature provided by Java that helps applications run faster and save time. By making threads run or work on different parts of the applications, the utilization of the CPU is done to the maximum. In a typical program there exist some parts that are independent of one another and hence can be executed with the help of threads that share a common memory space. This helps reduce the idle time of the CPU and use it more efficiently which is a boon for large scale applications that are made up of multiple servers and processors. In such case the processors' complete capacity can be utilized by executing applications with many threads.

THREAD LIFE CYCLE

A thread can be in different states or stages during its lifetime. A thread's life is controlled and managed by the JVM. The states of a thread are as follows:

- **New**: A thread starts it life in this state. A thread in this has been created but not started yet.
- **Runnable**: Once a thread is created it becomes a runnable thread. This means that it is a thread that is executing/running.
- **Waiting**: A thread in this state is waiting for another thread to complete its task. A thread can exit from this state only when another thread signals this thread to start again.
- **Timed_Waiting**: A thread in this state waits for another thread to complete its task for a specified period of time.
- **Blocked**: A thread in this state is blocked for the lock of the monitor.
- **Terminated**: A thread in this state is dead and has exited.

At any point of time, a thread can have only 1 state. The lifecycle of a thread is shown by the figure below:

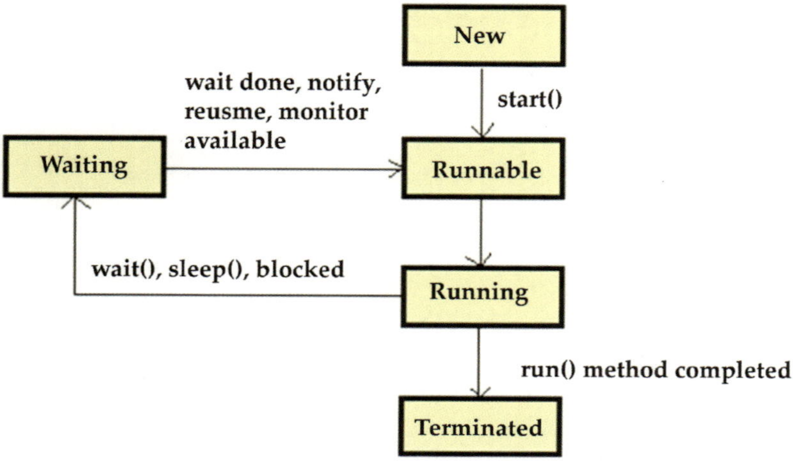

Once the thread is created, it is in the New state. On invoking the start() method on it, it moves to the runnable state. This new thread has not yet been picked up by the system scheduler to start running. The thread scheduler is a component of the JVM and it decides which thread should be chosen. Once it is picked up it goes into the running state and performs its task. This is done by the run() method. Once its task is done, it dies a natural death and exits. But, if during its execution if the sleep() or wait() is invoked on it, or if it is waiting for the I/O to be free. In these cases it goes into the waiting state. Once it is in this state, it can be revived again with the call of notify() that wakes up threads in sleep mode or by the timed wait duration elapsing or by the I/O operation that was blocking it being terminated. We shall see the working of threads in the upcoming section.

THREAD CREATION

In java, the thread class is the class that creates and manages threads. In java, we have two ways to create threads. The first way is to inherit/extend the Thread class. The second way is to implement the runnable interface. We shall now take a look at both the ways to create them.

- Extending the Thread class: By subclassing the Thread class, we inherit its methods and hence its behavior. This is depicted by the following example:

```
ThreadExample1.java

package com.java.threads;

public class ThreadExample1 extends Thread {

    public void run() {
        System.out.println("Running the Thread!");
    }

    public static void main(String[] args) {

        //create an instance of the class
        ThreadExample1 thread1 = new ThreadExample1();
        //start the thread
        //this method invokes the run() method
        thread1.start();
    }
}
```

The output generated is as follows:

```
Console    @ Javadoc
<terminated> ThreadExample1
Running the Thread!
```

Implementing the Runnable interface: Using this way, we implement the method run() provided by the runnable interface. This is shown below:

```
ThreadExample2.java

package com.java.threads;

public class ThreadExample2 implements Runnable {


    public static void main(String[] args) {

        //create an instance of the class
        ThreadExample2 object1 = new ThreadExample2();
        //create a thread object and pass the instance to it as a parameter
        Thread thread1 = new Thread(object1);
        //start the thread
        //this method invokes the run() method
        thread1.start();
    }

    @Override
    public void run() {

        System.out.println("Running the thread!");
    }

}
```

As we notice from the class ThreadExample2, the runnable interface has been implemented, the run() method has been overridden and the instance object has been passed to the thread class object as a parameter of its constructor. The output is as follows:

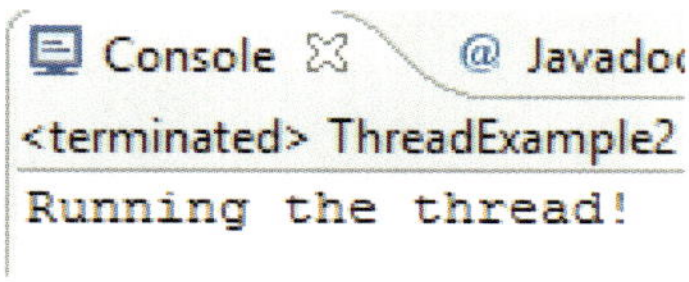

THE THREAD CLASS

Constructors

The thread class provides 8 constructors for creation of threads:

Table 21: Constructors of the Thread class

Constructor	Description
Thread()	creates a new thread object
Thread(String name)	creates a new thread object with the given name
Thread(Runnable r)	creates a new thread object with a runnable object (The class runnable/class that implements runnable)
Thread(Runnable r, String name)	creates a new thread object with a runnable object and gives it the specified name
Thread(ThreadGroup group, Runnable r)	creates a new thread object belonging to the specified thread group with a runnable object
Thread(ThreadGroup group, String name)	creates a new thread object belonging to the specified thread group and gives it the specified name
Thread(ThreadGroup group, Runnable r, String name)	creates a new thread object belonging to the specified thread group, with the specified name and a runnable object
Thread(ThreadGroup group, Runnable target, String name, long stackSize)	creates a new thread object belonging to the specified thread group, with the specified name and a runnable object and with the specified stack size

Methods of the Thread Class

The thread class provides many useful methods that help manipulate threads. Some of them are as follows:

Table 22: Methods of the Thread class

Method	**Description**
String getName()	This method returns the name of the current thread
void setName(String name)	This method sets the name of the Thread to the specified name
void run()	This is the starting point of entry for a thread, called by the start() method and executes the thread
void start()	This method causes the thread to begin execution by invoking the run() method
void sleep(long milliseconds)	This method causes the thread to stop running for the specified time
void getPriority()	This method obtain the priority level of the thread
int setPriority(int priority)	This method sets the priority of the thread to the specified priority
void join()	This method waits for a thread to end its execution
boolean isAlive()	This method returns true if the thread is still running
Thread.State getState()	This method returns the current state of the thread
boolean isDaemon()	This method returns true if the current thread is a daemon thread
void setDaemon(boolean b)	This method sets the current thread to be a daemon thread
void interrupt()	interrupts the thread.
boolean isInterrupted()	tests if the thread has been interrupted

EXAMPLES

Example 1: A simple example showing the use of some of the thread methods and constructors

ThreadExample3.java

```java
package com.java.threads;

public class ThreadExample3 implements Runnable {

    public static void main(String[] args) {

        ThreadExample3 object1 = new ThreadExample3();
        // create thread by passing a runnable object
        Thread thread1 = new Thread(object1);
        // create thread by passing runnable object and thread name
        Thread thread2 = new Thread(object1, "Thread2");
        // create thread by passing runnable object, thread group and thread
        // name
        Thread thread3 = new Thread(new ThreadGroup("Group1"), object1,
        "Thread3");
        thread1.start();
        thread2.start();
        thread3.start();
    }

    @Override
    public void run() {

        System.out.println(" Thread Name:" + Thread.currentThread().getName());
        System.out.println("Thread Id:" + Thread.currentThread().getId());
        System.out.println("Thread Group:"
                + Thread.currentThread().getThreadGroup());
        System.out.println("Thread Priority:"
                + Thread.currentThread().getPriority());
    }
}
```

As we can see, three different constructors of the Thread class are used. Methods of the thread class such getName(), getId(), getThreadGroup() and getPriority() are used. The output generated is as follows:

Console | Javadoc | Declaration | Problems

```
<terminated> ThreadExample3 [Java Application] C:\Program Files\Java\jdk1.8.0_131\bir
 Thread Name:Thread3
 Thread Name:Thread2
 Thread Name:Thread-0
Thread Id:11
Thread Id:12
Thread Group:java.lang.ThreadGroup[name=main,maxpri=10]
Thread Priority:5
Thread Group:java.lang.ThreadGroup[name=Group1,maxpri=10]
Thread Priority:5
Thread Id:10
Thread Group:java.lang.ThreadGroup[name=main,maxpri=10]
Thread Priority:5
```

Example 2: sleep() method

ThreadExample4.java

```java
package com.java.threads;

public class ThreadExample4 extends Thread {

    public void run() {
        for (int i = 1; i < 5; i++) {
            System.out.println(" Thread Name:"
                    + Thread.currentThread().getName() + " Counter:" + i);

            try {
                // invoke the sleep method for 2 seconds
                Thread.sleep(2000);
            } catch (Exception e) {
                System.out.println(e);
            }
        }

    }

    public static void main(String[] args) {

        // create threads
        ThreadExample4 thread1 = new ThreadExample4();
        ThreadExample4 thread2 = new ThreadExample4();

        thread1.start();
        thread2.start();
    }
}
```

The output generated is:

Console @ Javadoc Declaration

<terminated> ThreadExample4 [Java Application]

```
Thread Name:Thread-0 Counter:1
Thread Name:Thread-1 Counter:1
Thread Name:Thread-0 Counter:2
Thread Name:Thread-1 Counter:2
Thread Name:Thread-1 Counter:3
Thread Name:Thread-0 Counter:3
Thread Name:Thread-1 Counter:4
Thread Name:Thread-0 Counter:4
```

Example 3: Thread Priorities

In java, threads are assigned priorities which are represented by a number between 1 and 10. The scheduler schedules the threads as per their priority but this behaviour is dependent on the Jvm and the scheduling mechanism it uses. By default, threads are given a priority of 5. A total of 3 priorities are present which are constants of the thread class. They are as follows:

- static int MIN_PRIORITY: this value is 1

- static int NORM_PRIORITY : this value is 5
- static int MAX_PRIORITY: this value is 10

The priorities of the threads are set to NORM_PRIORITY or 5 by default if no priority has been assigned to it. But using the setPriority() method, the priority of a thread can be changed. The use of thread priorities has been explained in the class ThreadExample5.

ThreadExample5.java

```
package com.java.threads;

public class ThreadExample5 extends Thread {

    public static void main(String[] args) {

        // create threads
        ThreadExample5 thread1 = new ThreadExample5();
        ThreadExample5 thread2 = new ThreadExample5();
        ThreadExample5 thread3 = new ThreadExample5();

        // set priorities and start the threads
        thread1.setPriority(Thread.MIN_PRIORITY);
        thread2.setPriority(Thread.MAX_PRIORITY);
        thread1.start();
        thread2.start();
        // this thread is assigned the default priority
        thread3.start();

    }

    @Override
    public void run() {

        System.out.println("Thread Name:" + Thread.currentThread().getName());
        System.out.println("Thread Priority:"
                + Thread.currentThread().getPriority());
    }
}
```

As seen from the above example, three threads with three different priorities have been created. If no priority has been set for a thread, it is set to 5 by default as shown by the output below:

Console | @ Javadoc | Declaration

<terminated> ThreadExample5 [Java Application]

```
Thread Name:Thread-1
Thread Priority:10
Thread Name:Thread-2
Thread Priority:5
Thread Name:Thread-0
Thread Priority:1
```

An important/key point to note is that the start() method can be invoked only once on a thread. If we invoke it more than once, the thread reaches an illegal state and an IllegalStateException is thrown.

Example 4: Working of Threads using PipedReader and PipedWiter

PipedReaderWriterThreadExample.java

```
package com.trial.java.fundamentals;
import java.io.IOException;
import java.io.PipedReader;
import java.io.PipedWriter;
public class PipedReaderWriterThreadExample {
    public static void main(String[] args) throws IOException {

        PipedReader pipedReader = new PipedReader();
        PipedWriter pipedWriter = new PipedWriter();
        // Connect the reader and writer to form a pipe
        pipedReader.connect(pipedWriter);
        // Write data to the pipe
        Thread writerThread = new Thread(new Runnable() {
            @Override
            public void run() {
                try {
                    System.out.print("Writing the following data to the pipe:");
                    for (int i = 0; i < 5; i++) {
                        pipedWriter.write(i);
                        System.out.print(i);
                    }

                } catch (IOException e) {
                    e.printStackTrace();
                } finally {
                    try {
                        pipedWriter.close();
                    } catch (IOException e) {
                        e.printStackTrace();
                    }
                }
            }
        });
        // Read data from the pipe
        Thread readerThread = new Thread(new Runnable() {
            @Override
            public void run() {
                try {
                    int intToread;
                    System.out.print("\nReading the following data from the pipe:");
                    while ((intToread = pipedReader.read()) != -1) {
                        System.out.print(intToread);
                    }
                } catch (IOException e) {
                    e.printStackTrace();
                } finally {
                    try {
                        pipedReader.close();
                    } catch (IOException e) {
                        e.printStackTrace();
                    }
                }
            }
        });
        // Start the reader and writer threads
        writerThread.start();
        readerThread.start();
    }
}
```

The output is:

```
Console ⊠  Problems  @ Javadoc  Declaration
<terminated> PipedReaderWriterThreadExample [Java Application]
Writing the following data to the pipe:01234
Reading the following data from the pipe:01234
```

It should be noted that both ends (reader and writer) should not be handled by a single thread else deadlock may occur. If any of the threads stop working, the connection between the reader and writer or the pipe is said to be broken.

Example 5: Working of Threads using PipedInputStream and PipedOutputStream

```java
PipedInputOutputStreamThreadExample.java
package com.trial.java.fundamentals;
import java.io.IOException;
import java.io.PipedInputStream;
import java.io.PipedOutputStream;
public class PipedInputOutputStreamThreadExample {
    public static void main(String[] args) throws IOException {
        PipedInputStream pipedInputStream = new PipedInputStream();
        PipedOutputStream pipedOutputStream = new PipedOutputStream();
        // Connect the PipedInputStream and PipedOutputStream to form a pipe
        pipedInputStream.connect(pipedOutputStream);
        // Write data to the pipe
        Thread outputThread = new Thread(new Runnable() {
            @Override
            public void run() {
                try {
                    System.out.print("Writing the following data to the pipe:");
                    for (int i = 68; i < 72; i++) {
                        //write ascii characters to the pipe
                        pipedOutputStream.write((char) i);
                        System.out.print((char)i);
                    }
                } catch (IOException e) {
                    e.printStackTrace();
                } finally {
                    try {
                        pipedOutputStream.close();
                    } catch (IOException e) {
                        e.printStackTrace();
                    }
                }
            }
        });
        // Read data from the pipe
        Thread inputThread = new Thread(new Runnable() {
            @Override
            public void run() {
                try {
                    int charToread;
                    System.out.print("\nReading the following data from the pipe:");
                    while ((charToread = pipedInputStream.read()) != -1) {
                        System.out.print((char) charToread);
                    }
                } catch (IOException e) {
                    e.printStackTrace();
                } finally {
                    try {
                        pipedInputStream.close();
                    } catch (IOException e) {
                        e.printStackTrace();
                    }
                }
            }
        });
        // Start the threads
        outputThread.start();
        inputThread.start();
    }
}
```

The output generated is as follows:

```
Console ⊠   Problems   @ Javadoc   Declaration   Annot
<terminated> PipedInputOutputStreamThreadExample [Java Application]
Writing the following data to the pipe:DEFG
Reading the following data from the pipe:DEFG
```

SYNCHRONISATION

By the use of threads, a type of asynchronicity is added to our programs. When we use multiple threads there is a high chance that two threads may be reading/writing the same data. This may cause the data to be in inconsistent state and unusable. When many threads need to access the same resource which they share, there should exist a way in which we can assure/ensure that the resource is being accessed by just a single thread at a particular point of time. This is done with the help of synchronisation in Java.

We are familiar with the term 'monitor' in case of Operating Systems. It is an importance concept in terms of synchronisation in operating systems. In concurrent programming it is a functionality that allows threads to be mutually exclusive with the ability to block/wait until some condition is rendered true. Java supports the same concept to implement synchronisation. In java, each object is bound to a monitor. To achieve a lock on some data or an object in java, we make use of synchronized blocks or synchronized methods.

When a thread enters such a block/method, no other thread can access the data/object that has been synchronized. Any thread that wants to obtain access to the synchronized block must wait until the previous thread has exited the block.

When we want to synchronize an entire method we simply need to put the keyword 'synchronized' in its declaration as follows:

```
public synchronized void method1() {
}
```

But, when we want to use objects of a class that was initially designed without multithreading in mind, in a multithreaded context we can do this using a synchronized block. For example, if we need a particular operation to be synchronous, we can just add that statement in a synchronous block. The syntax is as follows:

```
synchronized(object)
{
   // statement/statements to be synchronized
}
```

To enable synchronized communication among threads, the thread class is made up of methods wait(), notify() and notifyAll(). As explained earlier, the wait() method causes the current thread to go into waiting state. The thread is forced to release the lock on the monitor. The notify() method on the other hand wakes up a single thread that is waiting on the monitor. The choice of which thread to be woken up is random. The notifyAll() method wakes up all the threads that are waiting for the monitor.

These methods must be invoked within a synchronized context, i.e. in a synchronized statement or synchronized method. This is because if a method/statement doesn't need to be synchronous/mutually exclusive to thread access, there should be no need to communicate between different threads and hence no need to use wait()/notify()/notifyAll(). This in turn means that the method can be access by multiple threads simultaneously.

This use of synchronization is explained by the following example: Consider a bank where a customer deposits and withdraws money. If his balance is negative, he shouldn't be allowed to withdraw money. In such a scenario, the wait() method can be called. This method will restrict the withdraw operation until the balance is positive. The notify() method can be called when the balance is positive to let the user know that he can now withdraw money.

ThreadExample6.java

```java
package com.java.threads;
public class ThreadExample6 {
    public static void main(String[] args) {
        final Bank acc = new Bank();
        acc.balance = 2000;
        new Thread() {
            public void run() {
                acc.withdraw(3000);
            }
        }.start();
        new Thread() {
            public void run() {
                acc.deposit(1500);
            }
        }.start();
    }
}

class Bank {
    float balance;
    public synchronized void deposit(float amount) {
        this.balance = this.balance + amount;
        System.out.println("Balance after desposit is:" + this.balance);
        notify();
    }
    public synchronized void withdraw(float amount) {
        if (this.balance < amount) {
            try {
                System.out.println("Insufficient funds to withdraw. Please deposit funds.");
                wait();
            } catch (Exception e) {
                System.out.println(e);
            }
        }
        this.balance = this.balance - amount;
        System.out.println("Balance after withdrawal is:" + this.balance);
    }
}
```

As seen from the class Bank, the methods withdraw() and deposit() are synchronized and use wait() and notify() to manage thread communication. The output is as follows:

```
Console  @ Javadoc  Declaration  Problems
<terminated> ThreadExample6 [Java Application] C:\Program Files\Java\jdk1.8.0_
Insufficient funds to withdraw. Please deposit funds.
Balance after desposit is:3500.0
Balance after withdrawal is:500.0
```

Initially, when we try to withdraw an amount higher than what is present, the thread is blocked until funds are deposited. Once, the funds are deposited, the thread is now able perform its task.

Static and Synchronized

The ‘synchronized’ keyword can be applied in a static context too. This can be done by using the synchronized keyword on the static method (Gosling, 2000). The syntax is as follows:

public static synchronized method1() {}

When we use the 'synchronized' keyword on a static method, the class is locked and not the object as in case of non-static synchronized blocks/methods. Hence, static synchronization must be used carefully as it could cause problems when mixed with non-static synchronization blocks. This is because, if a static synchronized method is called by a thread a class level lock is obtained. But, if another thread calls a non-static method and tries to access another object, it will be unable to access the object, as the entire class's lock has been obtained by the previous thread that invoke the static method.

So, the following declaration public static synchronized method1(){} of a class named Test is equivalent to the following:

synchronized(Test.class) {}

A simple method showing the use of static synchronization is shown below:

ThreadExample.java

```
package com.java.threads;

public class ThreadExample {

    public static void main(String[] args) {
        new Thread() {
            public void run() {
                Counter.count(10);
            }
        }.start();

        new Thread() {
            public void run() {
                Counter.count(100);
            }
        }.start();

        new Thread() {
            public void run() {
                Counter.count(1000);
            }
        }.start();
    }
}

class Counter {
    public static synchronized void count(int counter) {

        counter = counter + 100;
        System.out.println("Value of counter is:" + counter);
    }
}
```

The output generated is:

```
Console ⊠   @ Javadoc   Declaration
<terminated> ThreadExample [Java Application]
Value of counter is:110
Value of counter is:200
Value of counter is:1100
```

As we can see from the output, the threads have been executed in a mutually exclusive manner and hence the output is correct.

Static synchronization at class level

As mentioned above, the 'synchronized' keyword can be used at a class level as well. The Counter class used in the above example can be synchronized at class level as follows:

```
class Counter {
    public static void count(int counter) {

        synchronized (Counter.class) {
            counter = counter + 100;
            System.out.println("Value of counter is:" + counter);
        }
    }
}
```

Note that the wait() method is used without any parameters. But, a specific duration could be specified using the method void wait(long milliseconds).

The join() method

As explained in table 22, this method waits for the current thread to terminate. In other words, it stops all the executing threads until the thread that invokes the join method completes its execution. The use of the join() method is shown below:

```
ThreadExample7.java
package com.java.threads;

public class ThreadExample7 extends Thread{

    public void run(){
        try{
            Thread.sleep(1000);
            for(int i=0; i<5; i++)
            {
                System.out.println("Thread Name:" +Thread.currentThread().getName() + " Counter:" +i);
            }
        }catch(InterruptedException e){
            System.out.println(e);
        }
    }

    public static void main(String[] args) {

        ThreadExample7 thread1 = new ThreadExample7();
        ThreadExample7 thread2 = new ThreadExample7();
        ThreadExample7 thread3 = new ThreadExample7();
        ThreadExample7 thread4 = new ThreadExample7();

        thread1.start();
        try{
            //call the join method on thread1
            thread1.join();
        }
        catch(InterruptedException e)
        {
            System.out.println(e);
        }
        thread3.start();
        thread2.start();
        thread4.start();
    }
}
```

The output generated is as follows:

```
Console  @ Javadoc  Declaration
<terminated> ThreadExample7 [Java Application]
Thread Name:Thread-0 Counter:0
Thread Name:Thread-0 Counter:1
Thread Name:Thread-0 Counter:2
Thread Name:Thread-0 Counter:3
Thread Name:Thread-0 Counter:4
Thread Name:Thread-2 Counter:0
Thread Name:Thread-1 Counter:0
Thread Name:Thread-3 Counter:0
Thread Name:Thread-3 Counter:1
Thread Name:Thread-3 Counter:2
Thread Name:Thread-3 Counter:3
Thread Name:Thread-3 Counter:4
Thread Name:Thread-1 Counter:1
Thread Name:Thread-1 Counter:2
Thread Name:Thread-1 Counter:3
Thread Name:Thread-1 Counter:4
Thread Name:Thread-2 Counter:1
Thread Name:Thread-2 Counter:2
Thread Name:Thread-2 Counter:3
Thread Name:Thread-2 Counter:4
```

As seen from the output, the first thread, thread-0 is executed first and the rest of them are blocked until its execution is complete.

Similar to the wait() method, the Thread class provides us with another version of the join() method where we can invoke it on a thread for a specified period of time. It is as follows:

public void join(long milliseconds)

The previous example can be modified to use this method as follows:

```
thread1.start();
try{
    //call the join method on thread1
    thread1.join(500);
}
catch(InterruptedException e)
{
    System.out.println(e);
}
```

The rest of program remains the same. However, the output changes slightly as thread1 executes for half a second and then the other threads take over as shown below.

```
Console
<terminated> ThreadExample7 [Java Application]
Thread Name:Thread-0 Counter:0
Thread Name:Thread-0 Counter:1
Thread Name:Thread-0 Counter:2
Thread Name:Thread-0 Counter:3
Thread Name:Thread-1 Counter:0
Thread Name:Thread-0 Counter:4
Thread Name:Thread-2 Counter:0
Thread Name:Thread-2 Counter:1
Thread Name:Thread-2 Counter:2
Thread Name:Thread-2 Counter:3
Thread Name:Thread-2 Counter:4
Thread Name:Thread-3 Counter:0
Thread Name:Thread-3 Counter:1
Thread Name:Thread-3 Counter:2
Thread Name:Thread-3 Counter:3
Thread Name:Thread-3 Counter:4
Thread Name:Thread-1 Counter:1
Thread Name:Thread-1 Counter:2
Thread Name:Thread-1 Counter:3
Thread Name:Thread-1 Counter:4
```

The methods wait() and join() throw the InterruptedException. This exception is thrown when the thread is either waiting, sleeping or busy being blocked and it is interrupted during this state. If we want to know if a thread has been interrupted, the thread class provides us with a method interrupted() to check this. This method can be used to examine if a particular thread has been interrupted, and if it is the case, we can handle this exception as follows:

if (Thread.interrupted())

throw new InterruptedException();

In java, the process of thread interruption works with the use of a flag called as the interrupt status. If a thread is interrupted, this flag is set Once the static interrupted() method is called, this flag is cleared.

DEADLOCK

Deadlock is a scenario where two or more threads are blocked endlessly, waiting for one another (Goetz and Peierls, 2006). This happens when many threads acquire locks on two or more objects in a different order. This deadlock situation arises due to synchronization as it blocks the current thread as it waits for the lock. But due to this behavior it may wait forever. This is explained by the following example:

DeadlockExample.java

```
package com.java.threads;
class Thread1 extends Thread {
    public void run() {
        // this thread locks object1 first and then object2
        synchronized (DeadlockExample.object1) {
            System.out.println("Thread1 blocking object1");
            try {
                Thread.sleep(100);
            } catch (InterruptedException e) {}
            // waits forever to obtain a lock on object2
            System.out.println("Thread1 waiting for object2");
            synchronized (DeadlockExample.object2) {
                System.out.println("Thread1 blocking object1 and object2");
            }
        }
    }
}
class Thread2 extends Thread {
    public void run() {
        // this thread locks object2 first and then object1
        synchronized (DeadlockExample.object2) {
            System.out.println("Thread2 blocking object2");
            try {
                Thread.sleep(100);
            } catch (InterruptedException e) {}
            // waits forever to obtain a lock on object1
            System.out.println("Thread2 waiting for object1");
            synchronized (DeadlockExample.object1) {
                System.out.println("Thread2 blocking object1 and object2");
            }
        }
    }
}
public class DeadlockExample {
    // create two resources
    public static Object object1 = new Object();
    public static Object object2 = new Object();
    public static void main(String args[]) {
        // create and start the threads
        Thread1 thread1 = new Thread1();
        Thread2 thread2 = new Thread2();
        thread1.start();
        thread2.start();
    }
}
```

As seen from the program DeadlockExample, thread1 locks the object1 first while thread2 locks object2 first. After each thread acquires one lock; on object1 and object2 respectively by thread1 and thread2, they both wait indefinitely for the lock on the other object which results in a deadlock.

The output is as follows:

```
Console  @ Javadoc  Decla
DeadlockExample [Java Application] C:\Prc
Thread1 blocking object1
Thread2 blocking object2
Thread2 waiting for object1
Thread1 waiting for object2
```

One way to resolve a deadlock is to manage the order in which the locks on different objects are obtained. If we change the order of the locks in the above example, the deadlock is resolved. This is shown below:

```java
DeadlockExample.java
package com.java.threads;
class Thread1 extends Thread {
    public void run() {
        // this thread locks object1 first and then object2
        synchronized (DeadlockExample.object1) {
            System.out.println("Thread1 blocking object1");
            try {
                Thread.sleep(100);
            } catch (InterruptedException e) {}
            // waits forever to obtain a lock on object2
            System.out.println("Thread1 waiting for object2");
            synchronized (DeadlockExample.object2) {
                System.out.println("Thread1 blocking object1 and object2");
            }
        }
    }
}
class Thread2 extends Thread {
    public void run() {
        // this thread locks object1 first and then object2 like thread1
        synchronized (DeadlockExample.object1) {
            System.out.println("Thread2 blocking object2");
            try {
                Thread.sleep(100);
            } catch (InterruptedException e) {}
            // waits forever to obtain a lock on object1
            System.out.println("Thread2 waiting for object1");
            synchronized (DeadlockExample.object2) {
                System.out.println("Thread2 blocking object1 and object2");
            }
        }
    }
}
public class DeadlockExample {
    // create two resources
    public static Object object1 = new Object();
    public static Object object2 = new Object();
    public static void main(String args[]) {
        // create and start the threads
        Thread1 thread1 = new Thread1();
        Thread2 thread2 = new Thread2();
        thread1.start();
        thread2.start();
    }
}
```

The order of calling the locks on the objects has been changed. Now thread2 is blocked until thread1 completes its task which is shown by the output below:

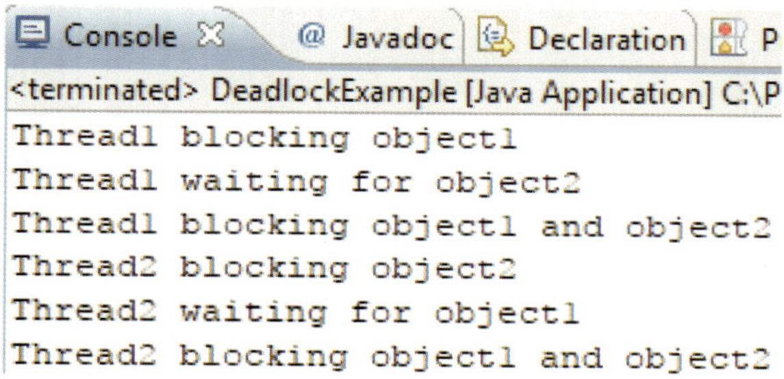

As shown in the output, thread1 and thread2 both execute successfully and complete their respective tasks.

In addition to deadlocks, multithreaded environments give rise to another two less common issues namely starvation and livelock.

Starvation, as its name suggests is when a thread literally starves for resources. This situation arises when a thread monopolizes a particular resource for longer periods of time, resulting in other threads waiting on the resource forever and ultimately being unable to move forward and complete its task.

Livelock is a peculiar issue in case of multithreaded environments. This issue occurs when two threads are responding to each other. This means that each thread knows that it is blocking the other and hence decides to take action and stops its work. But the other thread at the same time, decides to take action and stop its work. So, neither thread advances. Their states just keep changing constantly based on the other thread.

A simple real world example is when 2 people meet in a tiny cramped hallway, each person, being polite, moves to the side to let the other one pass. But, they move to same side at the same time. Then they keep moving from side to side without moving forward as they continuously move to the same side at the same time which results them in being indefinitely stuck.

THREAD POOLS

Java 5 introduces the java.util.concurrent packages that include advanced level concurrency features that are useful in case of multithreaded applications. We shall take a look at two special features provided by this package. They are as follows:

1. Executors

The basic multithreaded applications that we have seen so far create and use threads within the program on a small scale. But, if we imagine a large scale application that has over hundreds of threads, it seems more practical to separate the management of threads from the rest of the application logic. The java.util.concurrent package provides us with the executor interfaces that helps manage threads. Executors are capable of creating pools of threads so we do not need to create threads manually.

Three executor interfaces are provided as follows:

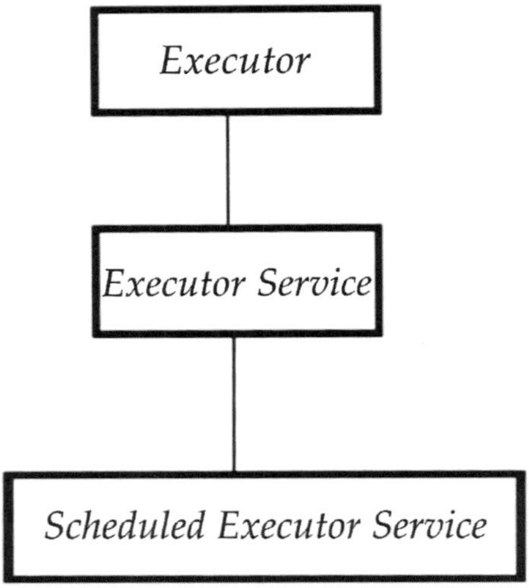

The Executor interface is the main interface and it has a sub-interface named ExecutorService and a sub- sub interface named ScheduledExecutorService.

The executor interface provides a method execute() to launch threads. This method takes a runnable object as a parameter.

The ExecutorService interface is the advanced version of the Executor interface offering many api's and services.

The ScheduledExecutorService is also an advanced interface based on the executor. It had additional methods that help schedule tasks repeatedly at fixed intervals of time.

Detailed discussion of the Executor interfaces is beyond the scope of this book. However, the book xyz by abc can be referred for further reading.

A simple example using the executor interface with the ExecutorService is shown below:

ThreadExample8.java

```
package com.java.threads;

import java.util.concurrent.ExecutorService;

public class ThreadExample8 implements Runnable {

    public static void main(String[] args) {
        // //create a pool of 5 threads using the newFixedThreadPool() method of
        // the Executors class
        ExecutorService executor = Executors.newFixedThreadPool(5);
        for (int i = 0; i < 10; i++) {
            Runnable worker = new ThreadExample8();
            // call the execute method of ExecutorService
            executor.execute(worker);
        }
        // shutdown the executor
        executor.shutdown();
    }

    @Override
    public void run() {
        System.out.println("Thread Name:" + Thread.currentThread().getName());

    }
}
```

The output of the above program is as follows:

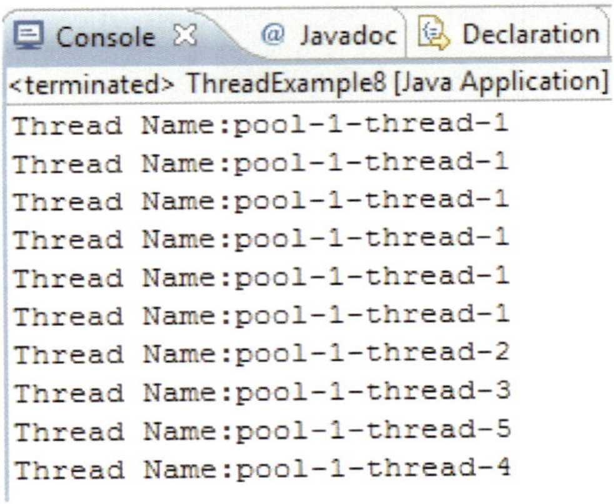

2. Atomic Variable

Although synchronization works well for multiple threads, in case of very large scale applications with millions of threads competing for the same resource, many threads are blocked and suspended to be resumed later. In addition to the overhead of synchronization, the threads that are waiting on the lock cannot do any other task until they finish their previous task. To avoid these issues, the concurrent package in java 5 has a functionality of Atomic variables. These variables have the property of atomicity. An atomic action is when an event happens completely or not at all.

The concurrent package support atomic actions on variables. It is like a small yet powerful toolkit that supports thread safe operations without use of locks and synchronized blocks/methods.

Some of the classes present in this toolkit are:

AtomicBoolean, AtomicInteger, AtomicLong, AtomicLongArray etc.

All the classes in this toolkit have a get() and a set() method. The reads and writes on objects of these classes are similar to the read/write operations on volatile variables. This means that any write/set operation always happens before a read/get operation. This is said to be 'happens-before'.

Consider a class with a variable i that we increment as follows:

AtomicExample.java

```
package com.java.threads;

public class AtomicExample {

    private int i;

    public void incrementI()
    {
        i++;
    }

    public void decrementI()
    {
        i--;
    }

    private int getIValue()
    {
        return this.i;
    }
}
```

A simple way to make the variable thread safe is synchronization. If we make the method synchronized, it becomes thread safe.

As this is a simple class, synchronization works to make it thread safe. But, for a complex class, we may be faced with the liveness issues such as starvation, deadlock or livelock.

So to simplify things, we can use an AtomicInteger in place of an Integer variable with having the need for synchronization. Hence, the above class now changes as follows:

AtomicExample.java

```
package com.java.threads;

import java.util.concurrent.atomic.AtomicInteger;

public class AtomicExample {

    private AtomicInteger i;

    public void incrementI()
    {
        i.incrementAndGet();
    }

    public void decrementI()
    {
        i.decrementAndGet();
    }

    private int getIValue()
    {
        return i.get();
    }
}
```

CONCURENT COLLECTIONS

The java.util.concurrent packages made a few changes to the Collections Framework as well. Some new classes and interfaces that support concurrent access and are thread safe have been added to the Collections Framework.

They are as follows:

1. Blocking Queue: This class inherits from the Queue Interface defines a *FIFO* queue data structure that blocks the thread if you try to add an element to an already full queue or if you try to pop an element from an empty queue (Collins, 2011).

Some of its implementations: ArrayBlockingQueue, DelayQueue, LinkedBlockingQueue, LinkedBlockingDeque , etc.

2. ConcurrentMap: This interface inherits from the Map interface and provides atomic operations. In a concurrentMap implementation, the remove or replace operations proceed only if a key is present and add a key/value pair only if the new key to be added is not present in the Map.

This interface has 2 implementations: the class ConcurrentHashMap and the interface ConcurrentNavigableMap

The ConcurrentHashMap is the concurrent/thread safe version of the HashMap. It has the same properties, functionality and behavior as that of a HashMap. The difference is that concurrent access is supported by the ConcurrentHashMap.

ConcurrentNavigableMap is an interface that inherits from the ConcurrentMap interface. This interface supports navigable Map operations such as returning the closest match for a given search target. A number of methods for locating elements have been provided by this interface.

The implementation class of the ConcurrentNavigableMap is the ConcurrentSkipListMap class. This class is a similar to a TreeMap. It could be said that it is a concurrent version of a TreeMap. It supports scalability, and sorts elements based on their natural order. Additionally, it implements a SkipList that is concurrent/thread-safe.

A SkipList is a data structure similar to a search algorithm, that performs very rapid search operations where a hierarchy of elements/sequences are maintained and each subsequence of elements skips a few elements. More information about skiplists can be found here.

CHAPTER 17

GARBAGE COLLECTION IN JAVA

In java, memory management is done with the help of an entity/module called as the garbage collector. Unlike similar OOP programming languages such as C or C++, the collector in java is automatic. The garbage collection process includes periodical checking of the heap memory, scanning them and checking which of the objects are in use and which of them aren't in use and then deleting the objects that are not used, thus freeing up memory space. In order to check if an object is still in use, the concept of referencing is used. If an object is in use it means that some part of the program still maintains a reference to the object. This means that the program still is making use of it and has a pointer linked to it, which in turn means that memory is still allocated to the object. An unreferenced object is one that is not used by any part of the program and hence is unreferenced and thus its memory space must be freed as it is no longer in use. Its memory in the heap can be reclaimed and assigned/re-allocated to new objects that will be created by the program. This unused object takes up space in the memory which can be reused in a better way. This is done by the garbage collector automatically, unlike other programming languages, where the allocation-de-allocation-reallocation process is manual and it is up to the user to manage memory. Leaving the responsibility to the user makes the program vulnerable to memory leaks and dangling pointers. All these issues have been eliminated in Java by its automatic Garbage collector.

WORKING OF THE GARBAGE COLLECTOR

The working of the GC is a simple three-step process that is described as follows:

Step 1: Marking

The very first and crucial step in the process of collection of unused objects is called as marking. This step involves identifying which parts of memory are in use and which of them are not being used anymore. The garbage collector scans the memory and marks all the objects that are referenced and unreferenced. As we can see in the figure below, all objects are scanned and then marked based on their usage. As shown below, the used objects are marked in red and the unused objects are marked in green. This marking process can take a lot of time as all objects need to be scanned.

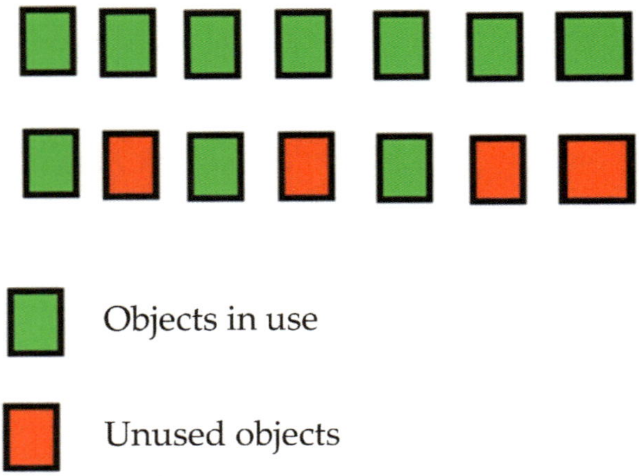

Step 2: Normal Deletion

The second step is simple deletion of the objects that are no longer in use. This action frees up space and now new objects can be allocated this freed up space.

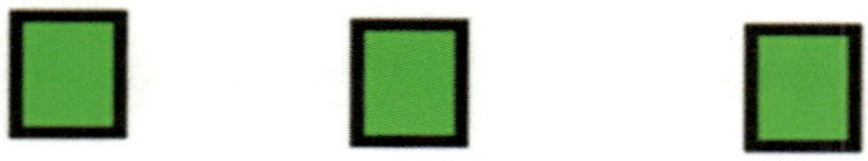

After deletion

Step 3: Compacting the Memory fragments

In addition to deletion of unused and unreferenced objects, the java garbage collector further makes use of algorithms/collectors that help defragment or compact the memory to form contiguous blocks of used/referenced objects. In this step, the objects that remain or the objects that are still in use are compacted together. This makes it easier and faster to allocate memory blocks.

This is shown in as follows.

After compacting

THE CONCEPT OF GENERATIONS

In java, one of the advantages is that the developer is not exposed to complexities of the memory allocation and release processes. The GC in java is a tool that helps free up memory space. But, in doing so, it makes certain assumptions with respect to the use of objects by the various java applications. This is reflected in certain fine tuning parameters of the GC that are adjusted to achieve better performance. While marking an object for garbage collection, the GC marks it if it isn't referenced anymore. The simplest way to mark any object is to iterate over all the possible objects and find every object. But, this approach is a little time consuming, especially in case of very large scale applications which is made up of many objects. This slows down the marking process because as more objects get allocated, the list keeps growing which results in the increase in time taken to iterate over all the objects.

In order to remedy this problem, the JVM has a number of object collection/memory recovery algorithms that are executed along with the collection on the basis of 'Generations'. Generational collection is based on the hypothesis that most objects in a program live for a short period of time. This conclusion was reached after empirical analysis of allocation data over several java programs. This analysis was done to find out ways and properties that help in minimizing the effort required to reclaim unused or unreferenced objects. Hence, in java the unused objects are classified into different generations based on the amount of time that they exist.

A simple example of data that is short lived is shown below. The following graph shows the distribution of objects' lifetime. It displays the amount of bytes allocated on the X axis against the lifetime of the bytes. As we can see, the lifetime of the objects is generally short.

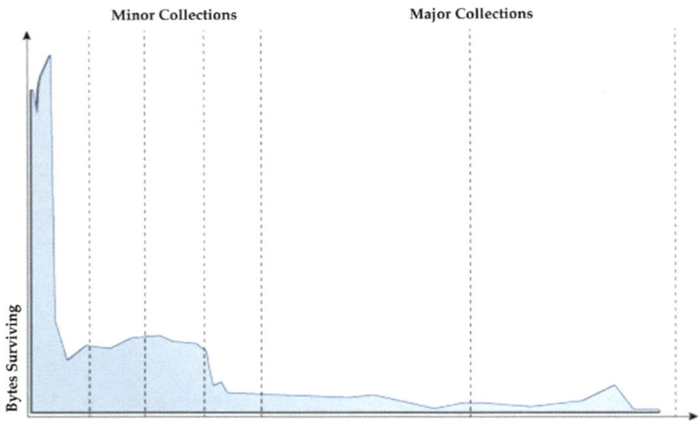

Figure 161: Distribution of an objects' lifetime: (Oracle.com, 2017)

In general it was found that most of the objects have a short life-span and this is clearly depicted by the help of the graph above. It shows a higher concentration on the left side which means that many objects don't survive for longer periods of time. Hence, the JVM divides the heap into small parts, namely generations. Based on the generations, objects are classified and marked accordingly by the collection algorithms.

The heap is divided into the following generations: Young, old/ tenured and Permanent.

The young generation comprises of all the newly created and allocated objects. When this part fills up with objects completely, a minor garbage collection event occurs. This event consists of collection of all unreferenced/unused objects in this generation. The assumption made here is that not many objects survive and thus can be collected quickly. For the objects that do survive, they age and are moved eventually to the old generation. This minor garbage collection event is a stop-the-world event, which means that all applications are stopped until the minor garbage collection terminates. Conventionally, an age threshold is set for this generation. If an object reaches that age, it is moved to the older generation.

The next generation is the Old/Tenured Generation which stores objects that survive for a longer period of time. This section comprises of objects that have survived the young generation. Eventually, after a period of time these objects need to be collected as well. This collection is a major collection and is yet another stop-the-world event. This process is a lot slower as compared to a minor collection and hence is not done often. The duration of the major collection is dependent on several parameters such as the time of GC and the collection algorithm used.

The next generation is the Permanent generation which consists of all the non-heap data. This pool of objects consists of the JVM data itself, such as classes and methods. Basically, the metadata of the classes and methods used in the application are stored by this generation. This heap space is filled up during runtime based upon the classes used by the program. When the jvm no longer references or uses these non-heap objects, they may get collected by the garbage collector. Whenever a complete garbage collection occurs, this generation is always included.

The generations are depicted below:

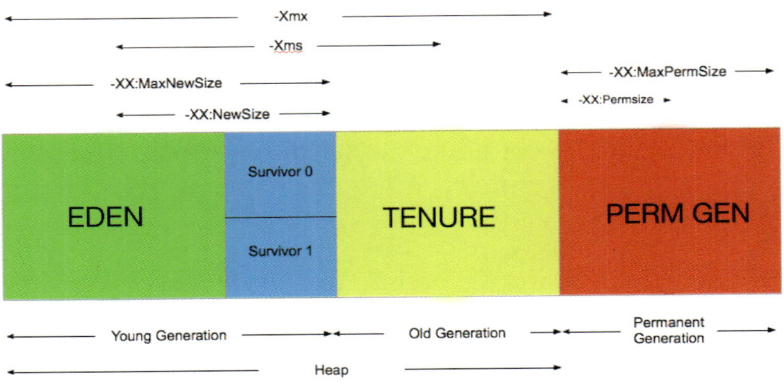

Figure 162: Generations (www.engineersbloc.com, 2017)

Now that we know of generations, we further take a look into how the objects age in the JVM and see how generational garbage collection works.

Initially the objects are newly created and allocated to young generation in the eden space. This space stores newly allocated objects. The survivor spaces, shown by the green sections in the figure below are initially empty.

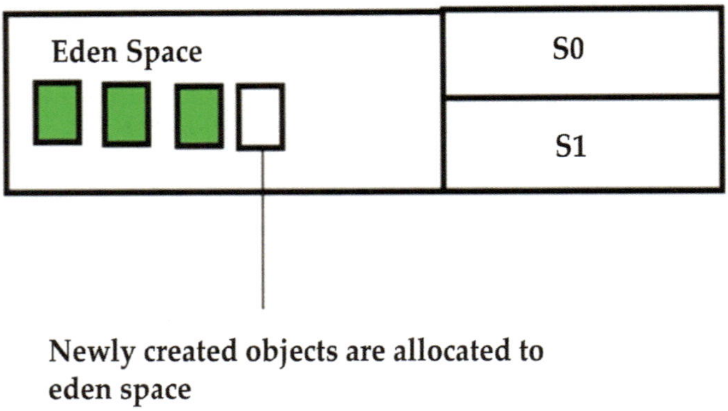

Once, the eden space is full, a minor garbage collection event is triggered by the jvm.

The objects that are currently in use are moved to the survivor space 0.The objects that are not used are deleted and the objects that do survive are moved to survivor space 0.

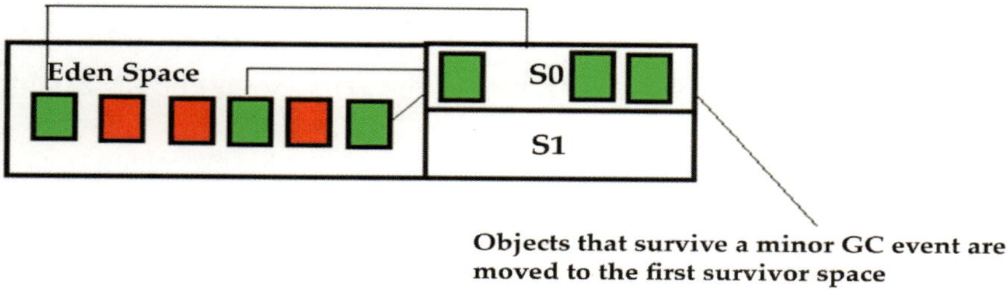

When the next minor collection event occurs after the eden space is full, this process is repeated. Objects in use from the eden space are moved to survivor space 0 and unused objects are deleted. But, this time, objects from the survivor space 0 that survive are moved and aged from the survivor space 0 are moved in Survivor space 1.

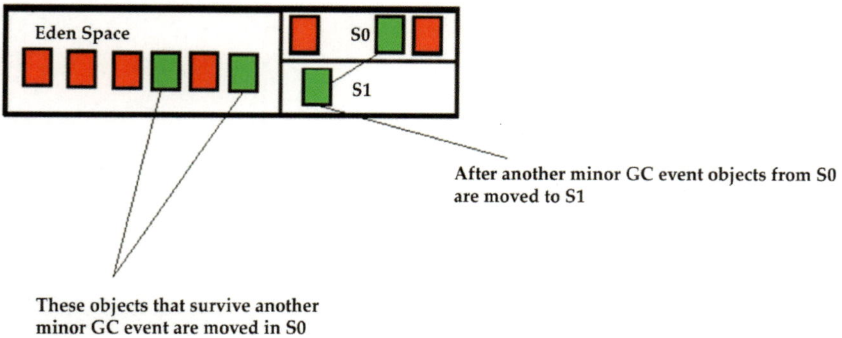

Once all the objects that survive move to the survivor space 1, the eden space and the survivor space 0 are cleared. Now a collection of differently aged objects are present in the young generation.

Notice we now have differently aged object in the survivor space. When another minor GC event occurs, the same process occurs: the objects that survive are aged, unused objects are deleted and after the age threshold is reached, the objects are moved into the succeeding survivor spaces.

As the jvm keeps triggering minor collection events, the objects will be further aged and promoted to the older generation. As this goes on, eventually the JVM triggers a major collection event that clears up space from the older generation and defragments the heap.

Further, several types of garbage collectors are available such as the parallel collector, the Mark and sweep collector. Additional information related to these collectors can be found at the Java Documentation (docs. Oracle.com, 2017).

CHAPTER 18

REFLECTION IN JAVA

Java is a powerful language that is capable of examining and modifying the properties of an object at runtime. Java allows a developer to inspect, analyse and modify objects and their types, fields and classes etc which is called as reflection. The JVM makes use of the java.lang.Class class and the java.lang.reflect package that has methods that one can use to examine the properties of an object at runtime. This class serves as the base class or point of entry for the reflection api. This class provides several methods that helps us retrieve metadata bout classes such as fields, methods and so on. Furthermore, using the reflection Api, the behaviour of a class can be modified as well.

REFLECTION API

This API is mainly in the following context:

- Reflection is used in Integrated Development Environments (IDE's) such as Eclipse, Netbeans etc. where a developer may need to list the members and fields of a class. This may help a developer write better and cleaner code.

- Another important area of application of reflection is in debuggers and testing tools as they need to inspect the private members of a class. This further helps in developing better test cases that ensure better code coverage.

Some useful methods of the reflection API are as follows:

Method[] getDeclaredMethods(): returns a list/collection of Method objects containing the declared methods of the current class.

Constructor[] getDeclaredConstructors(): returns the list of constructors of the class

Field[] getDeclaredFields(): returns a list of Field object with the fields of the class

Class<T> getSuperClass(): returns a reference of the super class of the current class

T newInstance(): creates a new instance of the class type

String getName(): returns the name of the class as a string

Class<T> getEnclosingClass(): returns an instance object of the class enclosing the current class. This is useful in case of nested classes (Collins, 2011).

Package getPackage(): returns the package the class is declared in

boolean isInterface(): returns true if the object is an interface

boolean isAnonymousClass(): returns true if the class is an anonymous class

int getModifiers(): returns the modifiers for the class encoded as an integer

boolean isArray(): returns true if the object is an array

T newInstance(): creates a new instance of the class

static class forName(String className): returns an instance of the class name it takes as an argument and loads it dynamically

EXAMPLES OF REFLECTION

The following examples demonstrate the use of the reflection API.

Example 1: Basic Java reflection API to obtain class information.

ReflectionExample1.java

```
package com.java.reflection;
import java.lang.reflect.Constructor;
import java.lang.reflect.Field;
import java.lang.reflect.Method;
public class ReflectionExample1 {

    int x;
    double y;

    public ReflectionExample1(int x, double y) {
        this.x = x;
        this.y = y;
    }
    public ReflectionExample1() {
        this.x = 0;
        this.y = 0;
    }
    public int getX() {
        return x;
    }
    public void setX(int x) {
        this.x = x;
    }
    public double getY() {
        return y;
    }
    public void setY(double y) {
        this.y = y;
    }
    public void display() {
        System.out.println("X:" + x + " Y:" + y);
    }
    class NestedClass {}

    public static void main(String[] args) {
        // get instance of the class Class
        Class classObject = ReflectionExample1.class;
        System.out.println(classObject);
        // get the list of classes declared within the class
        Class[] classList = classObject.getDeclaredClasses();
        for (int i = 0; i < classList.length; i++)
            System.out.println(classList[i].getName());
        // get the list of fields declared in the class
        Field[] fieldList = classObject.getDeclaredFields();
        for (int i = 0; i < fieldList.length; i++)
            System.out.println("Fields of the class:" + fieldList[i].getName());
        // get the list of the constructors declared in the class
        Constructor[] constructorList = classObject.getDeclaredConstructors();
        for (int i = 0; i < constructorList.length; i++)
            System.out.println("Constructors of the class:" + constructorList[i]);
        // get the list of methods declared in the class
        Method[] methodList = classObject.getDeclaredMethods();
        for (int i = 0; i < methodList.length; i++)
            System.out.println("Methods of the class:" + methodList[i]);
        // get the superclass of the class
        System.out.println("Superclass: " + classObject.getSuperclass().getName());
    }
}
```

The output generated is as follows:

```
Console
<terminated> ReflectionExample1 [Java Application] C:\Program Files\Java\jdk1.8.0_131\bin\javaw.exe
class com.java.reflection.ReflectionExample1
com.java.reflection.ReflectionExample1$NestedClass
Fields of the class:x
Fields of the class:y
Constructors of the class:public com.java.reflection.ReflectionExample1(int,double)
Constructors of the class:public com.java.reflection.ReflectionExample1()
Methods of the class:public static void com.java.reflection.ReflectionExample1.main(java.lang.String[])
Methods of the class:public int com.java.reflection.ReflectionExample1.getX()
Methods of the class:public double com.java.reflection.ReflectionExample1.getY()
Methods of the class:public void com.java.reflection.ReflectionExample1.display()
Methods of the class:public void com.java.reflection.ReflectionExample1.setX(int)
Methods of the class:public void com.java.reflection.ReflectionExample1.setY(double)
Superclass: java.lang.Object
```

Example 2: The newInstance() api

The newinstance() method creates an object of the class as it would have been created using the 'new' keyword with a default constructor. The object/class that is returned is always initialized. This method throws two Exceptions: InstantiationException and IllegalAccessException.

```
ReflectionExample2.java
package com.java.reflection;

public class ReflectionExample2 {

    int x;
    int y;

    public String toString() {
        return "x:" + x + " y:" + y;
    }

    public static void main(String[] args) {

        //create an instance using 'new'
        ReflectionExample2 object1 = new ReflectionExample2();
        System.out.println(object1);
        //get a Class object of the class ReflectionExample2
        Class classObject = ReflectionExample2.class;
        try {
            //create an instance using the newInstance() method
            ReflectionExample2 object2 = (ReflectionExample2) classObject
                    .newInstance();
            System.out.println(object2);
        } catch (InstantiationException e) {
            // TODO Auto-generated catch block
            e.printStackTrace();
        } catch (IllegalAccessException e) {
            // TODO Auto-generated catch block
            e.printStackTrace();
        }
    }
}
```

As shown by the output, a new instance of the class is obtained using two ways; using the new operator and the newInstance() method(). Both the ways generate the same result as shown by the output below.

```
Console    @ Javadoc
<terminated> ReflectionExample2
x:0 y:0
x:0 y:0
```

Example 3: Class.forName

This method returns an instance of the type Class and loads the instance dynamically. This method takes the fully qualified class name as a parameter and cannot be used for primitive data types such as int, float etc. (Shams and Edwards, 2013). This api is similar to the Class.class API which returns an instance of the class as well.

```
ReflectionExample3.java
package com.java.reflection;

public class ReflectionExample3 {

    public static void main(String[] args) throws ClassNotFoundException {

        Class classObject = Class
                .forName("com.java.reflection.ReflectionExample3");
        System.out.println(classObject.getName());
    }
}
```

The output generated is as follows:

```
Console    @ Javadoc    Declaration    Prob
<terminated> ReflectionExample3 [Java Application] C:\Pr
com.java.reflection.ReflectionExample3
```

Example 4: getMethods() and getDeclaredMethods()

ReflectionExample4.java

```
package com.java.reflection;
import java.lang.reflect.Method;
public class ReflectionExample4 {

    int x;
    double y;

    public ReflectionExample4(int x, double y) {
        this.x = x;
        this.y = y;
    }

    public void display(){
        System.out.println("x:" + x + " y:" +y);
    }

    public static void main(String[] args) {

        // get instance of the class Class
        Class classObject = ReflectionExample4.class;
        // get the list of the methods declared in the class
        System.out.println("-------getDeclaredMethods()-------");
        Method[] classMethodsList = classObject.getDeclaredMethods();
        for (int i = 0; i < classMethodsList.length; i++)
            System.out.println("Methods of the class:" + classMethodsList[i]);
        System.out.println("-------getMethods()-------");
        // get the list of methods in the class and its superclass
        Method[] methodList = classObject.getMethods();
        for (int i = 0; i < methodList.length; i++)
            System.out.println("Methods of the class:" + methodList[i]);
    }
}
```

A notable point is that there is a difference between the getDeclaredXXX() and the getXXX() api's as shown in the above example. The getDeclareMethods() method returns all the methods declared in the current class. The getMethods() method returns all the methods declared in the current class and the methods the current class inherits from its superclass which is the Object class in this case. The output is as shown below:

Console | Javadoc | Declaration | Problems

```
<terminated> ReflectionExample4 [Java Application] C:\Program Files\Java\jdk1.8.0_131\bin\javaw.exe
-------getDeclaredMethods()-------
Methods of the class:public static void com.java.reflection.ReflectionExample4.main(java.lang.String[])
Methods of the class:public void com.java.reflection.ReflectionExample4.display()
-------getMethods()-------
Methods of the class:public static void com.java.reflection.ReflectionExample4.main(java.lang.String[])
Methods of the class:public void com.java.reflection.ReflectionExample4.display()
Methods of the class:public final void java.lang.Object.wait() throws java.lang.InterruptedException
Methods of the class:public final void java.lang.Object.wait(long,int) throws java.lang.InterruptedException
Methods of the class:public final native void java.lang.Object.wait(long) throws java.lang.InterruptedException
Methods of the class:public boolean java.lang.Object.equals(java.lang.Object)
Methods of the class:public java.lang.String java.lang.Object.toString()
Methods of the class:public native int java.lang.Object.hashCode()
Methods of the class:public final native java.lang.Class java.lang.Object.getClass()
Methods of the class:public final native void java.lang.Object.notify()
Methods of the class:public final native void java.lang.Object.notifyAll()
```

Example 5: isInterface(), getModifiers() and isArray()

ReflectionExample5.java

```java
package com.java.reflection;

import java.lang.reflect.Method;
import java.lang.reflect.Modifier;

public class ReflectionExample5 implements interface1, interface2 {

    public static void main(String[] args) {

        int arr[] = new int[4];
        // get Class object
        Class classObject = ReflectionExample5.class;
        // obtain a list of interfaces
        Class[] interfaceList = classObject.getInterfaces();
        for (int i = 0; i < interfaceList.length; i++) {
            System.out.println("Interface Name: " + interfaceList[i].getName());
            // obtain the list of methods of each interface
            Method[] methodList = interfaceList[i].getDeclaredMethods();
            for (int j = 0; j < methodList.length; j++) {
                System.out.println("Method belonging to the interface " + interfaceList[i].getName() + ":"
                        + methodList[j].getName());

            }
        }
        // get Modifier of the class
        System.out.println(("Modofier of the class " + classObject.getName() + " is :"
                + Modifier.toString(classObject.getModifiers())));
        // use isArray() to check if the object is an areay
        System.out.println("isArray(): " + arr.getClass().isArray());
    }

    @Override
    public void method2() {}

    @Override
    public void method1() {}

    @Override
    public void method3() {}

}

interface interface1 {

    public void method1();

    public void method2();

}

interface interface2 {

    public void method3();

}
```

The output generated by the above class is:

Console | Problems | Servers | Properties

```
<terminated> ReflectionExample5 [Java Application] C:\Program Files\java\
Interface Name: com.java.reflection.interface1
Method belonging to the interface com.java.reflection.interface1:method2
Method belonging to the interface com.java.reflection.interface1:method1
Interface Name: com.java.reflection.interface2
Method belonging to the interface com.java.reflection.interface2:method3
Modofier of the class com.java.reflection.ReflectionExample5 is :public
isArray(): true
```

Example 5: Use reflection api on existing java classes such as Integer.

ReflectionExample6.java

```
package com.java.reflection;

import java.lang.reflect.Field;
import java.lang.reflect.Method;
import java.lang.reflect.Modifier;

public class ReflectionExample6 {

    public static void main(String[] args) {

        // get modifiers of the Integer class
        System.out.println(Modifier.toString(java.lang.Integer.class.getModifiers()));

        // display fields/variables of the Integer class in Java
        Field[] fieldList = java.lang.Integer.class.getDeclaredFields();

        for (int i = 0; i < fieldList.length; i++) {
            System.out.println("Field: " + fieldList[i]);

        }

        // display methods of the Integer class in Java
        Method[] methodList = java.lang.Integer.class.getDeclaredMethods();
        for (int j = 0; j < methodList.length; j++) {
            System.out.println("Method:" + methodList[j]);
        }
    }
}
```

The output generated is as follows:

Console ☒ Problems Servers Properties

<terminated> ReflectionExample6 [Java Application] C:\Program Files\java\jdk1.8.0_92\bin\javaw.exe (17 juil. 2017 à 10:47:13)

```
public final
Field: public static final int java.lang.Integer.MIN_VALUE
Field: public static final int java.lang.Integer.MAX_VALUE
Field: public static final java.lang.Class java.lang.Integer.TYPE
Field: static final char[] java.lang.Integer.digits
Field: static final char[] java.lang.Integer.DigitTens
Field: static final char[] java.lang.Integer.DigitOnes
Field: static final int[] java.lang.Integer.sizeTable
Field: private final int java.lang.Integer.value
Field: public static final int java.lang.Integer.SIZE
Field: public static final int java.lang.Integer.BYTES
Field: private static final long java.lang.Integer.serialVersionUID
Method:public static int java.lang.Integer.numberOfLeadingZeros(int)
Method:public static int java.lang.Integer.numberOfTrailingZeros(int)
Method:public static int java.lang.Integer.bitCount(int)
Method:public boolean java.lang.Integer.equals(java.lang.Object)
Method:public static java.lang.String java.lang.Integer.toString(int,int)
Method:public java.lang.String java.lang.Integer.toString()
Method:public static java.lang.String java.lang.Integer.toString(int)
Method:public static int java.lang.Integer.hashCode(int)
Method:public int java.lang.Integer.hashCode()
Method:public static int java.lang.Integer.min(int,int)
Method:public static int java.lang.Integer.max(int,int)
Method:public static int java.lang.Integer.reverseBytes(int)
Method:public int java.lang.Integer.compareTo(java.lang.Integer)
Method:public int java.lang.Integer.compareTo(java.lang.Object)
Method:public byte java.lang.Integer.byteValue()
Method:public short java.lang.Integer.shortValue()
Method:public int java.lang.Integer.intValue()
Method:public long java.lang.Integer.longValue()
Method:public float java.lang.Integer.floatValue()
Method:public double java.lang.Integer.doubleValue()
Method:public static java.lang.Integer java.lang.Integer.valueOf(java.lang.String,int) throws java.lang.NumberFormatException
Method:public static java.lang.Integer java.lang.Integer.valueOf(int)
Method:public static java.lang.Integer java.lang.Integer.valueOf(java.lang.String) throws java.lang.NumberFormatException
Method:public static java.lang.String java.lang.Integer.toHexString(int)
Method:public static int java.lang.Integer.compare(int,int)
Method:public static java.lang.Integer java.lang.Integer.decode(java.lang.String) throws java.lang.NumberFormatException
Method:static void java.lang.Integer.getChars(int,int,char[])
Method:public static int java.lang.Integer.reverse(int)
Method:static int java.lang.Integer.stringSize(int)
Method:public static int java.lang.Integer.sum(int,int)
Method:public static int java.lang.Integer.parseInt(java.lang.String) throws java.lang.NumberFormatException
Method:public static int java.lang.Integer.parseInt(java.lang.String,int) throws java.lang.NumberFormatException
Method:public static long java.lang.Integer.toUnsignedLong(int)
Method:public static int java.lang.Integer.compareUnsigned(int,int)
Method:public static int java.lang.Integer.divideUnsigned(int,int)
Method:static int java.lang.Integer.formatUnsignedInt(int,int,char[],int,int)
Method:public static java.lang.Integer java.lang.Integer.getInteger(java.lang.String,java.lang.Integer)
Method:public static java.lang.Integer java.lang.Integer.getInteger(java.lang.String,int)
Method:public static java.lang.Integer java.lang.Integer.getInteger(java.lang.String)
Method:public static int java.lang.Integer.highestOneBit(int)
Method:public static int java.lang.Integer.lowestOneBit(int)
Method:public static int java.lang.Integer.parseUnsignedInt(java.lang.String) throws java.lang.NumberFormatException
Method:public static int java.lang.Integer.parseUnsignedInt(java.lang.String,int) throws java.lang.NumberFormatException
Method:public static int java.lang.Integer.remainderUnsigned(int,int)
Method:public static int java.lang.Integer.rotateLeft(int,int)
Method:public static int java.lang.Integer.rotateRight(int,int)
Method:public static int java.lang.Integer.signum(int)
Method:public static java.lang.String java.lang.Integer.toBinaryString(int)
Method:public static java.lang.String java.lang.Integer.toOctalString(int)
Method:public static java.lang.String java.lang.Integer.toUnsignedString(int)
Method:public static java.lang.String java.lang.Integer.toUnsignedString(int,int)
Method:private static java.lang.String java.lang.Integer.toUnsignedString0(int,int)
```

REFERENCES

1. Webopedia.com. (2017). *What is Object-Oriented Programming? Webopedia Definition*. [online] Available at: http://www.webopedia.com/TERM/O/object_oriented_programming_OOP.html [Accessed 22 Jul. 2017].
2. development, J. (2017). *Java language basics*. [online] Ibm.com. Available at: https://www.ibm.com/developerworks/java/tutorials/j-introtojava1/index.html/ [Accessed 22 Jul. 2017].
3. Rolling Stone. (2017). *Steve Jobs in 1994: The Rolling Stone Interview*. [online] Available at: http://www.rollingstone.com/culture/news/steve-jobs-in-1994-the-rolling-stone-interview-20110117 [Accessed 22 Jul. 2017].
4. Horstmann, C. S., & Cornell, G. (2002). *Core Java 2: Volume I, Fundamentals*. Pearson Education.
5. Wu, C. T. (2006). *An introduction to Object-oriented programming with Java*. Tata McGraw-Hill Publishing Company Limited.

6. Gosling, J., & McGilton, H. (1995). The Java language environment. *Sun Microsystems Computer Company, 2550.*
7. Curtin, M. (1998). Write once, run anywhere: Why it matters. *Technical Article. http://java. sun. com/features/1998/01/wo.*
8. Eckel, B. (2003). *Thinking in JAVA*. Prentice Hall Professional.
9. Gong, L., & Ellison, G. (2003). *Inside Java (TM) 2 Platform Security: Architecture, API Design, and Implementation*. Pearson Education.
10. Shavor, S., D'Anjou, J., Fairbrother, S., Kehn, D., Kellerman, J., & McCarthy, P. (2003). *The Java developer's guide to Eclipse*. Addison-Wesley Longman Publishing Co., Inc..
11. Naughton, P., & Schildt, H. (1996). *Java: the complete reference*. Osborne/McGraw-Hill.
12. Tempero, E., & Biddle, R. (2000). Simulating multiple inheritance in Java. *Journal of Systems and Software*, *55*(1), 87-100.
13. Liskov, B., & Guttag, J. (2000). *Program development in JAVA: abstraction, specification, and object-oriented design*. Pearson Education.
14. Johnson, R. E., & Foote, B. (1988). Designing reusable classes. *Journal of object-oriented programming*, *1*(2), 22-35.
15. Gosling, J. (2000). *The Java language specification*. Addison-Wesley Professional.
16. Goetz, B., & Peierls, T. (2006). *Java concurrency in practice*. Pearson Education.
17. Collins, W. (2011). *Data structures and the Java collections framework*. Wiley Publishing.
18. Chan, P., & Lee, R. (1998). The Java Class Libraries, Volume 2: java. applet, java. awt, java. beans. The Java Series.
19. Shams, Z., & Edwards, S. H. (2013). Reflection support: Java reflection made easy. *The Open Software Engineering Journal*, *7*(1).
20. Serializable (Java Platform SE 8). (n.d.). Retrieved from https://docs.oracle.com/javase/8/docs/api/java/io/Serializable.html
21. javatpoint (2017). *Features of Java - Javatpoint*. [online] Available at: https://www.javatpoint.com/features-of-java [Accessed 22 Jul. 2017].

22. Applets Java: A Framework for Programming and Problem Solving", Kenneth A. Lambert and Martin Osborne, PWS Publishing, 1999, pp. 443-455.
23. How to explain multiple inheritance in Java - Stack Overflow. (2013). Retrieved from https://stackoverflow.com/questions/18328629/how-to-explain-multiple-inheritance-in-java
24. Exceptions (1995). Retrieved from https://docs.oracle.com/javase/tutorial/essential/exceptions/definition.html
25. Apps, S. (2017). *Checked and Unchecked Exceptions in Java*. [online] HackTrix. Available at: http://www.hacktrix.com/checked-and-unchecked-exceptions-in-java [Accessed 22 Jul. 2017].
26. Javamadesoeasy.com. (2017). *Exception handling, exception hierarchy in java*. [online] Available at: http://www.javamadesoeasy.com/2015/05/exception-handling-exception-hierarchy.html [Accessed 22 Jul. 2017].
27. Oracle.com. (2017). *Java Garbage Collection Basics*. [online] Available at: http://www.oracle.com/webfolder/technetwork/tutorials/obe/java/gc01/index.html [Accessed 22 Jul. 2017].
28. www.engineersbloc.com. (2017). *Tuning Java Garbage Collection for Performance*. [online] Available at: http://www.engineersbloc.com/collection/278/ [Accessed 22 Jul. 2017].
29. Docs.oracle.com. (2017). *Java Language Keywords (The Java™ Tutorials > Learning the Java Language > Language Basics)*. [online] Available at: https://docs.oracle.com/javase/tutorial/java/nutsandbolts/_keywords.html [Accessed 22 Jul. 2017].
30. "The Complete Reference Part 2 by Herbert Schildt".
31. The Path Class (The Java™ Tutorials > Essential Classes > Basic I/O). (2017). Docs.oracle.com. Retrieved 10 July 2017, from https://docs.oracle.com/javase/tutorial/essential/io/pathClass.html
32. Chan, P., Kramer, D., & Lee, R. (1999). *The Java Class Libraries: Supplement for the Java 2 Platform* Standard Edition (Vol. 1). Addison-Wesley Professional.
33. Friesen, J. (2015). *Java I/O, NIO and NIO. 2*. Apress.

INDEX